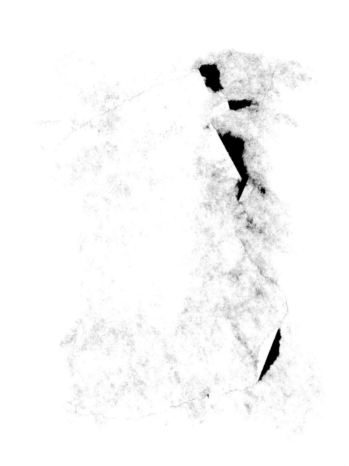

500

LITTLE-KNOWN
FACTS IN
U.S. HISTORY

GEORGE W. GIVENS

Bonneville Books
Springville, Utah

ISBN 13: 978-1-55517-947-9
ISBN 10: 1-55517-947-9

Published by Bonneville Books, an imprint of Cedar Fort, Inc.
925 N. Main, Springville, UT, 84663
Distributed by Cedar Fort, Inc. www.cedarfort.com

Cover design by Nicole Williams
Cover design © 2006 by Lyle Mortimer
Printed in the United States of America

10   9   8   7   6   5   4   3   2   1

Printed on acid-free paper

TABLE OF CONTENTS

FOREWORD

My father was a collector. If you had asked him to describe himself, he likely would have said "teacher" or "author." But nearly two years after his death, I believe "collector" more aptly defines his life. And I'm sure my mother would agree. After he passed away in June 2004, she was faced with the daunting task of finding places for his collections. She found a buyer for his gun collection. She sold or gave away much of his antique collection. She divvied up his book collection among her children (thanks, Mom), kept quite a few books for herself, and sold the ones that had no takers in the family. But the one collection she couldn't touch was his knowledge.

I imagine there were and are more brilliant men out there. There are more well-known and more prolific writers, more popular teachers (although I have to believe that's because not everyone had the chance to sit in one of Dad's classes), and greater thinkers. But I'm convinced that there was no one more hungry for knowledge than Dad. He drank it in like a parched man and devoured it as though starving. Thankfully, he never hoarded it. To anyone who would sit and listen for a few minutes, he would eagerly and excitedly share.

For him, books weren't vehicles to fame and adulation; they were the best way to spread his enthusiasm for learning. So when my mother came across this manuscript, turned down by one publisher when it was

written thirty years ago and then stowed away, she decided to find out if anyone out there would still be interested in sitting down and listening to my father again. Fortunately, Lee Nelson, Cedar Fort acquisitions editor, believes there are such people.

A history teacher for nineteen years, most of those in Arizona, Dad was passionate about this nation's beginnings and the men and women who played a role in those beginnings. David McCullough, author of *John Adams* and *1776,* among other titles, has said that if we are at all grateful for this country of ours, we should want to know about its founders. In the same sense, Dad always believed that the more vividly we could see our past, the more clearly we would see our present.

Most of us know the basic outline of American history, but God is in the details, whether as the conductor of events or in the strength of the people who lived through them. In the pages ahead, you will find hundreds of those details—some sad, some puzzling, some disturbing, and many humorous—that I hope will instill in you the same fascination with our past that my father held his entire life.

—Bobbie Givens Goettler

PART ONE

THE NEW WORLD
(1451–1778)

ALBERICA THE BEAUTIFUL (1451)

By one of those strange quirks of history, both Christopher Columbus and his patron, Queen Isabella of Spain, were born in 1451. To make the coincidence even stranger, another man just as closely connected with the New World was born in Florence that same year. Through a comedy of errors on the part of mapmakers and geographers, this man, Amerigo Vespucci, would have his name attached forever to this new land.

Vespucci did not discover America; in fact, he didn't discover any new lands at all. He was not a great writer, scholar, or philosopher. He was not even a great navigator. He had never been entrusted with a command of any kind. He did only one thing of note in his uneventful life. As a member of an expedition to the New World in 1499, he *recognized* the New World for what it was—a *new world*—and duly reported this information to Europe. As a result, and through no effort of his own, the Western Hemisphere would thereafter be referred to as "America's Land," or, simply, "America."

As innocent as he was of this honor, he was also innocent of historical slander that, for the next three centuries, erroneously portrayed him as a lying, cheating imposter. As late as 1856, Ralph Waldo Emerson wrote, "Strange that broad America must wear the name of a thief . . . the pickle-dealer (who) . . . managed in this lying world to supplant Columbus and baptize half the earth with his own dishonest name." Incidentally, it was a name that, had geographers translated it into Latin as was the custom, would have been "Alberica."

COLUMBUS KNEW HE WAS NOT FIRST? (1480)

Historians today feel it is not only possible that fishermen from Bristol, England, reached the North American continent in the 1480s, but also that Columbus was aware of this fact before he set out on his voyage in 1492. Soon after the return of John Cabot from his voyage to America in 1497, an Englishman named John Day wrote a letter to a Spanish "High Admiral," very likely Christopher Columbus, admiral of the ocean seas:

"It is assumed true that the cape of the before-mentioned land is the one found and discovered in other times by the people of Bristol and thought to have been an island, as your Lordship already knows."

Historians believe "in other times," although vague, refers to a previous generation—no later than 1480. The "people of Bristol" were fishermen, and the letter suggests that Columbus knew about their previous voyage. It will be a pretty safe thing to continue planning your Columbus Day vacations, however, until someone uncovers the name of the captain of that Bristol fishing vessel.

GLOBES, SPHERES, AND ORBS (1492)

Contrary to an idea popular a generation ago, Columbus didn't have to convince anyone of the shape of the earth. For two thousand years, learned scientists had reasoned that the earth was a sphere, if not a "whirling orb." A geographer who lived at the time of Christ, Strabo, had written, "If it were not for the immensity of the Atlantic, you could sail from Iberia (Spain) to India by keeping to the same parallel."

As a matter of fact, model globes had been around for some time by 1492. Martin Behaim, in Nuremberg, Germany, had recently finished a model globe showing Asia directly across the ocean from Spain. In the very courts that Columbus frequented to plead for funds stood statues of dead kings holding a scepter in one hand and the orb of the earth in the other. As early as 517 B.C., Hecataeus had mapped the earth as a sphere. So if Columbus's sailors were afraid of sailing off the edge of the earth, there was a communication gap somewhere!

COLUMBUS CLAIMS THE PRIZE (1492)

To encourage his sailors to want to keep sailing westward, Columbus announced an annuity of ten thousand maravedis offered by the sovereigns to the man who first discovered land. To this Columbus added his own prize of a silk jacket. Around 10 P.M. on the night of October 11, a seaman named Pedro Yzquierdo thought he saw a light and sang out, "Lumbre! Tierra!" Columbus, who thought he had seen a light shortly before this, replied, "I saw and spoke of that light, which is on land, some time ago." Although neither man had actually seen land, Pedro claimed the prize.

Several hours later, Martin Alonso Pinzon became the first man to actually see land and received as a prize five thousand maravedis, but the admiral himself claimed the sovereigns' major prize. Pedro Yzquierdo was enraged at what he considered this breach of promise and, upon his return to Spain, went off to Africa and became a Muslim.

COLUMBUS NOT CHEATED (1492)

It has often been said that Columbus was cheated out of his rightful reward in history because the New World was not named after him. Actually, he didn't know what he had discovered, remaining convinced until the day he died that the New World was a part of Asia—even obliging every member of his crew to take an oath before a notary that such was the case.

It was at this point that Amerigo Vespucci lost confidence in his Genoese countryman and decided to voyage to the New World himself. After intelligent and intensive explorations, Amerigo returned to Europe with news of a vast new continent, a "New World," creating more justified excitement than the discoveries of Columbus himself. It was with Amerigo's information that Waldseemuller, the Lorraine mapmaker, drew maps showing a New World and exalted Amerigo's name by placing it rightly on the new land mass. It is perhaps prophetic justice that America is named not after a fanciful dreamer but after a hardheaded businessman. It may also have been prophetic that Amerigo died on February 22, 1512—the day that would later be honored as the birthday of the father of Amerigo's land—George Washington.

ENGLAND'S CLAIM TO AMERICA (1497)

England's claim to North America was ironically based on the discoveries of a Venetian navigator, Giovanni Caboto, sailing under a patent from Henry VII of England. At least this is what history books tell us. But was John Cabot (the anglicized name) really Italian? Genealogy of the Cabot family shows absolutely no Cabots in Italy before the explorer, and the conclusion of historian L. V. Briggs is that the "Italian" Caboto was a member of the same family as the American Cabots, who descended from another John Cabot who migrated to Salem from the Isle of Jersey around 1700. This is also the tradition of the Boston Cabots and is probably comforting to Anglophiles. Incidentally, in addition to giving him a small pension, Henry VII rewarded Cabot with a gift of ten pounds sterling "to have a good time with."

EARLY KIDNAPPING (1524)

More than four hundred years before the famous Lindberg kidnapping, the first recorded kidnapping in what is now the United States took place along the mid-Atlantic coast. In 1524, according to a letter he addressed to Frances I, King of France, Giovanni Verrasano and his crew "tooke a childe [Indian] from . . . olde woman to bring into France, and going about to take . . . young woman which was very beautiful and of tall stature, we could not possibly, for the great outcries that she make, bring her to the sea; and especially having great woods to pass through and being farre from the ship, we purposed to leave her behinde, beareing away the childe only." So it was in one of their very first encounters with Native Americans that explorers treated them not as fellow humans but as trophies to be taken home.

THE "LOST COLONY" OF GUALDAPE (1526)

All students of American history are familiar with the "Lost Colony" of Roanoke off the North Carolina coast, 1587–90, but few are familiar with the "Lost Colony" of San Miguel de Gualdape in that same general vicinity, settled in 1526 by the Spanish, sixty-one years before the English made their attempt. In that year, six hundred Spanish settlers with African-American slaves, horses, and equipment made a settlement somewhere on the East Cost. Some historians place it south of Cape Hatteras; others place it on the James or Potomac River. The colony suffered disease, inner dissension, and Indian assaults before it was finally abandoned and the survivors returned to the West Indies. Although the people themselves did not disappear, as did those at Roanoke in 1587, the location of the colony remains undiscovered to this day.

SPORTING INDIANS ATTACK DESOTO (1540)

One of the most unusual conflicts between Indians and whites on the North American continent occurred between a small party of seven soldiers from Hernando DeSoto's army and a band of approximately fifty natives of Apalachee, Florida.

It was several weeks before the single Spanish survivor of the encounter was well enough to talk. When he did, he told a strange story. The seven conquistadores had become separated from the main army and were on foot when they met the fifty natives. Only seven Indians stepped forward to battle the Spaniards; the rest, in a sportsmanlike manner, moved away as spectators. Even with their armor, the Europeans were no match for the fast arrows and clubs of the Apalachees, who apparently felt themselves equal to any Christians who were not mounted on horses. The lucky survivor had nothing but praise for "the courtesy and valor of those Indians that day."

FIRST CHRISTIAN MARTYR (1542)

When Francisco Vázquez Coronado made his grand but profitless expedition through the American Southwest, he was accompanied by four Franciscan friars. The leader of this religious group, Fray Marcos, had made a short journey into the area in 1539 and issued glowing reports of golden cities that prompted the expedition. He was soon to be exiled from the expedition in humiliation when the group failed to find what he had promised. But one of the remaining friars, Juan de Padilla, was to go on to greater glory.

At the conclusion of the fruitless search for the seven cities of Cibola, the good friar's heart ached—not for the gold missed but for the souls of the poor Indians he had encountered. In 1542 he retraced 1,500 miles of the journey to live with the natives of Quivira, in Kansas, and teach them Christianity. Here these same Indians killed him—ironically, not because of their hostility but because of their jealousy upon hearing that he was leaving to work with other Indians. Thus, he became the first Christian martyr in what is now the United States.

"MRS. ROBINSON CRUSOE" (1543)

One of the most amazing footnotes to the European discovery of America concerns a French woman named Marguerite de la Roque, a passenger on Jean Roberval's expedition to the St. Lawrence River in 1542–43. Angered by her love affair with another man on board, Roberval marooned Marguerite and her old maid servant on one of the Harrington Islands. Her lover decided not to leave her and leaped overboard as the ships pulled away.

Within a short time, the man, Marguerite's newborn child, and her servant all died, leaving Marguerite to fend for herself like the well-known Robinson Crusoe—even fighting off bears and killing three in the process. Her stay on the island lasted for two and a half years before she was rescued by Breton fishermen and returned to France. History doesn't record whether Roberval ever learned of Marguerite's rescue or whether he might have intended it himself, but some authorities record that he died while on a second voyage to St. Lawrence in 1547.

AMERICA'S FIRST WONDER DRUG (1569)

Few are familiar with its history today, but one of the first, if not the first, money crop and object-in-trade in the English Colonies was sassafras root bark. In 1622 each Jamestown colonist was committed, under penalty of ten pounds of tobacco, to produce a hundred pounds of sassafras. Its popularity began with the writings of Doctor Nicolas Monardes in 1569: "It healeth opilations, it comforteth the liver and the stomach and doth disopilate; to give appetite to eat; in the headache, in griefes of the stomach; it causeth to cast out gravel and stones; it removeth the impediments that cause barrenness and maketh women to conceave; in the toothache; in the evil of the poxe and eville of the joints."

One record states that a group of Virginians were reduced to eating their dogs cooked in a soup of sassafras—a favorite tea in England. When a rumor started that it would retard old age, every ship headed for America was under pressure to return with a load. Legend arose that the odor would keep away sickness, evil, and vermin. Spoons were made of the wood, cradles were inlaid with it, and Bible boxes were constructed of it. It was even believed that ships with sassafras wood in their hulls would never be wrecked.

FIRST ATTEMPTED SETTLEMENT (1578)

The first English attempt to plant a permanent colony in America ended in disaster with none of the seven ships in the expedition ever reaching the North American coast. The year was 1578, twenty-nine years before success occured at Jamestown. That year Sir Humphrey Gilbert received a patent from Queen Elizabeth to settle land in America within a six-year period. With his half-brother, Sir Walter Raleigh, as captain of one of the ships, Gilbert set sail in November 1578 with a broken-down, ill-prepared, and ill-organized fleet, which was immediately scattered by bad weather. The last of the seven ships, Raleigh's *Falcon,* limped home in May 1579. None of the ships reached Norumbega, the name given to the North American coastline between the Hudson and Newfoundland.

DRAKE IN CALIFORNIA (1579)

On his extremely profitable trip around the world from 1577 to 1580, Sir Francis Drake took time to do a little exploring. His accounts tell how, after weeks of icy gales, he found refuge for the *Golden Hine* in a small cove on the West Coast—the cove probably referred to today as Drake's Cover, thirty miles from San Francisco. There, on June 17, 1579, he laid claim to "the Whole Land" in the name of Queen Elizabeth and "Herr successors forever" and named it Nova Albion, or New England. Three hundred and fifty years later, the brass plate with which he posted his claim was discovered by a private chauffeur who, unaware of what it was, discarded it. In 1936 the plate was rediscovered and identified as authentic.

The West Coast, which was to prove a treasure hoard of gold to North Americans three centuries later, was equally profitable in 1579. Capturing Spanish treasure ships along the Pacific coast, Drake returned to his queen a profit of 4,000 percent on her investment.

THE LOST COLONY (1587)

The story of the Lost Colony of Roanoke and its 119 settlers, including seventeen women and eleven children, left on the island of Roanoke at Cape Hatorask (Hatteras) by John White in 1587 is fairly familiar to most students of American history. Governor White returned from England in 1590 after an unexplained absence of three years to find that his daughter, his granddaughter Virginia Dare, and the other 117 settlers had disappeared. The only clue he found was the puzzling word "Crotoan" carved on a tree near the former settlement. The settlers' disappearance is a mystery that has excited the imaginations of generations of Americans. Less well known, perhaps, is what the Jamestown colonists learned twenty years later.

From the Indians they discovered that white people had been living with some nearby natives but had recently been massacred on orders of Powhattan. Only four men, two boys, and a young girl—who were under the protection of another friendly chieftain—had survived. Again, nothing more was discovered until the early 1700s, when travelers to Carolina were amazed to find a tribe of Indians in the vicinity of Hatteras who had gray eyes.

TOBACCO AS A MEDICINE (1588)

Thomas Harriot's *Breife and True Report of the New Found Land of Virginia* (1588) praised tobacco as a medicine that "purgeth superfluous fleame & other grosse humors, openeth all the pores & passages of the body: by which means the use thereof not only preserveth the body from obstructions: but also if any be, so that they have not beene of too long continuance, in short time breaketh them: whereby their bodies are notably preserved in health, and know not many grievous diseases wherewithall wee in England are oftentimes afflicted." It was claimed that smoking tobacco would heal gout and ague, cure hangovers, and reduce fatigue and hunger. It was also praised for its "cooling" effect.

SCURVY (1590)

A most common disease for sailors during the Age of Exploration, when America was the target of ship captains, was scurvy, caused by a deficiency of vitamin C. Horrific contemporary descriptions tell us what the disease was like: "It rotted all my gums," wrote one sufferer, "which gave out a black and putrid blood. I also used by knife on my gums, which were livid and growing over my teeth. . . . When I had cut away this dead flesh and caused much black blood to flow, I rinsed my mouth and teeth with my urine, rubbing them very hard. . . . And the unfortunate thing was that I could not eat, desiring more to swallow than to chew. . . . Many of our people died of it every day, and we saw bodies thrown into the sea

constantly, three or four at a time. For the most part they died with no aid given them, expiring behind some case or chest, their eyes and soles of their feet gnawed by the rats."

PANAMA CANAL FIRST PROPOSED (1599)

For some reason, history books often fail to mention the fact that the French explorer Samuel de Champlain started his career of exploration for Spain. In 1599, as captain of the *Saint Julien,* he sailed to the Spanish West Indies with the annual fleet, where he spent two years exploring the West Indies, Mexico, and Panama. Upon his return to Europe in 1601, he prepared a record, including charts and maps, of all he saw in the Spanish possessions. That record is now preserved in manuscript form at Dieppe, France. One of the most interesting portions of his manuscript includes a plan he worked out after sighting the Pacific from the Panama portage. It was a plan for a canal to connect the two great oceans "to shorten the voyage to the South Sea by more than fifteen hundred leagues." Like many ideas whose time had not yet come, it had to wait—more than three hundred years in this case.

"THOSE BIG-MOUTHED INDIANS" (1605)

In 1605 Captain George Waymounth guided his ship, the *Archangel,* along the New England coast, searching for a suitable haven for perse-cuted Catholics from England. He was not too successful, but his men did capture and bring back to England five Native Americans. These five men, their names unknown today, are credited with praising their homeland so much that the Europeans decided to take it for their own. Of course, European settlement was inevitable, but how much these five unnamed natives pushed it along will never be known.

Sir Ferdinando Gorges, who came into custody of three of these Indian braggards, spent a fortune and most of the rest of his life in colo-nizing projects in New England. He stated in later years that the acci-dent of acquiring those Indians "must be acknowledged the means, under God, of putting on foot and giving life to all our plantations." Even the Spanish ambassador in England reported to his government that those Indians were being trained "to say how good that country is for people to go there and inhabit it." The words of these poor Indians probably rank as the most successful real-estate pitch in history.

"THE MOST HISTORIC SPOT" (1607)

The British political scientist Sir James Bryce referred to it as "one of the great events in the history of the world—an event to be compared for its momentous consequences with the overthrow of the Persian empire by Alexander; with the destruction of Carthage by Rome; with the conquest of Gaul by Clovis; with the taking of Constantinople by the Turks—one might almost say with discovery of America by Columbus."

The event occurred on May 14, 1607, when 104 settlers left their three small ships in the James River and went ashore to build the tiny palisade that was to be England's first permanent settlement overseas. The site of the fort has long been washed away by the river, but the site of the rest of the small Jamestown settlement has been rightfully called "the most historic spot in the nation."

FORESTS OF EARLY AMERICA (1607)

As beautiful as they must have been, trees in the East created an extremely dark forest world so thick that the gloom depressed white men who passed through it. Some parts were called "the Shades of Death." The leaves created a shadow so deep that songbirds and many wild animals could not live in the heart of the forest. One early traveler reported journeying the better part of a day without seeing the sun, while another pioneer traveled a mile without finding a spot "the size of a hand" where sunlight could penetrate.

There was strange advantage to the thick forests. Poison ivy, which must have light, sought it above the treetops. Except for one mishap of Capt. John Smith, there is no record of ivy poisoning until well into the eighteenth century. When the forests were finally cleared, the trilobed leaves with their poisonous oil came down to earth, where victims could reach them.

These trees that shaped early America, stretching a thousand miles to the south and westward over an area as large as the Roman Empire, were so thick that it was said a squirrel could travel from the Ohio River to Lake Erie or from the Hudson River to Niagara Falls without touching the ground. Openings did exist, but it was still felt that this "climax forest" would supply the world forever.

CANNIBALISM IN VIRGINIA (1609)

Captain John Smith, leader and participant in the early Jamestown difficulties, wrote years later of the "Starving Time" experienced by the settlers in 1609. According to a biographer:

"Of five hundred [persons], within six months after Captain Smith's departure there remained not past sixty men, women and children, most miserable and poor creatures. . . . Nay, so great was our famine that a savage we slew and buried, the poorer sort took him up again and ate him; and so did divers one another boiled and stewed, with roots and herbs. And one amongst the rest did kill his wife, powdered (salted) her, and had eaten part of her before it was known, for which he was executed, as he well deserved. Now whether she was better roasted, boiled, or carbonadoed [broiled], I knew not; but of such a dish as powdered wife I never heard of."

Discovery of "a good quantity of meat, oatmeal, peas and beans" in the killer's quarters spoiled his story of hunger and revealed that the crime was one of anger. The cannibalism was intended somewhat to excuse the crime, but he burned for the murder nevertheless. "Anyway," as one author said in reference to the wife, "the poor soul was most foully slain and probably cared little whether or not she was eaten afterward."

"LADY" POCAHONTAS (1610)

The story of John Smith's rescue by Pocahontas is a good story but may not be good history. What is history, however, is the following: Pocahontas made several trips to Jamestown during its early years, was baptized Rebecca, dressed in English clothing, and won the heart of young John Rolfe, a respectable English planter. Persuaded after much soul-searching that he was moved not by "the unbridled desire of carnall affection" but "for the good of the plantations, for the honour of our countrie, for the glory of God, for my owne salvation, and for the converting to the true knowledge of God and Jesus Christ, an unbelieving creature, name Pokahumtas," Rolfe proposed and was accepted. Shortly thereafter, the Rolfes visited England, where Lady Rebecca was eagerly accepted into English society. Because of her royal Indian blood, she was granted an audience with the king, whereas her husband, a commoner, was not. She never returned to America but died at Gravesend as she was about to return home. Her son, Thomas, became the forefather of many of Virginia's first families.

POCAHONTAS'S SISTER (1614)

History doesn't tell us much about the younger sister of Pocahontas except that the governor of Virginia wished to marry her. Sir Thomas Dale, who had given John Rolfe permission to marry the older daughter of Powhatan, sent a request to the chief, along with an offer of beads, copper, fishhooks, knives, combs, and a grindstone for the hand of his twelve-year-old daughter in marriage. As badly as Powhatan wanted the grindstone, one white son-in-law was enough, so he turned down the governor's request. It was just as well, perhaps, for when Governor Dale returned to England two years later with Rolfe and Pocahontas, it might have proven embarrassing when he introduced his Indian child bride to his English wife and children who had remained behind in England.

COMMUNISM IN EARLY VIRGINIA (1614)

According to an agreement between the Jamestown settlers and the Virginia Company, signed in 1609, there was to be no private owner-ship of land until 1616, but all land was to be worked in common and food distributed according to need. Lack of individual initiative under this communistic system prompted Governor Dale to go to private land ownership in 1614. According to Ralph Hamor, one of the planters, the change was astounding:

"When our people were fed out of the common store, and laboured jointly together, glad was he could slip from his labour, or slumber over his taske he cared not how, nay, the most honest among them would hardly take so much true paines in a weeke, as now for themselves they will doe in a day: neither cared they for the increase, presuming that how-soever the harvest prospered, the generall store must maintaine them, so that wee reaped not so much Corne from the labours of thirtie, as now three or foure do provide for themselves."

HOLLAND UNSAFE FOR PILGRIMS (1615)

A major reason the Pilgrims decided to remove to America was that even Holland was not a safe haven for the Separatists. Catholic Spain was threatening Holland, and England was attempting control through diplomatic channels—and some not-so-diplomatic ones. William Brew-ster went into hiding after the English ambassador tried to seize him for publishing material critical of the Church of England (Anglican). For this same offense, the Reverend Alexander Leighton was fined 100,000 pounds, publicly whipped and pilloried, his ears cut off, his nose slit, and his face branded "SS" (Stirrer of Sedition). Then he was imprisoned for life.

Leighton, a Scottish minister, had published in the Netherlands an attack upon the Anglican Church. With this undoubtedly in mind, Mr. Brewster did not come out of hiding until the *Mayflower* was well out to sea on her "weighty voyage." We cannot help but admire the Dutch for the toleration they showed the Separatists in view of the fact that several years previous to the Brewster incident, Separatist exiles in Amsterdam had antagonized the Dutch Reform Church by gratuitously pointing out the errors in that church.

TOBACCO (1616)

Three and a half centuries before the U.S. surgeon general issued the first public warning about the dangers of cigarette smoking in January 1964, King James I had issued a warning that it was "a custome Loth-some to the eye, hatefull to the nose, harmefull to the braine, dangerous to the Lungs, and in the blake stinking fume thereof, nearest resembling the horrible Stigian smoke of the pit that is bottomlesse." Despite this royal warning, England imported 2,500 pounds of tobacco in 1616, and by the time of the American Revolution, more than 100 million pounds had been shipped from the Colonies.

JOHN SMITH AND THE PILGRIMS (1619)

The Pilgrim fathers were relative latecomers to the rockbound coasts of New England. Many European explorers had preceded the Pilgrims, notably Capt. John Smith of Jamestown fame. He had made several exploring trips along the New England coasts before 1620, possibly naming New England and Plymouth. In 1619 he even offered to pilot the Pilgrim adventurers to the New World, but his offer was refused. "My books and maps," he acidly noted, "were much better cheape to teach them, than my selfe."

On John Smith's map of New England can be found such names as Boston, Dartmouth, Cambridge, Southampton, Ipswich, Oxford, and even a place called Plimouth. The belief that the Pilgrims brought these English names to New England six years later is a historical myth.

VIRGINIA BLUE LAWS (1619)

"Blue laws," usually associated with the God-fearing Puritans of New England, were actually enacted first in the Jamestown Colony by the Virginia House of Burgesses at its inaugural 1619 session. One such law provided that "all persons whatsoever upon the Sabbath days shall frequent divine service and sermons, both forenoon and afternoon." To enforce church attendance in the earliest days of the colony, appointed officials actually went from house to house on the Sabbath, driving people ahead of them to the local Anglican Church. The law even provided for the death penalty for nonattendance, although it was never enforced. Swearing was forbidden, and those who offended a second time might have a bodkin (large needle) stuck through their tongue. If they still persisted, the penalty was death.

JAMESTOWN: FIRST WHITE WOMEN (1619)

To make their beachhead in Virginia more secure, members of the Virginia Company that settled Jamestown formed a subsidiary company whose purpose was to supply the settlers with wives. In 1619 ninety young women, certified as "pure and spotless," were put up at auction for 120 pounds of tobacco. All told, 140 women were sent to Virginia; by 1624 only thirty-five were still alive.

Contrary to what most history books tell us, however, these mail-order brides were not the first Englishwomen to settle in America. As early as 1608, seventy settlers had landed at Jamestown, including Mistress Forest, a gentlewoman, and Anne Burrows, her maid. Within a year Mistress Forest lost her maid to John Laydon, a laborer, and Virginia had its first Church of England wedding. America's first bride, incidentally, was fourteen years old.

THE MAYFLOWER'S END (1620)

Most of the story of the *Mayflower* and the Pilgrims is familiar—too familiar to repeat here. Part of it, however, is not familiar: Whatever happened to this historic ship? A replica of the original ship may be seen today in Plymouth Harbor, or at least what the builders believed is a replica. The replica, a gift from the English people in the 1950s, was designed after other cargo ships of the times and according to sketchy written descriptions by the Pilgrims.

Actually, there is a record of a ship called the *Mayflower* that brought more Pilgrims to America in 1629, but it was not likely the same ship because there were at least twenty *Mayflowers* of English registry in 1620. The last we hear of the original *Mayflower* was when she was lying at Rotherhithe in very poor trim, being valued at 138 pounds, with all her fittings and "one suit of worn sails." Some historians believe she was broken up that year, with some of her timber used to build a barn on a farm at Jordons in Buckinghamshire, about thirty miles outside of London.

EATING UTENSILS (1620)

Eating utensils were usually limited in early America to spoons and knives. Forks were not unknown, being brought to England from Italy during the reign of Queen Elizabeth, but they were considered an affectation in the Colonies. Consequently, the hands were often used in their place, and each individual had to be provided with water and napkins to clean them throughout the meal. Expert knife users who could balance slippery food on their knives while lifting it to their mouths were paid a certain degree of respect. Imagine eating peas with a knife! An old rhyme shows one solution:

> *I eat my peas with honey;*
> *I've done it all my life.*
> *It makes the peas taste funny,*
> *But it keeps them on my knife.*

SAINTS AND STRANGERS (1620)

Of the 104 passengers on the *Mayflower,* only forty-one were officially listed as Pilgrims—or Saints, as they called themselves. To have enough people to establish a colony, many members of the Church of England were recruited from around London—these recruits the Saints referred to as Strangers. Because of religious differences between the Pilgrims and the Strangers, there was constant bickering between the two groups and with the forty members of the crew. One of the ironies of history permitted the Strangers more lasting fame than the Pilgrims. None of the main characters of Henry Wadsworth Longfellow's *Miles Standish* were Pilgrims. Miles Standish himself was a Stranger, as were Priscilla Mullins and John Alden, a cooper hired by the Saints.

It is also interesting to note that the Mayflower Compact was written as a result of the conflict between the Pilgrims and the Strangers. By mistake, the *Mayflower* landed the colonists farther north than originally planned, the result being that their patent was invalid. The Strangers consequently questioned the authority of the Pilgrims to govern. William Bradford tells us that "mutiny threatened" until a compromise was reached in the Mayflower Compact by which it was agreed to enact "just and equall laws" for the benefit of all.

MAYFLOWER DESCENDANTS (1620)

So many people have claimed descent from the *Mayflower* passengers that it has been jokingly said that if all their claims were true, then the *Queen Elizabeth* couldn't have held all the original Pilgrims. Even presidents of the United States are not immune from making these claims, although it has been fairly well verified that at least six of our presidents can trace their ancestry back to the *Mayflower*.

John Adams and John Quincy Adams were descended from John Alden and Priscilla Mullins; Zachary Taylor from William Brewster and Isaac Allerton; Ulysses S. Grant from Richard Warren; William Howard Taft from Francis Cooke, of the Scrooby group; and Franklin D. Roosevelt from Francis Cooke, Isaac Allerton, Richard Warren, John Howland, and John Tilley.

Genealogists generally agree that about 750,000 Americans can lay claim to *Mayflower* ancestry.

COMMUNISM IN PLYMOUTH (1620)

The first settlers at Plymouth practiced communal ownership of land and goods, resulting, many historians believe, in their reluctance to work industriously for profit or gain. In 1620–21 heads of families were given a town lot and were required to build their own houses, but they worked the land in common and shared the crops. After experiencing a "Starving Time," such as was experienced in Jamestown, the company decided to change the system of land ownership. In 1624 each person in the colony was given his own private parcel of land for subsistence farming.

"This had very good success; for it made all hands very industrious, so as much more corne was planted than other waise would have bene by any means. . . . The women now wente willingly into ye field, and tooke their little-ones with them to set corne, which before would aledg weaknes,

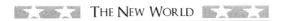

and inabilities; whom to have compelled would have bene thought great tiranie and oppression. . . . For this comunitie [communal life] was found to breed much confusion & discontent, and retard much imploymet that would have been to their benefite and comforte."

If Karl Marx ever read William Bradford's *History of the Plymouth Plantation*, it apparently had no influence on him.

A FORGIVING INDIAN (1620)

Capt. John Smith of Jamestown fame explored and mapped the New England coast in 1614 while fishing and trading with the natives. At the end of the season, Smith sailed for England with a load of goods and left his other ship, under the command of Thomas Hunt, to finish drying a load of fish for the Spanish market. As he was finishing the job, Hunt lured twenty-four friendly Native Americans on board and below deck, where he locked them up and sailed off with them to Spain. There he sold them as slaves, some of them eventually ending up in the hands of sympathetic friars, who released them.

One of the freed Indians was returned to England, and circa 1620 he sailed to New England with a fishing fleet. There he was left off at the site of Plymouth, his former home, only to find that he was the sole survivor of his tribe—all the others having perished in a plague that swept New England in 1617. A few months later when the Pilgrims landed, this Indian, who could speak English, was able to help the Englishmen survive the harshness of the New World. Known as Squanto, he had apparently forgiven the white men for his six years of forced slavery and exile.

A DUEL AT PLYMOUTH (1621)

Dueling is most commonly associated with the Andrew Jackson era. It is incongruous to picture the Pilgrims dueling, but dueling had its beginning in America in 1621. On June 18 of that year, less than a year after they landed, two Pilgrim servants by the names of Edward Leister and Edward Dotey were brought before Governor Bradford for illegally dueling. The governor issued the following decision:

"The Second Offense is the first Duel fought in New England, upon a Challengeat Single Combat with Sword and Dagger between Edward Dotey and Edward Leister, Servants of Mr. Hopkins; both being wounded, the one in the Hand, the other inn the Thigh; they are adjudg'd by the whole Company to have their Head and Feed tied together and so to lie for twenty-four hours, without Meat or Drink; which is begun to be inflicted, but within an Hour, because of their great Pains, at their own and their Master's humble request, upon Promise of better Carriage, they are Released by the Governor."

A Bounty to Settle Boston (1623)

Not ignoring the fact that the Puritans of Massachusetts Bay came to the New World because freedom of opportunity and religion were lacking in England, it is nonetheless interesting to note that the Massachusetts Bay Company felt compelled to offer a bounty for settlement—in this case, clothing. It might be argued that the clothing given to each male settler was done altruistically, but the following list would strike most observers as an inducement:

"Four pairs of shoes, four pairs of stockings, a pair of Norwich garters, four shirts, two handkerchiefs, a green cotton waist coat, a leather belt, a woolen cap, a black hat, two red knit caps, two pairs of gloves, a mandillion or cloak lined with cotton, and an extra pair of breeches."

Something must have worked because between 1630 and 1640, 198 ships arrived in Massachusetts Bay from England with 16,000 settlers.

Preparing Meat in Early America (1625)

For unknown reasons, the English and early Americans insisted that their meat be finely cut before serving. It was not until the 1620s that large pieces of meat were served at meals. One interesting sixteenth-century recipe for cooking meat reads: "Y-mynce it, smyte them on gobbets, hew them on gobbets, chop on gobbets, hew small, dyce them, skern them to dyce, kerf it to dyce, grind all to dust, smyte on peces, parcel-hem; hew small on morselyen, hack them small, cut them on culpons."

Because they lacked means of preserving meat, settlers used spices heavily. To many of our colonial forefathers, however, this was only a halfway measure—they also perfumed their meat.

Peter Minuit, the Scoundrel (1626)

Peter Minuit's purchase of Manhattan Island from the Indians for sixty guilders' (twenty-four dollars) worth of trinkets has gone down in American history as the greatest real-estate bargain of all time. Little else is known about the transaction. As the second and probably the most effective director of New Amsterdam, appointed in 1626 by the Dutch West Indian Company, Minuit was also probably its most unpopular director. As a Huguenot, he came under much criticism by the Puritanical Dutch Reform Church. The first minister, the Reverend Jonas Michaelius, angrily wrote back to Amsterdam that the governor was a liar, a rogue, a profane swearer, a fornicator, and in short, "a slippery fellow who . . . is a compound of all iniquity and wickedness." By 1632 the governor was replaced—perhaps not too wisely because he went to work for the Swedes and a few years later helped establish a competing colony on the Delaware River.

PLAYTIME AT JAMESTOWN (1627)

Within two decades after the founding of Jamestown Colony, children were playing in the homes and streets of that frontier settlement. As difficult as it may be to picture these young English children or their elders ever having time to play games, artifacts unearthed in the ruins are evidence of many typical seventeenth-century pastimes.

Excavated ivory fragments appear to be parts of dice and chessmen. Other typical games were undoubtedly tick-tack, backgammon, Irish, and cards such as trump, primero, piquet, saint, and decoy. Despite laws against it, gambling was practiced in card games such as putt (put) and a game known as cross and pile (similar to heads and tails). Men also enjoyed hunting for sport as well as meat, and there was apparently time for singing and dancing.

Fireplace tile pictures show children skating, using a yo-yo, bowling, spinning tops, fishing, rolling hoops, swinging, wrestling, skipping rope, playing skittles, sledding, boxing, and riding a hobby horse. It appears that children's games, like the children themselves, haven't really changed much in the past three centuries.

WATER OR BEER? (1630)

One of the reports most likely to discourage Europeans from going to America was that there was nothing to drink there but water. A major complaint by settlers at Jamestown was that when they asked for beer they were given water, "which is contrary to the nature of the English." The Old World belief still held strong that water was chilling, weakening, and generally deleterious because of its cooling and diluting properties.

Governor Bradford of Plymouth admitted that as good as New England water tasted, it could never take the place of beer for true-born Englishmen. Water was also a matter of social status because beer obviously cost more than water. Family members forced to drink water were marked as paupers reduced to consuming the poorest of nature's offerings.

John Hammond, the author of an early description of Maryland, declared that the best way to tell a good housewife from a bad housewife was whether the family drank beer or water—only a "sloathful and careless" wife would inflict water upon her husband. The colonists' aversion to water, incidentally, extended also to bathing in it.

AMERICA'S FIRST EXECUTIONS (1630)

America didn't have to wait long for its first execution, coming as it did the first year the English settled in Virginia. Captain George Kendall, one of the original members of the first council of the 1607 Jamestown Colony, "was put off from being on the Council and committed to prison [on board the *Discovery*]; for that it did manyfestly appear he did practize to sew discord between the President and Council." Shortly thereafter, upon seizing the ship and attempting to sail for home, abandoning the rest to the "furie of the Savages, famine, and all manner of mischiefs and inconveniencies," he was halted by cannon fire from shore and removed. For this act of mutiny, Kendall was stood up against the palisade and shot.

Even in a utopian society such as was attempted at Plymouth, man's base instincts will surface, as was also evidenced by the documented execution on September 30, 1630, of John Billington, one of the signers of the Mayflower Compact. According to a report, he was "found guilty of willful murder, by plaine and notorious evidence, and was for the same accordingly executed." He had waylaid a man with whom he had formerly quarreled and shot him, and "as it was ye first execution amongst them, so was it a matter of great sadness unto them."

FOOD CARGO ON ARBELLA (1630)

On June 12, 1630, the *Arbella*, flagship of the little fleet bearing Governor John Winthrop and his company of Puritans, dropped anchor in Massachusetts Bay. In addition to the colonists, the cargo was of significant interest. The following cargo list is from the inside cover of the manuscript journal of Governor Winthrop:

"In Arbella—forty-two tuns of beer (10,000 gallons), fourteen tuns of drinking water, two hogsheads Syder, one hogshead Vinegar, sixteen hogsheads meat, beef, pork, and beef tongues, six hundred pounds haberdyne (salt cod), one bbl. salt, one hundred pounds suet, 20,000 bisquit—15,000 brown, 5,000 white, 1 bbl. flour, thirty bu. oatmeal, eleven firkins butter, forty bu. dried pease, 1½ bu. mustard seed."

Staples for at least a year were the minimum requirement. The year 1629 saw published a "catalogue of such needful things as every planter doth or ought to provide to go to New England: as named for one man . . . eight bushel of meal, two bushel of pease, two bushel of oatmeal, one gallon of aqua-vitae, one gallon of oil, two gallons of vinegar, one firkin of butter. Spice—sugar, pepper, cloves, mace, cinnamon, nutmegs, fruit. Also there are divers other things necessary to be taken over to this plantation as books, nets, hooks and lines, cheese, bacon, kine, goats and c."

Drinking Water? Don't Believe It! (1631)

Water intended as a beverage was viewed with deep distrust by early English and colonial forefathers—and probably for logical reasons. Knowing practically nothing of germs and sanitation, they undoubtedly often became sick from drinking impure water. Consequently, beer and cider were the usual thirst quenchers at meals and throughout the day, even for small children. At meals, children were sometimes given a little wine with which to drink to the health of their elders. In one family the formula was "health to papa and mama, health to brothers and sisters, health to all my friends." As late as 1719 an eight-year-old girl from Barbados at school in Boston wrote to her father complaining that her grandmother, who was boarding her, made her drink water. The father responded, insisting that she be given beer or wine as befitted her social station.

A rumor even circulated that the early Puritan governor Winthrop drank water daily and by preference, but the rumor was not generally believed.

Tree Size in Eastern Forests (1632)

Early explorers found plant life in the Eastern forests extremely thick and of unimaginable size. Oaks were "far greater and better" than in England. White cedars, which still grow there, are today small trees but at that time rose seventy to eighty feet, whereas maples were so large that keels eighty-eight feet long could be hewn from a single trunk. White pines grew 150 feet high with trunks six feet through. Sycamores in Pennsylvania had fifteen-foot trunks, which when lying hollow on the ground could and did serve as ready-built cabins for whole families of early settlers.

The great sycamore, largest of the deciduous trees, grew so large that after age and decay had hollowed it, pioneer families seeking shelter could spend the night inside the trunks. One such tree in Ross County, Ohio, was used as a two-horse stable. In the same vicinity was a wild grapevine sixteen feet in circumference that had three branches, each eight feet around, and when finally cut into firewood made eight cords.

TEMPERANCE IN EARLY AMERICA (1634)

The first tavern opened in Boston in 1634, and within five years laws were passed to control drinking. Influenced by John Winthrop's belief that "the common custom of drinking to one another is a mere useless ceremony," the practice of drinking healths was forbidden. Like Prohibition, it could not be enforced and was repealed in 1645. Other laws were passed restricting the amount that could be consumed. Beer, cider, and so forth were restricted to one quart per customer between meals but as much as wanted at meals. Such restrictions suggest some apparently rather heavy drinking practices. Hard liquors such as sack, a strong and heady drink sold by the cask, could be consumed only at home.

Among the Dutch, those who practiced "unreasonable night-tippling" or "intemperate drinking on the Sabbath" were heavily fined. Of course, the 1656 law that made it an offense to drink on the Sabbath also made it illegal to sow, mow, bowl on the green, build, play tick-tack or cards, fish, hunt, dance, take a jaunt in a carriage or boat, or do any smithing, sawing, or bleaching. It wasn't until the eighteenth century that tavern restrictions were relaxed, allowing them to became the social centers they often are today.

A PURITAN INVENTORY (1635)

The sparse home furnishings of the early colonists is best illustrated by one of the earliest village inventories on record—that of widow Sarah Dillingham of Salem. Her inventory is quite ample for the times, and it had taken her more than fifteen years to accumulate these items:

"2 bedsteads in the parlor [many were pallet beds made up on the floor], 1 large neste of boxes, 1 small do., 1 cubert, 1 sea chest, 2 joyned chairs, 1 round table, 1 desk, 1 bande box, 1 case of bottles, 2 boxes, 1 warming pan, 2 jugs, 3 pans, 1 tray, 2 baskets, 25 saucers, 6 porringers, 2 chamber pots, 7 spoons, 1 trevett, 1 fire shovel, 1 tongs, 1 grett iron potthookes, 1 pair bellowes, 1 dark lanthorne, 1 brasse pott, 1 morter, 1 iron pott, 1 frying pan, 2 kettles, 2 skillets, 1 iron ladle, 1 chest, 2 hoes, 1 hatchet, 1 scythe."

HARVARD UNIVERSITY (1636)

John Harvard did *not* found Harvard University, as is commonly believed. The Puritans founded it collectively in 1636 with a public grant of four hundred pounds for the purpose of training young ministers of the gospel. The university, however, honors the name of John Harvard, a butcher's son and a graduate from Cambridge University. He died in 1638 of tuberculosis, bequeathing a modest sum of money along with four hundred books—his entire library—to the institution. Little did young Harvard dream of the fame to be attached to his name for this modest act of charity. And even less could he have dreamed that his little library of four hundred books would one day increase to more than eight million.

A NATION DESTROYED (1637)

As a result of the killing of an Indian trader named John Oldham by the Pequots in 1636, the Massachusetts Colony sent an expeditionary force into Pequot country to punish the Indians. Thus began a war in which the English colonists set out to exterminate the Pequot nation. In one battle alone they killed more than seven hundred men, women, and children, capturing only seven and allowing only seven to escape. When the war ended in 1637, all surviving Pequots were either enslaved by the English colonists or absorbed by other Indian tribes.

And who was John Oldham, whose death prompted all of New England to go to war? He had immigrated to Plymouth in 1623, but the following year he was banished from that colony for failing to conform to the religious laws of the colony. He was English, however, and at the time that fact justified the destruction of an entire Indian nation.

AN EARLY COLONIAL DRAFT (1637)

Contrary to the beliefs of many people today, conscription is a well-established American institution, dating back almost three and a half centuries. In the war against the Pequot Indians, the Massachusetts Bay legislature enacted on April 18, 1637, draft legislation calling for 160 men from the towns of Massachusetts "according to the portion underwritten"—the quotas ranging from twenty-six for Boston; eighteen for Salem; seventeen for Ipswich; and three for Marblehead.

About this same time, Connecticut authorities conscripted an "army" of ninety men, which they placed under the command of Capt. John Mason. It was this Connecticut army that won the first "major" war in American history—the Pequot War—when they attacked and massacred more than seven hundred Pequots near the Mystic River, not only ending the war but also effectively destroying the Pequots as an Indian tribe. This massacre become known in American history as the Great Swamp Fight, but, of course, Native Americans didn't write the history books.

EARTHQUAKE AT PLYMOUTH (1638)

With earthquakes being most common to the West Coast of North America, it is difficult to associate them with early eastern America. Such is the case, however, as revealed in William Bradford's *History of the Plymouth Plantation*. Bradford describes an earthquake occurring on Friday, June 1, 1638, at 2 P.M. one day at Plymouth:

"However, it was very terrible for ye time; and as ye men were set talking in ye house, some women and others were without ye doors, and ye earth shook with ye violence as they could not stand without catching hold of ye posts and pails stood next them, but ye violence lasted not long. And about halfe an hower, or less, came an other noyse & shaking, but neither so loud nor strong as ye former, but quickly passed over, and so it ceased."

Although this was the first earthquake recorded in what would become the United States, it apparently prompted several Indians to describe to Roger Williams an earthquake that occurred in 1558 at Providence. Neither of these quakes or a more famous quake in 1663 did much damage, simply because the population was sparse, and the homes were not as prone to earthquake damage as modern homes.

THE LOG CABIN (1638)

The log cabin, contrary to the belief of many, was not the structure erected by the early English settlers. It was not until around 1638 that the Finns and the Swedes introduced it in New Sweden, on the banks of the Delaware River. The French in Canada were building log cabins thirty years before this time, but they had no influence on the English settlers. By the Delaware River method, logs were shaped and notched on both sides, and the interstices were "chinked" with a mixture of wood chips, clay and moss. The roof was usually constructed of bark. This basic design was known among Swedish and Norwegian Vikings as far back as A.D. 800. Because of the availability of materials, ease of construction, and strength against attack, the log cabin became the most common type of house throughout frontier America, except in the Great Plains where there were no trees.

There is today on Cape Ann a log house called the Old Witch House with no daubing at all—its eight-inch logs squared so well that a knife cannot be slid between them. After three hundred years it is still so sound that it could serve as a defense against even modern weapons.

A FREE MAN'S OATH (1639)

The following "Oath of a Free-Man" was the first printed piece produced in colonial America. Stephen Daye, the printer, set up the first printing press in the English Colonies in Cambridge, Massachusetts, in 1639.

"I (A.B.) being by God's providence, an Inhabitant, and Freeman, within the Jurisdiction of this Commonwealth; do freely acknowledge my self to be subject by the Government thereof: And therefore do here swear by the great and dreadful Name of the Ever-living God, that I will be true and faithfull to the same, and will accordingly yield assistance & support thereunto, with my person and estate as in equity I am bound; and will also truly endeavour to maintain and preserve all the liberties and priviledges thereof, submitting my self to the wholesome Lawes and Order made and established by the same. And further, that I will not plot or practice any evil against it, or consent to any that shall do so; but will timely discover and reveal the same to lawfull Authority now here established, for the speedy preventing thereof.

"Moreover, I doe solemnly bind my self in the [s]ight of God, that when I shall be called to give my voyce touching any such matter of this State, in whichFreemen are to deal, I will give my vote and suffrage as I shall judge in mine own conscience may best conduce and tend to the publik weal [will] of the body, without respect of persons, or favour of any man. So help me God in the Lord Jesus Christ."

THE FIRST "PUBLIC" SCHOOLS (1639)

Public schools are better defined by public support than by universal attendance. As such, public schools in this country go back much further than is commonly believed. On May 20, 1639, the town of Dorchester, Massachusetts, established by vote direct taxation of the residents for the support of education:

"It is ordered the 20th of May 1639, that there shall be a rent of twenty pounds a year forever imposed upon Tomson's Island to be paid by every person that hath property in the said island according to the proportion that any such person shall from time to time enjoy and posses there."

Eight years later, the colony of Massachusetts passed a law requiring "every township in this jurisdiction, after the Lord hath increased them to the number of fifty householders, shall then forthwith appoint one within their town to teach all such children as shall resort him to write and read, whose wages shall be paid either by the parents or masters of such children, or by the inhabitants in general," which is what the town of Dorchester had done already.

HARVARD GETS A NEW PRESIDENT (1640)

Firing a university president because of college violence was not unique to the 1970s. It happened with Harvard's first president, Nathaniel Eaton, but in his case it was not the students who were violent. He was asked to resign for beating up one of his assistants with a club "big enough to have killed a horse." In addition to this tendency to harsh discipline, which might very well be considered an asset among college administrators today, his wife confessed that the students had received bad food and were even forced to make their own beds.

Under the new president chosen in 1640, Harvard prospered, and its first graduating class of nine young men departed Harvard in 1642.

"COLORED" HOUSES (1640)

Nearly all houses in colonial America were built of wood, especially in early New England. The reason is obvious: availability of lumber. But few houses were painted. This would have been contrary to the simplicity of Puritan or Protestant religious philosophy. Consequently, the streets had a brownish, drab appearance that was relieved somewhat by the gaily colored tavern signs or shop signs. The first painted homes were called "colored" homes and were looked upon as curiosities. Neighbors considered the owners to be putting on airs.

The Chesapeake area seems to be the section of English America where houses were first painted—with lime whitewash to counteract mildew. In New England "colored" houses appeared first in Rhode Island toward the end of the 1700s. There red, yellow, and gray-blue were as predominant as white.

WORD MEANINGS CHANGE (1641)

The Bill of Rights forbids cruel and unusual punishment. Most North Americans today have an idea of what that means—inhumane treatment, such as torture. Torture, however, has not always been considered inhumane, at least not by the Puritans. In the Massachusetts Body of Liberties, 1641, we find this right:

"No man shall be forced by torture to confess any crime against himself nor any other *unless* it be in some capital case, where he is first fully convicted by clear and sufficient evidence to be guilty, after which, if the cause be of that nature, that it is very apparent there be other conspirators or confiderates with him, *then he may be tortured, yet not with such tortures as be barbarous and inhumane*" (emphasis added). We are certainly left wondering what humane torture would be.

RELIGIOUS TOLERATION IN MARYLAND (1641)

Despite the fact that all of the leaders of the colony of Maryland were Catholic and the servants and the small landowners were Protestant, toleration was, for the most part, strictly enforced. Just how far religious toleration extended is indicated by an event that occurred at St. Mary's in 1641.

After mass was celebrated in the only church in town, the Catholic chapel, the Protestant servants and farmers were permitted to read the Book of Common Prayer there for their own service. In a moment of intolerance, prominent Catholic Thomas Gerrard took away the prayer books and locked the Protestants out of the building. For this rash act, a jury composed predominantly of his fellow Catholics fined him 500 pounds of tobacco. The fine was set aside for the support of a Protestant minister, when one became available.

OFFENSIVE AND DEFENSIVE WARS (1641)

The issue of sending citizens off on wars of offense did not arise for the first time over the Vietnam conflict. The Massachusetts Body of Liberties dealt with this same question in 1641 and certainly more forthrightly than is the custom today. Right number 7 stated:

"No man shall be compelled to go out of the limits of this plantation upon any offensive wars which this Commonwealth or any of our friends or confederates shall voluntarily undertake. But only upon such vindication and defensive wars in our own behalf or the behalf of the counsel and consent of a Court General, or by authority derived from the same."

Unfortunately, the inclusion of the word "vindication," suggesting revenge or punishment, makes possible almost any kind of war and totally negates any meaning the right might have had.

TREASON IN RHODE ISLAND (1642)

In the early 1640s, during a dispute between Massachusetts Bay and the towns of Rhode Island, four men from the Rhode Island plantations offered their land and allegiance to the Bay Colony. One of these four men even secretly received an unexplained fee from the Massachusetts Court—believed by later historians to be a payment for helping turn the Providence Colony over to its northern neighbor. This was probably one of the first, if not *the* first instance of colonial treason. This is not so unusual, but perhaps the man's name is—Benedict Arnold, the great-grandfather of the Revolutionary War traitor.

PURITAN CHRISTMAS (1644)

In 1644 Christmas was officially abolished by an act of the English Parliament, controlled by Puritans. New Englanders made it a point to work on Christmas, just as they ostentatiously ate meat on Fridays. In fact, in 1640 Massachusetts imposed a fine of five shillings upon anyone who observed Christmas by fasting, feasting, or refusing to work. To do otherwise would jeopardize chances of salvation. On Christmas Day 1621, Governor William Bradford confiscated the "implements" of some servants who took the day off for entertainment, telling them that if it was against their consciences to work on Christmas, it was against his to let them make merry. To be at labor, a Judge Samuel Sewall once spent Christmas Day rearranging the caskets in the family vault.

Is it any wonder the Puritans disliked the unpopular Gov. Edmund Andros. Only five days after taking over as governor in 1686, he mocked the Puritans' refusal to celebrate Christmas, which to them smacked of popery, by attending church services twice on that day. Thus it was that in some parts of rural New England, Christmas remained unobserved until after the Civil War.

Never on a Sunday (1645)

Pilgrims commonly believed that a child was always born on the same day of the week that it was conceived, which led to many embarrassments for those whose children happened to be born on Sunday. Many New England ministers even refused to baptize infants born on Sunday because of their parents' sin of not keeping the Sabbath holy on a day nine months previous.

One Pilgrim minister seemed to take great delight in orating on the subject from his pulpit—that is, until his wife presented him with twins on the Sabbath immediately after the morning sermon. Unfortunately, historical records are mute as to the explanation he offered his congregation, but we can be quite sure his future sermons dealt with other topics.

Rules for Praying Indians (1646)

Only sixteen years after the Puritans settled Massachusetts Bay, they had apparently converted enough Indians to set down rules for their conduct, which they did, at Concord, Massachusetts, in November 1646. Following are excerpts taken from Vaugh's *New England Frontier*.

- There shall be no more Powwowing amongst the Indians. And if any shall hereafter Powwow, both he that shall Powwow, & he that shall procure him to Powwow, shall pay 20s apiece.
- They desire that no Indian hereafter shall have any more but one wife. That when Indians doe wrong one to another, they may be lyable to censure by fine or the like, as the English

are. That they pay their debts to the English.

- That they doe observe the Lords-Day, and whosoever shall prophane it shall pay 20s. That there shall not be allowance to pick lice, as formerly, and eate them, and whosoever shall offend in this case shall pay for every louse a penny.
- Whosoever shall play at their former games shall pay 10s.
- Whosoever shall commit adultry shall be put to death.
- They shall not disguise themselves . . . nor shall they keep a great noyse by howling.
- No Indian shall come into any English mans house except he first knock.

BOSTON GROWS UP (1648)

As the first half-century of life in the English Colonies drew to a close, Massachusetts boasted the largest town of any of the Colonies. Although Boston was a far cry from the sophisticated city it was destined to become, it had nevertheless come of age by 1648.

Hogs were forbidden to roam the streets without being rung and yoked; goats were banished from the town completely. A town ordinance forbade the playing of ball in the streets by both men and boys. Privies had to be twenty feet back from the highway, and when stables were cleaned, the manure could no longer be pitched into the street. An additional bit of legislation in this early American drive against pollution forced butchers to find some place other than the dock to throw their "stinking garbage . . . that such loathsome smells might be avoyded." The town where "Cabots talk only to the Lowells and Lowells talk only to God" had indeed grown up.

INDIANS ASK FOR MERCY FOR WHITES (1650)

Five French officers ambushed an Iroquois hunter at Pointe Claire in Lac St. Louis in 1650 and took his moose skins after killing him. The crime was discovered through identifying marks on the skins, and the five officers were brought before a military council for trial. Upon being found guilty, all five were led out to be shot. Friends of the slain Indian witnessing this sample of justice were astonished and actually pleaded for mercy for four of the whites. They felt that justice would be served through the death of only one of the men, but the authorities insisted that all five deserved death. The Indians thereupon redoubled their pleas for

mercy, even offering presents to the French if they would release four of the murderers—all to no avail. All five were executed.

NAKED ARMS FORBIDDEN (1650)

During the first century of colonization, all of the Colonies adopted laws concerning the quality and kind of clothing that could be worn by people of different classes. These laws had a twofold purpose: to prevent vain expenditures on finery and to preserve the necessary distinctions between the social classes. In Boston there were laws to prevent the wearing of silver, gold, silk laces, ruffs, girdles, and beaver hats. Being fond of bright colors, Puritans took to making slashes in their sleeves to allow the bright colors of their undergarments to show. The Massachusetts General Court found it necessary to pass laws limiting the people to one slash in each sleeve and to provide that "no garment shall be made with short sleeves, whereby the nakedness of the arms may bee discovered." In 1651 the court decreed that those who affected a style of dress above their station should be punished. One woman, hauled into court for overdressing, went free after she proved that her husband was making two hundred pounds.

THE "GENTLE" PURITANS (1650)

The list of Puritan capital offenses, though less lengthy than the list in Europe, would shock the average twentieth-century American. In the mid-1600s, John Cotton drew up the following list of capital offenses for his colony:

1. Blasphemy
2. Idolatry
3. Witchcraft
4. Consulters with witches
5. Heresy
6. Worship God in graven image
7. Willful perjury
8. Profaning the Lord's Day
9. Treason
10. Reviling of magistrate
11. Rebellion, sedition, or insurrection
12. Rebellious children
13. Murder

14. Adultery
15. Incest
16. Sodomy
17. Buggery
18. Pollution of a woman known to be in her flowers
19. Whoredom
20. Man-stealing

This was not unusual in the Colonies. The Quakers, known for their humanitarianism, at one time labored under the threat of death for committing fourteen offenses.

PATERNALISM VS. PRIVACY (1650)

Domestic privacy or the idea that a man's home is his castle was almost unknown in seventeenth-century New England. Certain musical instruments were forbidden in the home, diet was regulated by law, and unmarried persons, regardless of age, were forbidden to live alone or in pairs. Entertaining strangers or even relatives from out of town was sometimes considered a serious offense. Tithing men who kept order in the meetinghouses by expelling stray dogs, waking those who dozed, and punishing unruly children also were put in charge of groups of ten families—checking on how each family spent its time and seeing that they got to church. They were also charged with inspecting taverns, alerting selectmen as to any disorderly conduct, including idleness, and warning undesirables to leave town.

Whether most colonists considered all of this an invasion of privacy or necessary paternalism is not readily known, but it is doubtful that they were as concerned with privacy as their twenty-first century counterparts.

TOBACCO AS MEDICINE (1650)

John Josselyn expressed an opinion commonly held in the Colonies concerning the benefits of tobacco:

"The vertues of Tobacco are thes, it helps digestion, the Grout, the Tooth-Ace, prevents infection by scents, it heats the cold and cools them that sweat, feedeth the hungry, spent spirites restoreth, purgeth the stomach, killeth nits and lice; the juice of the green leaf healeth green wounds, although poysoned; the Syrup for many diseases, the smoak for the Phthisick, cough of the lungs, moist cause, good for all bodies cold and moist taken upon a full stomack it precipitates digestion, immoderately taken it dryeth the body, enflameth the bloud, hurteth the brain, weakens the eyes and the sinews." Such claims were not really necessary. It seems that everyone—old and young, rich and poor—smoked tobacco, usually in long clay pipes.

JUST A SIMPLE WEDDING (1650)

The earliest colonial weddings were performed by almost any civil officer, even captains of militia, but ministers, by law, were prohibited from performing marriage rites. The reason for such a law is not clear to historians, but they believe that it stemmed from the Puritan revolt against the gorgeous flummery of the established Church in England.

The ceremony itself was the essence of simplicity in keeping with Puritan philosophy, consisting primarily of prayer. Presents were few; only relatives were expected to give them. But there were no limits to the food and drinks served after the ceremony. A simple but delightful conclusion to the wedding activities was the "stealing of the bride," with the husband searching frantically for his new wife, hidden usually not far away.

After the marriage, it was the custom for the newly married couple to celebrate for one full season of the moon (about one month), during which they drank mead, a liquor made from honey. From this original "honey month" arose the delightful phrase and custom of the honeymoon.

BILLY GRAHAMS OF YESTERYEAR (1650)

Modern ministers who would like to add spice to their sermons should take a lesson from their Puritan forebears, who were anything but the cold, aloof men of God most commonly pictured.

One minister who had been having trouble with some unruly singers in the choir chose a most appropriate hymn the following Sunday. Scowling at the choir, he boomed out the hymn beginning, "And are you wretches yet alive and do you yet rebel?" In a similar situation to a choir that wouldn't cooperate with the parson began a hymn, "Let those refuse to sing who never knew our God."

A visiting clergyman, preaching in a shabby church in a barren and stony parish, sneeringly read out the beginning of the next hymn: "Lord, what a wretched land this is, that yields us no supplies!" His intent was frustrated, however, when the choirmaster announced in a loud voice the tune to which the hymn was to be sung, "Northfield," the name of the minister's own home and parish.

In York in 1700, when the Reverend Mr. Moody noted a finely dressed young man coming in during prayer, he at once exclaimed, "And O Lord! We pray Thee, cure Ned Ingraham of that ungodly strut." The next classic example belongs to the Reverend Mr. Miles, who, in praying for rain, said, "O Lord, Thou knowest we do not want Thee to send us a rain which shall pour down in fury and swell our streams and carry away our hay-cocks, fences, and bridges; but, Lord, we want it to drizzle-drossle, drizzle-drozzle, for about a week, Amen."

THE PINE TREE SHILLING (1652)

One of the first steps toward a uniform legacy currency in the early Colonies was the Pine Tree shilling. In 1652 the Massachusetts General Court gave Mr. John Hull, father-in-law of the well-known Judge Samuel Sewall, a thirty-five-year contract to mint the coins, for which he was to receive fifteen pence for every twenty shillings he turned out—no limit stipulated. Needless to say, it was a fantastic bargain for Hull, and the court later tried several times to get out of the contract, but to no avail. An indication of how well Hull, who lived to a ripe old age, fared under this contract was his wedding gift to his daughter—her weight in Pine Tree shillings.

A CURIOUS COLONIAL TABLE (1654)

Trenchers, or hollowed-out wooden plates, were common in early America—two people often eating from one trencher. Alice Morse Earle, in her charming book *Home Life in Colonial Days,* tells of an interesting old table board she once saw. In the early New England days, tables did not have legs but rested instead on trestles (similar to modern sawhorses) so that they literally were table-boards, as they were called. Earle saw one made of six-inch oak with the trenchers scooped out around the edge. After each meal the board was lifted off the trestles, washed and dried, and laid back down, ready for the next meal.

PURITAN EQUALITY (1653)

Yankee Puritans, whose ideal was "a church without a bishop, and a state without a king," evidently had a genius for democracy. All people—men, women, children, Indians, servants, and slaves—were admitted to their meetinghouses and in the early days were compelled to attend its services. Once inside, however, distinctions among them were strictly enforced. In early structures, especially the larger ones, there was a small upper gallery, close to the eaves, where any man with red or black skin was obligated to worship the Lord in safe isolation from the white congregation below. Even the rest of the seating gave evidence of aristocratic feelings, "foreseats" being reserved for the best. A committed deacon periodically assigned all the members seats on the basis of age, wealth, birth, learning, and public service, but not necessarily in that order.

Alice Morse Earle notes, "We can imagine the deacons loosening their tongues over the tavern flip and punch and arguing confidentially over the standing, the wealth, and the temper of the various parties to be seated." Not only were pews in church assigned by order of social ranking, but also students in college were listed in the catalog and seated at commons in the order of their rank. Obviously, colleges have not always been a chief agency of democracy.

"HANG THE BOOKS!" (1654)

Being rare, books in colonial America were highly cherished possessions—but not all books. That greatest of all civilized crimes, book burning, was not unknown to our ancestors. They did add a little twist to the public burnings, however. In 1654 the public hangman in Boston marketplace burned the writings of two self-proclaimed prophets, John Reeves and Ludowick Muggleton, and two years later some Quaker books were destroyed in the same manner. In 1707 a "libel on the Governor" did not warrant quite such a final fate; instead, it was hanged by the hangman. Twenty-one years before the Revolutionary War, the authorities were still burning books—*The Monster of Monsters,* an attack on the Massachusetts Court, suffering that fate in King Street. However, the authorities outdid themselves the following year in Connecticut. There an offending publication was sentenced to be "publickly whipt according to Moses Law with forty stripes save one, then Burnt." That must have hurt!

BUT NO SEAT BELTS! (1655)

Only thirty-five years after the Pilgrims landed at Plymouth, Boston had a speed law, possibly the first in America. The town records states:

"Whereas greatt inconveniences may accrew to the towne and inhabitants thereof, especially children, by persons irregular riding through the streetes of that towne, and galloping. It is therefore ordered that if any person shall bee seene to gallop through any streete of the town after this day, except upon dayes of military exercise, or any extraordinary case require, every such person shall pay two shillings, six pence . . . and it shall bee lawful for any person to make stop of such horse or rider till the sayd fine be paid."

ASSAULTS ON INDIANS (1655)

Justice for the American Indian was extremely tardy in its arrival, but at times the early colonists made the attempt. Colonial records reveal several cases of assaults on Native Americans by whites, often resulting in rather stiff punishment for the colonists. Plymouth authorities in 1655 fined and stocked one of their colonists for attempting to collect a debt from a native by seizing a child and goods as collateral. A more interesting case in 1667 involved the "barbarous and inhuman act" of digging up the skull of a Sagamore and carrying it about on a pole. For this a Bay Colony man was fined, stocked, imprisoned, and required to repair the grave and rebuild its stone marker. Only eighteen years after the landing of the Pilgrims, three of their number were hanged in Plymouth for the murder of a Narragansett youth. This act of justice, commented Gov. William Bradford, "gave them all and the countrie good satisfaction."

"WARNING OUT" (1655)

In contrast to the southern Colonies, which became noted for hospitality extended to total strangers, the New England Colonies set up laws limiting the stay and conduct of visitors in a community. The local sheriff called upon visitors to determine their business and then warned them of the necessity of conducting themselves in an industrious, godly, and sober manner or face expulsion. This was known as a "warning out."

Once, a widow in Dorchester was not permitted to entertain her son-in-law from another town. In another instance, a woman was fined for keeping her daughter as a guest for more than a week. In the latter case the daughter could not return to her own home because of bad weather.

Even tavern keepers were required to submit a stranger's name to the selectmen, who, if they determined the stranger might be detrimental to the community, could warn him out of town. Two hundred years later in the Wild West, "detrimental" meant a possible physical threat posed by a stranger in town. In early America, however, the most likely danger was a ne'er-do-well ending up on the town welfare roles.

GIANT COLONIAL SEAFOOD (1656)

The giant fish story is an American pastime, but what about other types of seafood? Have there been giants there also? The Dutch traveler Adriaen Van der Donck in 1656 referred to five- and six-foot-long patriarchal lobsters caught in New York Bay. William Eddis, in his *Letters from America* in 1792, verifies this but claims the incessant cannonading during the Revolution drove them all away from the coast, and none was caught after the war. There were also reports from Virginia of crabs large enough to furnish a meal for four men, and there were countless reports of giant oysters along the American coast. Van der Donck in 1656 makes mention of foot-long oysters. Stratchey, in his *Historie of Travaile* into Virginia, says he saw oysters thirteen inches across. It was seafood such as this that saved the starving Jamestown colonists in 1609.

Yes, and the fish were included in these reports also. Sir Thomas Dale, the Virginia governor, caught five thousand sturgeons in one cast of a seine. Some of the early colonists reported sturgeon twelve feet long.

THE BLUE LAWS (1656)

The so-called blue laws of New England received their first widespread notoriety in a historically inaccurate book by the Reverend Samuel Peters, *A General History of Connecticut, by a Gentleman of the Province,* published in 1781. These laws, an elaboration of "Moses his Judicialls," were enacted by the Saints of New Haven in 1656. Although Peters fabricated some laws that never existed, they were nevertheless exceedingly harsh, proscribing the death penalty for blasphemy, idolatry, witchcraft, murder, false worship, incest, adultery, sodomy, bestiality, man-stealing, giving false witness, reviling the magistrates, and the cursing or smiting of parents by children more than sixteen years of age.

Bibliolatry could scarcely be carried further, even by reference to Deuteronomy. The New Jersey Presbyterians, however, went just as far in their Calvinism. In 1661 they passed a law that provided that any "sonne or daughter above and of sixteen years not being distracted (demented) who shall beate or curse their father or mother shall be put to death without mercy."

History has not revealed any children who suffered the death penalty for striking or cursing their parents, but New England records do indicate such instances as a rebellious child being forced to work for his father as a prisoner with a lock on his leg.

A PERSISTENT MARTYR (1657)

In the early days of Quakerism in America, adherents seemed to delight in traveling to Massachusetts, there to preach and subsequently suffer punishment under the harsh Puritan laws so that they might receive their martyr's crown. One of the most persistent of these seekers was Christopher Holder, the "valiant apostle of New England Quakerism," who traveled to Salem in 1657 to preach and, as he expected, be seized by the authorities. Because he had been expelled once before, this time he was taken to Boston to be punished. He and a fellow Quaker were given thirty lashes with a three-cord knotted whip and then confined to a bare cell for three days and nights without bedding, food, or water.

Next they were imprisoned during nine weeks of a New England winter without comfort of fire, during which time they were whipped twice each week. Holder survived this ordeal but apparently didn't feel the crown was yet his. He returned to Massachusetts the following year, where authorities obliged him by cutting off one of his ears. This apparently satisfied him: there is no record of him returning.

A TYPICAL INDENTURE (1659)

There were, of course, many variations in the terms of servant indentures, but one made in 1659 between Edward Rowzie, a Virginia planter, and Bartholomew Clarke of Canterbury, England, was probably typical. For a term of four years (a more common indenture might be a little longer), Clarke agreed to work for Rowzie, to keep his secrets, and to obey his just and lawful commands: "Fornication he shall not commit, nor contract matrimony with any woman . . . at cards, dice or any unlawful games he shall not play." His master also agreed to teach his servant the "mystery, art, and occupation of a planter" and to supply "competent meat, drink, apparel, washing, lodging with all other things fitting to his degree and in the end thereof, fifty acres of land to be laid out for him, and all other things which according to the custom of the country is or ought to be done."

The "all other things" were understood to be two outfits of simple clothing and enough grain to support him for a year. It was possible for many servants to build up their estates by raising cattle, tobacco, and other goods on land owned by their masters. Thus, many servants completed their service as well-to-do planters.

SALEM MINISTER QUARTERED (1660)

Upon the expulsion of Roger Williams from Massachusetts Bay, his position as minister in Salem was filled by Hugh Peter. Mr. Peter is well known in American history for his contributions to the survival of the New England Puritan colony, being one of the most influential colonial leaders in soliciting favors from Parliament for Massachusetts. He was also one of the founders of Harvard University. Unfortunately for him, he decided to return to England to participate in the trial and execution of Charles I.

In 1660, after Charles II was put on the throne, Peter was arrested. On October 16 he was taken to Charing Cross, London, and hanged until he choked. Cut down while still alive, his private members were cut off, he was sliced open, his entrails and heart were "drawn" out and held before his eyes before being thrown into the fire, his head was cut off and set on London Bridge, his body was quartered and hung at the gates of the city—all as a moral lesson to others who might consider treason against His Majesty. Mr. Peter should have stayed in Salem.

BEGINNING OF SLAVERY (1661)

The first blacks brought to America, beginning in 1619 in Jamestown, Virginia, were not slaves in the modern sense of the word. The term *slave* was used indiscriminately at that time to refer to various persons of servant or inferior status. They were treated as indentured servants, and after several years they were given their freedom. There is on record at least one African-American who bought and held in servitude a white European. Because the need for labor remained high in America, however, many planters started considering the possibility of keeping blacks in perpetual bondage for the following reasons: They were physically stronger than

Indians, heretofore used as slaves; they were inexpensive; they could not easily escape and blend into the population; they were unprotected by any strong government; and finally, the supply seemed limitless.

Thus, in 1661 the state of Maryland, pressured by white planters, enacted a law that stated, "All Negroes and other slaves shall serve Durante Vita" (for life). Within the next ten years, such laws became universal in the colonies, or at least the practice did. Two hundred years later, the nation had to resort to a major war to undo laws like the act of the Maryland legislature.

THEY NEEDED WARMING WORDS (1662)

The ability of the Puritans to withstand the winter cold of their meeting-houses has long been a matter of amazement among their descendants. Women were permitted the use of foot warmers, but the men had to suffer through four-hour sermons while water froze in the baptismal basin, bread froze on the communion plate, and the ministers expounded in their heavy coats and gloves. No wonder the Puritans viewed with mixed emotions the warning words of that heated level described in Wigglesworth's famous poem of 1662, "The Day of Doom":

> God's fierce ire kindleth the fire,
> And vengeance feeds the flame—
> With piles of wood and brimstone flood,
> That none can quench the same.

Somehow, these dire warnings may not have seemed as threatening in the cold New England meetinghouses as the ministers intended.

THE OLDEST PROFESSION (1670)

An unusual but revealing side of colonial life is revealed by the extent of prostitution in early America—most of the professionals being located in Northern cities. It was not that Southerners were more moral, but there was such an abundant supply of female slaves who furnished a chattel type of prostitution with which white women couldn't compete. The "soiled doves" did all right in the North, however, Boston being well-supplied as early as 1670. The early founders of Philadelphia lived in riverbank half-cellars that soon became the red light district.

New York, however, probably offered the largest selection to adventure-seeking young men. By the time of the American Revolution,

New York was not only a hotbed of Toryism but also a hotbed of prostitution. Roughly 2 percent of the population were members of the world's oldest profession. Five hundred strong, most of them resided in an area known as Holy Ground because Trinity Church owned it.

SPIRITING (1670)

The scarcity of free labor in the English Colonies led the Founding Fathers to resort to other methods of acquiring the necessary workers. The most common kind was the voluntarily bound or indentured servants. In addition, there were slaves, insolvent debtors, paupers, and criminals who were sentenced to long terms of service in America in lieu of prison sentences in England.

Another unfortunate class was made up of those who had been kidnapped in the British Isles and sold to planters in the Colonies. The chief victims were children, often lured into the hands of their kidnappers by sweets and other inducements. This practice became prevalent during the reign of Charles II and was known as spiriting. Most of the spiriting took place in London and Bristol; at one time the ladies of the court and the mayor of Bristol were suspected of sharing the profits of this dirty business. E. Channing, in his *History of the United States,* says that "in 1670 as many as ten thousand persons were spirited from England in one year." Spiriting was obviously a booming profession. One practitioner actually kidnapped (kid-nabbed) five hundred persons in one year.

TRIAL BY JURY? (1670)

The colonial leader who granted so much freedom in his colony in America had good reason: he had suffered so much from lack of it in England. Upon finding his meeting hall closed by authorities in August 1670, William Penn, along with associate William Meade, preached in an English street. They were soon hauled into court for "disturbance of the peace." Trial by jury was guaranteed them, but when jury members returned a verdict of not guilty, they were threatened with fines, torture, and being "locked up without Meat, Drink, Fire, and Tobacco" until they returned with a verdict that satisfied the court. When the defiant jury returned with the same verdict for the fifth time, each juryman was fined forty marks and imprisoned, along with the defendants, until they paid the fine.

William Penn never forgot this lesson in English "justice," and when he founded Pennsylvania he determined that such justice would not exist in his colony.

NO "WANTON DALLYANCES" (1670)

The Sabbath in colonial New England, beginning on Saturday night and ending at sundown on Sunday, was made so sacrosanct that no labor whatsoever was permitted, including cooking, cleaning house, making beds, traveling, enjoying recreation, participating in "wanton dallyances," or even engaging in "unnecessary and unseasonable walking in the streets and fields." A couple in New London, Connecticut—John Lewis and Sarah Chapman—were charged in court with "sitting together on the Lord's Day, under an apple tree in Goodman Chapman's Orchard." Captain Kemble of Boston was condemned to sit two hours in the stocks for "lewd and unseemly behavior." His offense consisted of kissing his wife in public on the Sabbath after he had returned to Boston from a three-year sea voyage.

A man who had fallen into the water and absented himself from church to dry his only suit of clothes was found guilty and "publicly whipped." Other equally drastic laws prohibited the people from walking, driving, or riding horseback on Sunday, unless they went to church or to the cemetery. George Washington, as a newly elected president, was once stopped in Connecticut while on his way to church and asked for his license to travel upon the Lord's day.

FIRST MAIL SERVICE (1673)

Contrary to popular belief, it was not Benjamin Franklin who organized or founded the American Postal Service. He should be given credit, however, for putting it on a regular and trustworthy basis. The first mail service in the Colonies actually started before Franklin was born.

It began, appropriately enough, on January 1, 1673, with regular service between New York and Boston. The postman carried on his first trip two portmanteaus filled with letters and parcels, stopping once in Hartford to change horses. He delivered his mail to an inn in Boston where citizens could look over the mail and pay for those letters addressed to them. (For the first several years of mail delivery, it was the recipient, not the sender, who paid the postage, which was not cheap.)

The ground trip for "the post" from New York to Boston took about one month. Only nineteen years after the Pilgrims landed, the home of Richard Fairbanks was set aside by the Massachusetts authorities as a post office for the deposit of all mail "brought from beyond the seas, or . . . to be sent thither." Fairbanks was paid a penny for the transmission of each letter.

CHILDREN'S NAMES (1674)

Choosing a child's name appeared to pose a special problem for the colonial Americans—finding names that were significant or appropriate for certain conditions. Most names seemed to be chosen for the glory of God or with thought and hopes for the child's future.

Some of the most common names were Abigail ("father's joy"), Hannah ("grace"), and Zurishaddai ("the Almighty is my rock"). Others were Comfort, Deliverance, Temperance, Peace, Hope, Patience, Charity, Faith, Love, Submit, Endurance, Silence, Joy, Receive, Hoped For, and so forth. Some of the children of Roger Clap's large family were Experience, Waitstill, Preserved, Hopestill, Wait, Thanks, Desire, Unite, and Supply. One colonist in Narragansett had fifteen children named Parvis, Picus, Piersus, Prisemus, Polybius, Lois, Lettice, Avis, Anstice, Eunice, Mary, John, Elizabeth, Ruth, and Freelove.

THE SPORT OF "KINGS" (1674)

Horseracing, the sport of kings, is today limited in this country by the simple law of economics. Such was not always the case. Laws were enacted in the seventeenth century to ensure that the sport would be limited to gentlemen. In 1674 the York County court in Virginia ordered: "James Bullocke, a Taylor, having made a race for his mare to runn w'th a horse belonging to Mr. Mathew Slader for twoe thousand pounds of tobacco and caske, it being contrary to the Law for a Labourer to make a race, being a sport only for Gentlemen, is fined for the same one hundred pounds of tobacco and caske."

Seventeen years later in the same state, when Gov. Francis Nicholson declared an annual field day and offered prizes, he specifically limited entrees to "the better sort of Virginians only."

The New York colony seemed more democratic. Richard Nichols, the first English governor of New York, established the first regularly run horse race in America at Hempstead Plains, Long Island, in 1665. He gave a cup to the owner of the fastest horse, whoever owned it, for the main purpose of "the bettering of the breed of horses, which through neglect has been impaired."

WIGS AND KING PHILIP'S WAR (1676)

Despite the "Godly Laws" of the Puritans and Calvinists against the wearing of wigs, many individualists adopted the custom in the 1600s, bringing down upon their powdered heads thunder from the New England pulpits. Many people attributed the 1676–77 Indian uprising led by Metacom—a son of Massasoit who was nicknamed King Philip by the British—to the Lord's displeasure upon seeing His people's ill content with the hair He had given them. By the turn of the century, however, even the clergy was starting to wear them. When Cotton Mather himself appeared in a periwig, the fashion was here to stay—at least until the Revolution against England and English fashion.

The wearing of wigs was not the only cause of King Philip's uprising, which took the lives of hundreds of New Englanders. John Cotton laid the blame for the colonial disaster upon the children, even calling them together for a sermon over being "haughty in spirit, in countenance, in garbe, and fashion . . . Stubborne and rebellious against God and disobedient to parents." Another pastor in Duxbury declared that the war was a just punishment "for our dealing with the Quakers."

REBELLION AND DYSENTERY (1676)

When Nathaniel Bacon's rebellion against royal authority failed in Virginia in 1676 upon the leader's death from dysentery, the royal governor, William Berkeley, exacted terrible reprisals. Bacon led the uprising because he wanted the Indians punished for some minor depredations. In May 1676 he slaughtered and plundered the friendly Occaneechee Indians—by mistake! Then, turning upon the incensed governor, Bacon forced a commission from him to continue his war, after which he led his small army against another friendly tribe, the Pamunckeys. He then laid siege to and burned Jamestown but died shortly after from dysentery contracted in the trenches around Jamestown, whereupon Berkeley rounded up the remaining rebels and hanged thirty-seven of them.

"That old fool," fumed Charles II, "has hanged more men in that naked country than I have done for the murder of my father." Finally, the governor himself, reprimanded and called home by his royal master, died before further action could be taken against him, ending a tragic series of events that accomplished more harm than good but is often pointed to with pride as the first organized resistance to British authority in the English Colonies.

KING PHILIP'S REMAINS (1676)

Frightened by how close King Philip's Indian allies had come to obliterating the English colonists throughout New England, the settlers went to great lengths to make examples of those who took up arms against God's chosen people. Philip, killed by another Indian, was denied burial. His head and hands were cut off, and his body was quartered and left for the wolves. As a warning, his head was exhibited on a pike at Fort Hill in Plymouth for more than twenty years, becoming a ghastly birdhouse. Increase Mather delightedly carried away the jawbone of "that blasphemous leviathan." For many years, one of Philip's hands, pickled in a pail of rum, was carried about New England by the Indian who killed him.

All the hostile Native Americans captured in the war (as well as many who were friendly) were sold into slavery. For some time an argument raged as to the fate of the nine-year-old son of Philip, with the majority of the Pilgrim leaders favoring death. Finally "compassion" ruled, and the child was shipped off to spend the rest of his life in chains in Bermuda.

LONG HAIR IN COLONIAL TIMES (1680)

Many early ministers preached against long hair for men. The Reverend Mr. Rogers preached on the "Disguisement of long ruffianly hair," as had President Charles Chauncy of Harvard. Mr. Wigglesworth argued most logically on the subject countless times. The General Court referred to this offense on the list of existing evils—that "the men wore long hair like women's hair," while the women were complained of for "cutting and curling and laying out of hair, especially among the younger sort."

A long-haired Salem man was charged with a misdemeanor and fined ten shillings. Long hair was only one of the many fashions and habits that brought forth denunciations from the pulpit. Meddling, gossiping, tavern visiting, health drinking, chaise owning, hooped petticoats, gold-laced coats (unless owned by gentlemen), and pointed shoes were also denounced.

SUNDAY ENDURANCE (1680)

On their voyage across the Atlantic, one group of Puritans had to listen to at least one, and sometimes as many as three, sermon each day for ten weeks. One passenger called to account for fishing on the Lord's Day protested that "he did not know when the Lord's Day was; he thought every day was a Sabbath day, for, he said, they did nothing but pray and preach all the week long." Two visitors in Boston in the 1680s reported that prayers lasting for two hours were held for a sick minister, after which three other ministers took turns preaching the rest of the day, relieving each other alternately when one was exhausted. The normal Sabbath meetings were taken up with three- to four-hour sermons in the morning, a short break for lunch, and equally long sermons in the afternoon.

The listeners were not inhuman; after all, they did object on occasion. The most outspoken were Quakers who sneaked into the services. There are reports of Quaker women screaming out, "Parson, thou art an old fool . . . thy sermon is too long. Sit down!" More subtle was a congregation in one parish that developed a habit of simply walking out when the sermon dragged on. The minister ended this, however, by announcing that he would preach to the sinners first and the saints at the end. After that they all stayed to the bitter end.

"GOOD AND WHOLESOME LAWS" (1681)

Our Puritan ancestors never seemed to tire of drawing up lists of prohibited "carnall delights," such as attending plays, dancing around a Maypole, bowling on the green, playing at shuffleboard, and engaging in quoits, dice, and cards. A tight-rope exhibition was once kept out of Boston "lest the said divertissement may tend to promote idleness in the town and great mispense of time." In 1681 a French dancing master was ordered out of town lest "profane and promiscuous dancing" corrupt the morals of the citizens. Believing that "an hour's idleness is as bad as an hour's drunkenness," the Massachusetts General Court enacted laws against beachcombing and rebuked "unprofitable fowlers"—that is, bad shots who wasted their time and powder on birds. For a time even tobacco was included in the ban. The first man to be sentenced to the stocks in Boston was the very man who was contracted to build them. He was convicted of padding his bill for making the stocks.

A TEACHER'S DUTIES (1682)

A somewhat detailed teacher's contract signed at Flatbush, Long Island, in 1682 tells us much about colonial schools. A bell called students together at 8 A.M. and recessed school for lunch at 11:00 A.M., opened again at 1 P.M. and closed for the day at 4 P.M. Morning and afternoon sessions began and closed with prayer, and Wednesdays and Saturdays were devoted to the study of common prayers and the catechism. Pay for the teachers (usually in produce) amounted to three guilders a quarter for a "speller or reader" and four guilders for a "writer."

His contract specified duties outside of teaching: ringing the church bell on Sundays, leading the singing, reading the Bible at church services, and sometimes giving the sermon itself. He acted as sexton, providing water for baptisms, supplying bread and wine for communion, and even sweeping out the church. He delivered invitations to funerals, carried messages, visited and comforted the sick, and sometimes dug graves.

As some rural teachers might say today, "What's new?"

WHO WAS THE "CHIEF SCAMP"? (1682)

William Penn was to find religious bigotry almost as great in the New World as in the Old. When Cotton Mather learned that Penn was on his way to America in 1682 as the "chief scamp" of "one hundred or more of the heretics and malignants called Quakers," he and the Massachusetts General Court came up with a cunning plot that he revealed in a letter to John Higginson. The brig *Porpoise* was to ambush the Quaker ship near Cape Cod and sell the "whole lot to Barbados, where slaves fetch good prices in rum and sugar, and we shall not only do the Lord great good by punishing the wicked, but we shall make great good for His minister and people."

History records no encounter between these ships, so apparently Penn eluded the *Porpoise* on his own ship named, ironically, *The Welcome*.

WITCHCRAFT IN PENNSYLVANIA (1683)

William Penn and the Quakers are remembered in American history for their advanced thinking in regard to religious freedom—all settlers in Pennsylvania were granted absolute religious freedom. In an age when the mother country listed two hundred offenses for which the penalty was death, Penn's colony listed two: murder and high treason. Several decades before the sister colony of Massachusetts hanged nineteen women for the crime of witchcraft, Penn was presented with a witchcraft case in his "colony of tolerance." Unfortunately for the women of the Bay Colony, the Salem magistrates did not possess the same humor William Penn did. When an old woman confessed that she was a witch, Penn informed her that he knew of no law (unless it was gravity) against riding through the air on a broomstick. The case was dismissed in a gale of laughter.

THE WALKING PURCHASE (1686)

Known for his fair dealings with the original inhabitants of Pennsylvania, William Penn made a deal with the Delaware Indians in 1686 for some land in the fork of the Delaware and Lehigh Rivers, whose length was "as far as a man can go in a day and a half." That turned out to be forty miles, as walked by Penn. Fifty-one years later the Delawares agreed to a new lease on this tract with Penn's descendants. The same walking agreement was made, but this time the Delawares were dealing with Penn's son, Thomas, a man with a greedy reputation. Thomas employed experts, one of whom walked off 66.5 miles within the time period. Unfortunately for the Indians, the story doesn't end there. Thomas called in the Iroquois to expel the Delawares when they complained of his trick. Later, however, Penn had to relinquish the northern part of the territory to the Iroquois, who then occupied the land and refused to give it back to Penn.

OF GOATS, CHEESE, AND CANDLES (1687)

Because of the shortage of coined money in the English Colonies for the first two centuries, and because of the confusion resulting from so many kinds of paper currency, the Americans resorted to various standard commodities to take the place of money. This was referred to as "country pay" or "truck," and it dominated the economy. In 1687 John Winthrop Jr. bought a house using goats instead of money. As late as 1800, the books of a shoemaker in Massachusetts show him receiving from one family over the years his pay in salt, hay, mutton, corn, tallow, wood, fowl, candles, wheat, and a horse for hire.

Beaver skins were a common form of exchange in the Colonies, as was Indian wampum, musket balls, or any other commodity that enjoyed wide usage and had commercial value. One of the more interesting units of exchange was the nail. So many nails of a certain length were valued at so many pennies. From this practice we derive the present practice of referring to nails as 6d (penny), 8d, and so forth.

Another interesting practice that resulted from shortage of specie was the clipping of coins—filing or clipping off the edges of silver or gold coins that went through a colonist's hands until enough metal was accumulated to be of trade value. From this practice we derived the phrase, "I've been clipped!"

"FREEMEN" AND "GOODMEN" (1690)

Freemen in early New England were the aristocracy of their times—only they had the right to vote, hold office, and qualify for certain other privileges. To be a freeman, a citizen had to be a member of the Puritan church, be an industrious and law-abiding person, and be worth at least two hundred pounds in property or money, or have an income from having invested that amount. He then qualified for the title of "Mister," whereas those not qualifying were called "Goodmen." The wife of a Goodman was known as "Goodwife" or "Goody."

Goodmen and their wives were restricted from wearing clothing that was reserved for gentlemen and their ladies, such as silks or ornamental decoration on their clothing with silver, gold, or lace thread. The term "Goodwife" or "Goody" was still applied to the bed makers at Harvard University as late as the twentieth century.

"OLD CEDAR" MEETINGHOUSE (1690)

This meetinghouse, successor to the first one in Boston, had an interesting existence. Here, Gov. Edmund Andros, unable to obtain lawful permission for its use, forced an entrance on Good Friday. The following Sabbath he caused the communion service of the Church of England to be celebrated for himself and his associates while the Puritan congregation was kept waiting impatiently outside. Every Sunday for the next two years the owners of the meetinghouse were forced to share it with those whose forms of worship they detested.

It was in this same house, in 1697, that Judge Samuel Sewall stood with bowed head and listened to the reading of his public confession of sin for having sent innocent people to their deaths for witchcraft five years before. It was also in the shadow of this meetinghouse on a cold January Sabbath in 1706 that a son was born to a poor tallow chandler. Before the service had ended, the infant, bathed and swaddled, was borne into the meeting and up to the waiting minister who, dipping his fingers into the icy water of the baptismal basin, baptized him Benjamin Franklin.

LOCKE ON EDUCATION (1690)

The English philosopher John Locke contributed more than just a philosophy of government to the early Americans. Many ancestors of Americans were raised according to his *Thoughts on Education,* published in England in 1690. Many might have died as a result of it also. In it, he advised that a child's feet be washed daily in cold water and "to have his shoes so thin that they might leak and let in water." The well-known Josiah Quincy suffered as a result of this advice. When only three years old, he was frequently taken from his warm bed in winter, as well as in summer, carried to a cellar kitchen, and dipped three times in a tub of cold well water.

Locke also prescribed milk and warm beer for children. He warned against melons, peaches, plums, or grapes for children, and he suggested a hard bed of quilts rather than feathers. It's amazing that the colonists accepted his advice on government!

EDUCATION BY THE ROD (1691)

Colonial teachers, and usually parents, believed in strict discipline in early American schools. The usual method was the birth rod, as well as related variations.

One teacher invented an instrument he called a "flapper," a large piece of leather with a hole in the middle and fastened to a pliable handle. Each stroke on the bare skin raised a blister the size of the hole. Just as brutal was the tattling stick, a cat-o'-nine-tails with leather straps. Another master whipped the soles of his students' feet. One ingenious teacher split the end of a small branch, placed the culprit's nose in the split end, and forced him to stand for a time in humiliation.

In a dame school, tapping the head with a heavy thimble was called "thimble-pie." Particularly humiliating was yoking two students together with an instrument similar to an ox yoke—especially if the two were a boy and a girl. A wooden gag tied in the mouth like a bit was called a "whispering stick." Dunce stools and dunce caps with heavy leather spectacles were quite common. A unipod, a stool with one leg that could be quite tiring to sit on, was also used. Some students were forced to stand with large cards around their necks that said, "Tell-tale," "Bite-finger-baby," "Lying Ananias," "Idle-Boy," and "Pert-Miss-Prat-a-Pace."

WITCHES AND PURITANS (1692)

Contrary to the commonly accepted belief, no witches were ever burned in New England. In 1692 nineteen persons were hanged as witches at Salem, and one man was pressed to death because the Puritans of Salem took seriously the Bible's warning, "Thou shalt not suffer a witch to live." Burning was common in England at this time, with hundreds of people suffering the death penalty there. The hysteria was short-lived in New England, whereas witches were still being executed in the old country as late as 1722. All in all, the severity of Puritan laws, as usually related in school textbooks, was never as great as those in England, where it was not uncommon to impose the death penalty on twelve-year-old children for simple theft.

One New England magistrate heard a Plymouth man accusing his neighbor of witchcraft and then slapped the accuser with a heavy fine for malicious slander. Unfortunately, the Salem judges were not so enlightened. During the hysteria of 1691–92, they even hanged two dogs.

PENN PROPOSES UNITED NATIONS (1693)

Throughout his life Penn was entangled in financial and political difficulties, finding human weaknesses, greed, and corruption on all sides of him. Strangely enough, however, he did not seem to despair of the ultimate goodness and potential of his fellow man. This philosophy was evidenced in "An Essay Towards the Present and Future Peace of Europe," which he wrote in 1693.

In short, this document was a plan for a United States of Europe with a world court where the nations of the world could submit their disputes for arbitration. His plan also included a united nations army for crushing any aggressor nation. If Penn beheld the modern prototype of his dream today, he would still be frustrated to see the same human greed and bigotry stifling world peace and freedom.

EARLY MARRIAGE (1695)

The so-called carefree life of the unmarried youth was a rarity in early New England. Both social and legal pressure was exerted to force couples into marriage at the earliest possible age. Colonel Byrd speaks of his daughter, the beautiful Evelyn, as an "antique virgin" when she was only twenty years old. A writer in early New England refers to a young woman of twenty-five as an "ancient maid." The governor of New Hampshire married a widow after she had only six days in which to mourn the loss of her first husband, and in Virginia a widow used part of the meat prepared for the funeral of her first husband at the wedding feast given on the occasion of her second marriage.

Bachelors were often pressured into marriage by being forced to live where the court could impose a special tax on them. In Eastham, Massachusetts, a 1695 law ordained that "every unmarried man in the township shall kill six blackbirds or three crows while he remains single." They would not be allowed to marry until they had complied with the order.

Even into the nineteenth century, early marriage still persisted. Twenty-seven-year-old grandmothers were frequently found in North Carolina, and girls of the higher classes were married at thirteen. Early travelers to Oregon report seeing married women in the woods along the Columbia River still playing with their dolls.

COLLECTING SCALP BOUNTY (1697)

Toward the end of King William's War, Indians from Maine attacked the small Massachusetts settlement of Haverhill, carrying off Mrs. Hannah Dustin, her week-old baby, and its nurse. When the baby's crying annoyed its captors, they smashed its head against a tree. Biding her time, Mrs. Dustin planned her escape while being forced northward. One night the opportunity arose. Silently, she, the nurse, and a young captive boy stole hatchets from the sleeping Indians and fell upon them. Only two escaped, and Hannah calmly proceeded to scalp the ten they had killed. Within days she and her friends showed up back in Massachusetts where she collected a fifty-pound bounty for the scalps.

"DOG MAIL" (1698)

Although mail delivery in early America was not too regular, it was nevertheless ingenious at times. At the little frontier post of Chambly on the Richelieu River lived a dog who apparently had a "girlfriend" at La Prairie, another little hamlet several miles away on the St. Lawrence River. When it was discovered that the dog made frequent visits to his La

Prairie friend, authorities decided to turn him into a "post-dog," tying bundles of letters to his collar whenever he made the trip. For this service he was put on the roll call of the local fort and issued an official soldier's ration. We wonder what enticement was used to get the dog to make the return trip.

FIRST ANTI-SLAVERY TRACT (1700)

Samuel Sewall, one of the more famous and most interesting figures of colonial history, is best known for his *Diary*, kept over a period of about fifty years. His lesser-known work, *The Selling of Joseph*, written in 1700, was the first antislavery tract in America. In it he stated:

"It is most certain that all men as they are the sons of Adam, are coheirs; and have equal right unto liberty and all other outward comforts of life. . . . God hath said, 'He that stealeth a man and selleth him, or if he be found in his hand, he shall surely be put to death,' Exod. 21:16. . . . What louder cry can be made of that celebrated warning, 'Caveat emptor!'"

Sewall's farsightedness was also evident in his public confession of error for the part he played as a judge in the Salem witchcraft trials. He parts the curtain in a most interesting aspect of colonial values—an aspect seldom credited to the Puritans.

FROM PURITAN TO MOTHER SUPERIOR (1703)

One of the opening conflicts of Queen Anne's War, the second colonial war in America between England and France, was the attack by a band of Abnaki Indians on the small Maine village of Wells, where about forty colonists, mostly women and children, were either slaughtered or led away as captives to Canada. One of these captives was a seven-year-old Puritan girl by the name of Esther Wheelwright, a girl with a most unusual future. She wound up in the household of the Canadian governor, who promised to return her to her home. A Canadian priest with money for the purpose, however, bought her from the marquis for 1,400 livres in order, as Esther later told her relatives, "to make her a nun." In the convent of the Ursulines, where she eventually ended up, she lived an apparently contented life: the Puritan girl in her later years became Mother Superior of the convent.

FROM PURITAN TO SQUAW (1704)

The French and Indian attack upon Deerfield, Massachusetts, during Queen Anne's War is probably one of the most often-repeated Indian atrocity tales in American history. Less well known is the story of Eunice Williams, one of the 111 captives herded back toward Canada by the marauders. One of the seven children of Reverend and Mrs. Williams, she saw two of her brothers and sisters killed in the village and her mother, weak from childbirth, brained on the trail. Eunice survived, but as far as her father was concerned, she would have been better off dead. She eventually became an Indian squaw, and many years later she visited her father, now back in Deerfield, with her Indian husband. She had no desire to leave her Indian ways, but one of her grandchildren went on to become a student at Dartmouth in the early days of that college. Years later this same grandson attempted to pass himself off as the lost son of Louis XVI, but that is another story.

THE FIRST NEWSPAPER (1704)

Two attempts at publishing newspapers in the English Colonies were made in 1685 and 1690, but both were short-lived. The last attempt, *Publick Occurrences,* was closed down by colonial authorities. Fourteen years later the first successful newspaper appeared in Boston. The *Boston News-Letter* was a weekly printed on both sides of a single sheet—about seven by eleven and one-half inches. Its publisher, a postmaster named Campbell, acquired his news from the post riders around New England or the sea captains and sailors—most of it several weeks or months old. For example, the first issue, which purported to cover news from April 17 to April 24, 1704, included news from the *London Flying Post* printed in December 1703. Its largest circulation reached three hundred copies. Ironically, publication ceased with the evacuation of Boston by the British troops just as the greatest news events in the history of the world were beginning.

"COUGHING AND CHAWING" (1705)

The chewing of tobacco is not an American invention, and it is not likely that much pride would result from claiming it. Amerigo Vespucci first observed the juicy cud and its associated spitting among the Caribbean Indians. It is more than likely that lower-class working whites adopted the habit so they could enjoy their tobacco while both hands were occupied with labor. Whatever the case, the habit was firmly entrenched in the English Colonies by 1700. The well-known colonial traveler Madam Knight observed that the country folk in Connecticut "keep Chewing and Spitting as long as their eyes are open."

A museum in Saratoga Springs, New York, features an interesting kneeling cushion-footstool-cuspidor combination used by addicted forefathers in 1774. As the Jacksonians made the common man a hero, the habit reached such proportions that thousands of Americans and most Europeans became disgusted by the habit that made such a mess of so many homes and public buildings. By 1860 nearly all of the tobacco from Virginia and North Carolina was made into chewing tobacco. One author, perhaps with some exaggeration, stated, "No single other thing, not even Negro slavery, did so much . . . to encourage the supercilious Europeans to label the new nation barbaric." The last spittoons were removed from federal buildings in 1945.

COLONIAL DISEASES (1707)

The high mortality rate among early Americans came from the "unruly distempers" that struck down thousands of people. These diseases were primarily malaria, dysentery, typhoid fever, yellow fever, consumption, cholera, diphtheria, typhus, measles, whooping cough, scarlet fever, fluxes, and smallpox. Dysentery was known at that time as "camp disease" because of its prevalence among soldiers. In the measles epidemic of 1713, Cotton Mather lost five members of his family, including his wife, in only two weeks. It is somewhat ironic that Mather might have prevented his family from dying of smallpox but not measles. In 1707 he acquired an African slave who taught him the trick of inoculation for smallpox. In the smallpox epidemic of 1721, Mather made use of his new-found knowledge despite furious objection by the community.

Malignant fever, now known as influenza, ravaged the Colonies in epidemic proportions in 1732, 1760, and 1772. Diphtheria seemed to be the worst, however, especially among children. In 1735–37 five thousand New Englanders died of the so-called throat distemper. One couple, John and Mercy Wilson of Andover, Connecticut, lost eight children within a week.

"CHRISTIAN" HOLIDAYS (1708)

Judge Samuel Sewall should be alive today to see the increasing commercialization of Christmas and other holidays. On April 1, 1708, he wrote a letter to two prominent schoolmasters in Boston warning them of the "defiling and provoking nature" of scholars playing April Fool's jokes. Eleven years later he was still concerned about the same subject when he wrote in his diary of "playing idle tricks because 'twas first of April; they were the greatest fools that did so. New England men came hither to avoid anniversary days, the keeping of them, such as the 25th of December." (This is an interesting new reason for the settling of the Colonies.) Among the Puritans, Christmas was associated with the "Lords of Misrule," riot and drunkenness. Although adopted rather early and celebrated widely outside of New England, it was the middle of the nineteenth century before it was regarded as a day of joy and goodwill throughout rural New England.

Contrary to popular belief, the first New England Thanksgiving was not observed by the Pilgrims but by the Popham colonists at Monhegan thirteen years previously. When the Pilgrims did celebrate their Thanksgiving, it was a day of gratitude but also a day of joy and recreation.

OCCUPATIONS (1709)

The number of immigrants arriving in Philadelphia in April, June, and July 1709 was reported by one observer to number 1,838. According to this same observer, this number included:

56 bakers
14 tanners
3 hatters
87 masons
7 stocking weavers
8 lime burners
124 carpenters
6 barbers
2 engravers
68 shoemakers
4 locksmiths
3 brick makers
99 tailors
98 cloth and linen weavers

2 silversmiths
29 butchers
82 coopers
48 blacksmiths
45 millers
2 glass blowers
3 potters
13 saddlers
6 turners

The rest of these mainly German immigrants were husbandmen, the ancestors of the prosperous Pennsylvania Dutch farmers of today.

One hundred years earlier at Jamestown, Capt. John Smith would have bargained his very soul to receive such immigrants. There would more than likely have been no "Starving Time" had the British sent such workers rather than "gentlemen."

CARVING MEAT IN EARLY AMERICA (1710)

Carving meat was more than just a well-bred accomplishment in some of the early American Colonies: it was an art. Thousands of terms were applied with exactness to different cuts of fish, fowl, and meat. One author wrote:

"How all must regret to hear some Persons, even of quality say 'pray cut up that Chicken or Hen,' or 'Halve that Plover,' not considering how indiscreetly they talk, when the proper Terms are, 'break that Goose,' 'thrust that Chicken,' 'spoil that Hen,' 'pierce that Plover.' If they are so much out in common Things, how much more would they be with Herons, cranes, and Peacocks."

Who said our ancestors were the ill-bred riffraff of Europe?

ABOVE AND BELOW THE SALT (1710)

Midway down the length of colonial dining tables stood a large container of salt to be used with meals. Its purpose was also to indicate a rigid social distinction between those who sat "above the salt" and those who sat "below the salt." Those of inferior status, such as servants, possibly children, Indian guests, and so on, sat below the salt and were forbidden by custom from speaking unless addressed by persons above the salt. They were also required to rise silently and leave the room as soon as they finished eating. The quality and amount of food was the same at both ends of the table, but the prestige certainly was not.

A large saltcellar—or saler, as it was also called—"Sett in the myddys of the tabull" and was also used in college dining halls. Harvard University still has a "great silver salt," given to it in 1644, which was used to separate the graduates and faculty from the undergraduates.

QUEBEC SAVED BY INCOMPETENCY (1711)

One of those little-noticed footnotes in history concerns an incompetent English naval officer, his name now forgotten, who was responsible for Quebec, and possibly for all of New France, remaining in French control for an extra half century.

In the summer of 1711, a huge Anglo-American invasion force sailing in a fleet of seventy vessels moved into the mouth of the St. Lawrence River, heading for an unaware and unprepared Quebec. As darkness and fog moved in, an officer reported land but neglected to say the land was not ahead but astern. The admiral ordered the fleet turned "away" and then went to bed. The fleet was soon piling up on the rocky shores of the St. Lawrence. Before it got light, eight transports and two supply ships were sunk. A French messenger later reported to Quebec that he saw "about 1,500 to 1,600 dead bodies of which about a score were women, part of whom had infants in arms." He also reported "dead horses . . . 300 to 400 great iron bound casks." The expedition was still mighty and could have continued, but panic ruled and the great invasion collapsed.

FELONS TO AMERICA (1713)

It has been estimated that one-twenty-fifth of all immigrants coming to America between 1607 and 1775 were criminals. Between the close of the War of the Spanish Succession in 1713 (which lessened the British government's demand for felon soldiers) and 1775, approximately thirty thousand convicts, at least one-third of them women, arrived in America, mostly in the Chesapeake area. Forced exile was illegal in Great Britain, but the authorities did grant pardons or exempt from trial those who agreed to ship out to the American Colonies as purchasable labor for a term of seven to fourteen years. Americans protested and passed restrictive laws against this practice, usually to no avail. Benjamin Franklin suggested that the Colonies respond by returning shipments of rattlesnakes.

He said England's practice of emptying its jails into America was worse than "emptying their jakes [privies] on our tables."

Using America as a dumping ground for convicts gave the British the image of Americans as a race of convicts. Dr. Samuel Johnson referred to them in Revolutionary times as such and said they "ought to be thankful for anything we allow them short of hanging." Even after peace was signed, England sent over a shipload of convicts for sale. Old habits died hard.

FLOGGING (1715)

The whipping post was an integral part of the landscape of most communities. Colonial Boston had three main ones. Many magistrates favored tying the culprit to the tail of a cart and whipping him throughout town because it provided a maximum of publicity. The lash was justified in the Bible. According to the colonists, "Stripes, or whipping, is a correction fit and proper in some cases . . . when stripes are due: it is ordered that not above forty stripes shall be inflicted at one time: Deuteronomy 25:3."

In early Virginia "launderers and laundresses" who gave old, torn linen for good linen or who threw out "the water or suds of fowle clothes in the open streets" were whipped. Failure to conform after repeated whippings could result in being sold into bondage in the West Indies. A pretty general idea of colonial discipline can be imagined from the fact that a Sunderland, Massachusetts, schoolhouse built in 1793 had a whipping post set firmly in the schoolhouse floor. Flogging was permitted by law in Delaware until as late as 1953.

PLEADING THE CLERGY (1715)

The severity of the criminal code in England and the Colonies was often lessened by permitting first offenders charged with crimes other than murder, rape, arson, burglary, or robbery to "plead their clergy." Originally, this privilege was granted only to the clergy to protect them from secular courts. Gradually this privilege was extended to all who could read and eventually to women and illiterates. Instead of being sentenced to death or a long prison sentence, the culprit was perhaps branded on the thumb. This not only marked him for life but also prevented him from pleading his clergy a second time.

John Adams made use of "Pleading the Clergy" for his clients, the two Englishmen found guilty of manslaughter during the Boston Massacre. Accepting Adams's plea, the court ordered the two soldiers branded on the thumbs with the letter M and released.

SLAVERY IN THE NORTH (1715)

Proslavery factions in the South always maintained that the absence of slavery in nineteenth-century Yankee land had less to do with morality than it did with an institution that had simply proven economically unprofitable in the North. The prevalence of slavery in earlier days north of the Mason-Dixon line appears to validate this point.

As early as 1715, two thousand Boston inhabitants were slaves, and twenty-five years later one-fourth of the population of New York City was black. Clergymen of the Church of England owned slaves. Even the pious Cotton Mather, when presented with a slave by his congregation, thankfully recorded the event in his diary as "a smile from Heaven." The first Englishman to trade in slaves was Capt. John Hawkins, a devout Christian who named his slave ship *Jesus.* Capt. John Newport, who traded in slaves in the eighteenth century, composed the well-known hymn "How Sweet the Name of Jesus Sounds" while waiting in his ship off the coast of Africa for a cargo of slaves.

THE "SCARLET LETTER" (1715)

The wearing of letters to denote one's crime as a punishment was as old as the twelfth century. "A" stood for "adulterer," "B" for blasphemer or "burgler," "D" for "drunkard," "I" for "incestuous marriage," "T" for "thief," and so on through the alphabet to "V" for "venery." Variations on this theme were found throughout the Colonies. In New England a white woman "suffering an Indian to have carnal knowledge of her" had an Indian cut in red cloth sewed upon her right arm, and she "enjoyed to wear it twelve months." If the offender was a repeater or a member of the lower class, the letter was branded on the forehead. If Hester Prynne in *The Scarlett Letter* had been of the servant class, she wouldn't have gotten off so easily. An eighteenth-century adulterer was sentenced to receive twenty-one lashes, serve seven years in prison, and be branded on the forehead with an "A" for the third offense.

The Massachusetts Abstract of the Lawes required an adulterer to be "set on the Gallowes an Hour with a Rope about their neck, and other end cast over the Gallowes. And in the way from thence to the common Gaol, to be Scouraged, not exceeding Forty Stripes And forever after to wear a Capital A of two Inches long of a contrary Colour to their Cloathes."

"CRUEL AND UNUSUAL PUNISHMENT" (1716)

This is a relative term: what would be considered as such now certainly was not considered cruel and unusual in colonial America. As Calverton claimed, "No extreme of punishment or degree of servitude was considered too severe in suppressing insubordination on the part of the lower classes." Penalties for minor offenses were fines, whippings (although one case in Virginia shows 120 lashes inflicted), duckings (which could prove fatal), and confinement in stocks, pillory, and bilboes (the discomfort and humiliation would not be considered minor today).

For serious offenses the ears might be nailed to the pillory and then cut off at the end of the appointed time. An example of a serious offense would be "malicious and scandalous speeches against the government." Other punishments cruel by today's standards would be branding on the thumb, cheek, or forehead, or boring the tongue through with a hot iron. As an unusual punishment indicating the power of the Mosaic law, those guilty of slander or unchastity would have to acknowledge their fault while standing in church with a sheet wrapped around them.

IDLENESS (1717)

Critics of the welfare state might profit or learn from reading Puritan laws concerning the curse of idleness. A two-and-one-half shilling fine might be imposed on anyone passing more than an hour drinking in a public house during working hours. Continued idleness might bring a whipping on the bare back. For the third offense the culprit was whipped to the town boundaries, turned over to the authorities of the next town to be whipped through that township, and so on. When the whipping was to end, the law neglected to say. The colonial American was constantly reminded of the sin of idleness, from the hornbook ("The Idle Fool Is Whip't at School") to Poor Richard ("Leisure is the time for doing something useful").

Later in the eighteenth century, punishment by whipping was replaced by forced labor or commitment to the workhouse. With such incentives, it is not too surprising to read what Gabriel Thomas, a successful promoter of immigration, had to say about idleness. In Pennsylvania there were "no Beggars to be seen (it is a Shame and Disgrace to the State that there are so many in England), nor indeed have any here the least Occasion or Temptation to take up that Scandalous and Lazy Life."

WOMEN'S RIGHTS IN EARLY AMERICA (1719)

Law and custom in colonial America relegated women to an inferior status. Under common law a married woman had no existence apart from her husband; she was his chattel to do with much as he pleased. She could not make a contract, bring suit or be sued, execute a deed, administer an estate or will, or exercise legal rights over her children. In all colonies outside of New England, the law specified how much punishment a husband could inflict upon his wife. When he beat her, his stick could be no larger than a finger in diameter. He was forbidden to kill or permanently incapacitate her, no matter what the provocation.

Women were expected to defer to their husbands in the selection of their clothing. They could join churches but not speak in them. In colonies under the Church of England, divorce was almost impossible. From 1664 until the American Revolution, not a single divorce was granted in the colony of New York. Women could be severely punished for committing crime. One woman who killed her husband was burned to death. In 1720 a woman in Philadelphia was hanged for burglary. For the capital crime of practicing witchcraft, women suffered more than men. Most of the victims of the witchcraft mania in Salem were women. By definition a witch was a woman, although a few wizards were hung. Among the hazards of growing old in colonial America was the fear of being taken for a witch.

THE "CASKET GIRLS" (1719)

In 1719 the first consignment of "Casket Girls" reached Louisiana. These "mail-order brides," whose name derived from the small chests (caskets) in which they carried their clothes, were imported into Biloxi and New Orleans by the Compagnie des Indes as wives for the French settlers. Their place in history has been made secure by reason of their virtue—most previous importees were picked up off the streets of Paris and collected from houses of correction. The Casket Girls, to the contrary, were recruited from church charitable institutions, and their virtue was practically guaranteed. As a result, later Louisianans would go to great lengths to prove descent from these poor but virtuous girls rather than the more numerous prostitutes who arrived in the early days.

THE PROLIFIC ALDENS (1719)

A great-grandson of the original John and Priscilla Alden was born in 1719 and lived to be 102. During his five score years, he was responsible for increasing New England's population with 19 children, 62 grandchildren, 134 great-grandchildren, and 7 great-great-grandchildren—172 surviving him.

In a cemetery in Connecticut appears another record of fruitfulness: "Here lies the Body of Mrs. Mary, wife of Dr. John Buell, Esq. She died Nov. 4th, 1768. Age 90 having had 13 children, 107 Grand Children, 274 Great G. Children, 22 Great G.G. Children 416 Total, 336 Survived her."

The firstborn of John and Priscilla, who later became the well-known Capt. John Alden, was one of those accused of witchcraft at Salem in 1791 but, through the help of influential friends, escaped the colony until the hysteria blew over.

COLLEGE DISCIPLINE (1720)

Strict discipline was enforced in the colonial college. Students were held to systematic habits and a conventional standard of behavior by the regulations of the governing bodies. They were required to rise early, attend all lectures and recitations, indulge in no questionable conduct, and show proper deference to their superiors. At Harvard, discipline was maintained for a long time by flogging, but after 1734 violations of college rules were punishable only by fines, usually for such heinous crimes as slipping away from school to attend a play.

New ideas coming out of the Revolution brought about an increased amount of student unrest and more discipline problems on college campuses than at any other time until the 1960s. Students drove the faculty away from commencement exercises at Columbia in 1811. Yale students in 1841 destroyed all of New Haven's fire equipment after beating up the firemen. Amherst students seized control of the local government in 1827 after voting as a bloc and then, according to legend, specified that the new town hall be 160 feet by 8 feet. The University of North Carolina in 1851 had an enrollment of 230 but handled 282 cases of student delinquency. But perhaps the most ironic and most disquieting disturbance was at

Jefferson's beloved University of Virginia in 1836. Rioting there resulted in armed troops being called in to patrol the campus.

HAZARDS OF THE ATLANTIC CROSSING (1720)

Between 1607 and the Revolutionary War, a colonist's chances of surviving the Atlantic crossing was no better than 25 percent. Much has been made of the horrors of the Middle Passage for African slaves, and it is not to belittle those horrors to suggest that early American immigrants suffered nearly as much. Henry Laurens, a South Carolina merchant, wrote in 1760 of the Irish immigrants coming to Charleston: "I never saw an Instance of Cruelty in Ten or Twelve years (or experience of the slave trade) equal to the cruelty exercised upon these poor Irish."

Passengers on board the *Mayflower* in 1620 averaged a living space of seven by two-and-one-half feet, with no deck privileges. Conditions were worse a hundred years later, when English law in 1720 required a space of six by one-and-one-half feet per adult immigrant with none allotted for children. Is it any wonder that only ten years previous to 1720, out of a cargo of 3,000 German Palatines shipped from England to New York in ten ships, 720 died during the voyage or soon after landing? The ultimate in voyage fatalities apparently occurred in 1618 among 200 Separatists on the way to Virginia from Amsterdam. One hundred fifty died en route.

FRANKLIN AND MATHER AT ODDS (1721)

Benjamin Franklin, known for his liberalism, and Cotton Mather, known for his conservatism, on one occasion found their roles switched. It occurred during a smallpox epidemic in Boston in 1721–22 soon after James Franklin, with the help of his brother Benjamin, started the *New England Courant,* one of the first newspapers in New England. Cotton Mather demanded public inoculation, and passions were running high; at one point a bomb was thrown into Mather's house. The Franklin newspapers opposed this radical new practice of inoculation. Mather, of course, was proven right; after the epidemic was over, it was discovered that for those who had received the inoculation (around three hundred), survival ran nine times greater than for those not inoculated. Although Franklin's autobiography gives other reasons for his departure for a new life in Philadelphia a short time later, being proven wrong in a public controversy may have had significant influence on his desire to leave town. When smallpox returned to Boston in 1792, nearly half of the city's twenty thousand inhabitants had been inoculated

AMERICAN VS. EUROPEAN PHYSICIANS (1724)

In general, seventeenth- and eighteenth-century colonial doctors were superior to their European counterparts, paradoxically because they knew less about the medical practices of the times. While learned European physicians were administering indigestible concoctions of human excreta, urine, worms, and so on, Puritans with no knowledge of these complicated formulas were prescribing rest, good food, and fresh air. (Virginia pharmacists were sending their apprentices into the woods to find native remedies.)

The result was that the healing course of nature was less disturbed and, in many instances, actually aided. This is not to say that American medicine was free of nauseating or harmful practices. Governor John Winthrop prescribed a paste made of wood lice, and as late as 1724 Boston physicians were advising the swallowing of "Leaden Bullets" for "that miserable Distemper which they called the Twisting of the Guts." Cotton Mather reported one such treatment in which the bullet entered the lung of a patient: "I think I should endure abundant, before I tried such a remedy."

FUNERAL "GIFTS" (1725)

Although Puritan births and marriages occasioned little festivity, funerals were a different matter. They became the occasion for a reunion of friends and kinfolk for feasting and giving of gifts to the mourners. At great expense to the givers, mourners seemed to compete to see who could collect the greatest number of rings, scarves, and gloves. In time, funerals tended to become an opportunity for the conspicuous display of wealth rather than grief. In 1717 at the funeral of Andrew Belcher, ninety dozen pairs of gloves were distributed among the mourners. "None of any figure but what had gloves sent 'em," recorded Samuel Sewall in his diary. In 1738 Gov. Jonathan Belcher of Massachusetts gave 1,000 gloves in honor of his wife. Not to be outdone, Peter Faneuil, a wealthy Boston merchant, sent out 3,000 gloves as a mark of respect for his uncle.

One minister, Andrew Eliot of Boston, kept track of the gloves and rings he received at weddings, christenings, and funerals; in thirty-two years he received 2,940 pairs of gloves, all of which he sold to a milliner. The cost of a funeral was consequently quite high at times. That of Waitstill Winthrop—including escutcheons, hatchments, scarves, gloves, rings, bell-tolling, tailor's bills, and so forth—totaled more than 600 pounds—one-fifth of his estate. Popular funeral rings were often decorated with a coffin that contained a full-length skeleton lying in it.

CHILDREN AT FUNERALS (1725)

Colonial children were familiar with death, not only because it was so prevalent in their times but also because of their universal attendance at all funerals. With so few social events and so little entertainment, a funeral developed into an important social function in any community, reuniting friends and relatives, providing an outlet for pomp and show, and giving way to much feasting and drinking. So that their children might understand or appreciate the nearness of heaven and hell, parents encouraged children to attend all funerals. Little boys and girls were even encouraged to be pallbearers at the funerals of their playmates. Finally, a crisis arose in Boston when the large and noisy throngs of children and servants who followed the coffins through the streets forced authorities to forbid funerals on the Sabbath because the disturbance profaned the Lord's day.

FRANKLIN'S JUNTO (1727)

In 1727 Philadelphia, Benjamin Franklin established a club for young artisans and tradesmen for "mutual improvement," modeled after similar neighborhood improvement societies started by Cotton Mather. Their main purpose was similar to the purposes of present-day service clubs, such as Rotary and Kiwanis. Franklin's Junto, taking its nature from its founder, was inclined more toward serious topics. And what were the raging topics of debate in eighteenth-century Philadelphia?

- "Is it justifiable to put private men to death, for the sake of public safety or tranquility, who have committed no crime? As, in the case of the plague, to stop infection; or as in the case of the Welshmen here executed?"
- "If the sovereign power attempts to deprive a subject of his right (or, which is the same thing, of what he thinks his right) is it justifiable to him to resist, if he is able?"
- "Whence comes the dew that stands on the outside of a tankard that has cold water in it in the summertime?"

THE "HONEST LAWYER" (1728)

The legal profession in early America rated, as far as most people were concerned, even lower than the medical profession. In 1698 Connecticut classed lawyers with common drunkards and limited their number to eleven in the entire colony. Rhode Island forbade them to be elected to the House of Deputies. Vermont publicly called them "bandits." In Massachusetts, as late as 1768, only twenty-five men were practicing law, and up and down the seaboard it was the same story. In 1658 lawyers had been totally ejected from the colony of Virginia, where law was looked upon in much the same manner as it was by New Englander John Hull: "very much like a lottery—great charge, little benefit."

By the time of the American Revolution and with the establishment of courts, the legal profession began to gain status. Men such as Patrick Henry also gave the profession status, but seventy-five years earlier the populous colony of New York counted only seven lawyers in its midst—one was a former dancing master, one was a glover, and two were transported criminals. An early tavern called "The Honest Lawyer" pictured a man without a head.

BUNDLING (1730)

Bundling was normally a form of courtship, practiced in the early Colonies from Pennsylvania to Maine, in which young couples lay on or in bed, fully dressed (usually), and often with a centerboard wedged between them. Even visitors overnight might be bedded down with the farmer's daughter. This form of courtship was most widely practiced among the poorer classes and reflected a shortage of beds, privacy, candles, and firewood. Although accepted and even encouraged by parents, it was not always innocent and was the target of many reformers. Even so, it lasted the better part of two centuries, beginning with the earliest New England settlements. It did not die easily, being a matter of court record as late as 1845 among the Pennsylvania Dutch. During the stormy controversy over bundling, even poets had their say. One supporter wrote:

> *Since in a bed a woman and maid*
> *May bundle and be chaste,*
> *It does no good to burn out wood*
> *It is a needless waste.*

A detractor answered:

> *A female meek, with blushing cheek*
> *Seized in some lover's arms*
> *Has oft grown weak with Cupid's heat,*
> *And lost her virgin charms.*

PURITAN LOVE MAKING (1730)

"The pattern of love-making [among the Puritans] was as rigid as that of their cuffs and collars," according to one writer, and parental consent was a must. Illicit relations were a defiance of the conventions and a violation of the law. But we must assume from the colonial records of illegitimate births that much went on without the consent of parents. If a man should win the affections of a young lady without the consent of her parents, he was liable to punishment by fine, imprisonment, or flogging. Records indicate numerous instances in which punishment was enforced. Consent for marriage was usually obtained as a result of negotiations carried on by the parents in a very businesslike manner—so businesslike that in South Carolina the newspapers sometimes stated in figures the fortune of the bride-elect. Once a father gave permission, he legally could not interfere to break up the engagement. One young New England swain took advantage of this law and sued the girl's meddling father for loss of time spent in courting.

"OUR COUNTRY'S GRANDMOTHER" (1732)

George Washington was born in 1732 to a generous saintly woman named Mary Ball Washington. True or False? The description, despite popular stories to the contrary, couldn't be further from the truth. Letters still existing between mother and son show her to have been a selfish, complaining, and vulgar woman. She was such a self-centered and exacting mother that her children, although they did their duty by her, gave her little love and avoided her as much as possible. She opposed everything Washington did for the public good, seeming to favor only what he could do for her. Throughout the Revolutionary War she pestered him with complaining letters, suggesting, even at the darkest moments of the war, that her son cared nothing for her and that she was starving. As a young man, George wanted to join the Royal Navy as a midshipman, but the selfishness of his mother prevented him. For this we should be grateful;

such a career would undoubtedly have put America's Father on a different course in life.

LOGGERHEAD (1732)

A drink called "flip" was a common alcoholic drink served hot in early America. It was made of home-brewed beer, sweetened with sugar, molasses, or dried pumpkin, and flavored with a liberal dash of rum. The mixture was heated by stirring it with a red-hot poker called a hottle, flip dog, or loggerhead—part of the equipment at every fireside. Sitting around the fireside drinking flip would more times than not result in heated discussions or argument in which the loggerhead was picked up and waved about to emphasize a point or to awe an opponent. Thus arose the expression "to be at loggerheads."

THE LIFE THE PEOPLE LOVED (1733)

Partly due to the fear of drinking water, excessive drinking of alcoholic liquors was virtually a universal habit. In most communities the total abstainer was looked upon with suspicion by his neighbors to the point of ostracism. It is reported that alcoholism was especially high among the ministry, resulting, to some degree, from the obligation ministers felt to accept drinks offered them in each home they visited. Ministers visited their parishioners extensively in the nation's early days. More than a century later, ministers were apparently still imbibing freely. In 1836, 300,000 took a pledge of total abstinence. It is not recorded how many refused.

The mixtures swilled in early America were enough to make modern drinkers shudder. Combinations such as gin or rum with beer, for example, were likely to quickly induce a form of temporary paralysis. One author describes the general attitude of the colonists toward drinking: "Rude plenty combined at times with great toleration for heavy drinking was the life the people loved." But perhaps the following lines are the best indication of the esteem in which alcoholic beverages were held at that time:

> *There's but one Reason I can Think,*
> *Why people ever cease to drink,*
> *Sobriety the cause is not,*
> *Nor fear of being deam'd a Sot*
> *But if Liquor can't be got.*

WELFARE STATISM (1735)

Both supporters and detractors of government-guaranteed subsistence might be surprised to find out how old government largesse is in America. "Rules for the year 1735," as recorded by Francis Moore, keeper of the stores, shows how the government in London provided for all settlers in Georgia:

"They will give to such persons as they send upon the charity. To every man, a watch-coat; a musket and bayonet; a hatchet; a hammer; a handsaw; a shod shovel or spade; a broad hoe; a narrow hoe; a gimlet; a drawing knife; an iron pot, and a pair of pot-hooks; a frying pan; and a public grindstone to each ward or village. Each working man will have for his maintenance in the colony for one year (to be delivered in such proportions, and at such times as the Trust shall think proper) 312 lbs. of beef of pork; 104 lbs. of rice; 104 lbs. of Indian corn or peas; 104 lbs. of flour; 1 pint of strong beer a day to a man when he works and not otherwise; 52 quarts of molasses for brewing beer; 16 lbs. of cheese; 12 lbs. of butter; 8 oz. of spice; 12 lbs. of sugar; 4 gallons of vinegar; 24 lbs. salt; 12 quarts of lamp oil; and 1 lb. spun cotton; 12 lbs. of soap."

Similar amounts were allowed for women. The paternalistic policy did not work, however. Before long, the trustees conceded that the poor "who had been useless in England, were inclined to be useless in Georgia likewise," and total welfare was abolished.

SCOLDS AND GOSSIPS (1737)

Early colonial courts took it upon themselves to reform "common scolds"—women who indulged in malicious gossip, scolded their husbands in public, slandered their neighbors, and otherwise disturbed the community peace. The ducking stool was the most common punishment. For couples that were quarrelsome, instead of divorce, which might be the modern solution, the offenders were tied back to back and immersed in cold water. Another common punishment for scolds went back to the Middle Ages—a metal bridle called a brank, which fit over the head with vicious prongs that fit into the mouth to keep the "tongue from wagging." Some wives went further than simply scolding their husbands. In 1737 Salem, Dorothy Talbie, for "frequent laying hands upon hir husband to the danger of his Life," was bound and chained to a post "till shee manefest some change in hir course." Another wife, "Joan, wife of

Obadiah Miller of Taunton, was presented for 'beating and reviling her husband, and egging her children to help her, bidding them knock him in the head, and wishing his victuals might choake him.'"

BANKING IN EARLY AMERICA (1738)

In colonial times banks did not exist in America, and excess money was shrewdly invested in silverware. Not only was it easier to track down than money if it was stolen, but it also served a utilitarian purpose of adding beauty to the home and could be used on special occasions to impress distinguished visitors. It could also be quickly turned into money, if needed. If there were no banks holding large sums of money, just how were public projects like churches, colleges, canals, turnpikes, orphanages, and so forth financed? The answer was found in the lottery, which, ironically, made a comeback in the latter half of the twentieth century—and for the same purpose. In 1781 Congress granted a charter to the Bank of North America, a Philadelphia institution. This was the first incorporated bank in the United States.

JENKINS'S EAR (1739)

Wars have begun and men have died for silly and insignificant reasons—like the war that began in 1739 between Spain and England, gradually merging into the War of the Austrian Succession (King George's War in the Colonies). Much rivalry existed in the Georgia-Florida-Caribbean area with attacking British ships that carried on illicit trade with Spanish-controlled areas. English prime minister Robert Walpole managed to keep British tempers cool and things under control until Capt. Robert Jenkins, a British smuggler, showed up in British territory minus one ear, which he claimed had been cut off by the Spaniards. That was the final straw, and war was declared in June 1739.

As is so often the case when incidents of this nature take place, a thorough investigation was not conducted. Had it been, it would have been discovered that the incident—if true at all—had taken place eight years previously.

JOHN ADAMS THE FARMER (1740)

John Adams never forgot during his lifetime that he was a farmer. In case he was ever tempted, he had his diary to remind him. In it he described his endless rounds of toil as a youth:

"Sometimes I am at the orchard ploughing up acre after acre, planting, pruning apple trees, mending fences, carting dung; sometimes in the pasture, digging stones, clearing bushes, pruning trees, building walls to redeem post and rails. . . . Sometimes I am at the old swamp, burning bushes, digging stumps, cutting ditches across the meadows and against my uncle; and am sometimes at the other end of town, buying posts and rails to fence against my uncle and against the brook."

It seems likely that such toil encouraged further study. He went on to Harvard.

THE GOAT AND THE COMPASS? (1740)

The strange names on American tavern signs in early America were often new forms of Old World tavern names—largely renamed due to ignorance of the original spelling or meaning. For example, the early American "Cat and Wheel Inn" has been traced to the "Catherine Wheel" in London (from St. Catherine's Wheel, referring to the way a Saint was martyred). The "Goat and Compass" derives from the motto "God Encompasseth Us." The "Bacchanalian" was downgraded to the "Bag O'Nails." The "Pig and Carrot" tavern sign comes from Paris, where it was the "Pique et Carreau" (spade and diamond). The "Bell Savage" sign showing an Indian and bell was derived from the French novel about a beautiful girl from the wilderness, La Belle Sauvage. One of the most interesting American tavern signs shows a mouth painted over a bull—the "Bull and Mouth"—making crude sense to us until we learn of its origin: the Battle of Boulogne Mouth (harbor), which was fought in the days of Henry VIII.

FRANKLIN'S LONG LIFE (1741)

Benjamin Franklin, by contemporary odds, should have died in 1741. In that year he was thirty-five, which was the average lifespan for a colonial American in the mid-eighteenth century. Fortunately for the world, he lived another half century, thanks in part to this intelligent approach to bodily health. He was a great advocate of walking for exercise, going everywhere he could on foot. He also urged moderation in food and drink, although he suffered from gout in his old age. At a time when night air was considered dangerous, he slept with his windows open. He and

John Adams once shared a room together, and as advanced as Adams was in his thinking, he was horrified when Franklin threw open a window at night. When Adams started to object, Franklin began a lecture that soon put Adams to sleep—the window still open.

LARGE FAMILIES IN EARLY AMERICA (1742)

With an abundance of land and a scarcity of labor in the early Colonies, children were an asset and large families were common. Sir William Phips, governor of Massachusetts, was one of twenty-six children, all born of the same mother. Robert Carter of Virginia had seventeen children. Charles Carter of Shelby had twenty-three children by two marriages. Ben Franklin came from a family of seventeen. Chief Justice John Marshall was the first of fifteen brothers and sisters. The all-time American mother must be the South Carolina woman who brought thirty-four children into the world. In 1742 a New England woman died leaving 5 children, 61 grandchildren, 182 great-grandchildren, and 12 great-great-grandchildren.

It was possible, however, for a family to be too large in early America—that is, if the authorities felt the excessive size was a drain on a family's resources and a threat to its solidarity. Apparently the size of Francis Bale's family struck the town fathers that way. History doesn't tell us the size of his family, but the authorities "advised him to dispose of two of his children," which probably meant to place them with wealthier neighbors. When his wife objected, "they p'swaded him to p'swade his wife to it."

THE IROQUOIS MAKE A DEAL (1744)

When the Iroquois Indians saw the British and the French contending over land on the basis of who was there "first," they saw their opportunity. If this was the criterion, they argued, then obviously the land all belonged to them. Strangely enough, the British accepted the justice of this and immediately saw an opportunity to outsmart the French. Meeting with the Iroquois in July 1744, the governors of Maryland, Virginia, and Pennsylvania made a deal with the Iroquois for all of the land west of the frontier and north of the Ohio, the Iroquois reserving the land they actually occupied—what is now upstate New York. These colonial agents did even better than Peter Minuit, the man who bought Manhattan Island for twenty-four dollars' worth of trinkets. For this vast area they paid the Iroquois only $2,400, thinking themselves sharp bargainers. However, like the Dutch, the English were taken by Indians, who had no valid claims to the property they sold. The colonists soon found themselves fighting other Indians for every inch of land they believed they had legally purchased.

SCALP BOUNTIES (1744)

At the opening of King George's War in 1744, the Massachusetts General Court declared open season on Indians and offered a reward for scalps. Just why the court did this is difficult to understand because the Indian menace by this time was remote. Alden Vaughn in *New England Frontier* claims that "by 1750 the Indian had almost disappeared from the New England scene." Nevertheless, only thirteen years after the bounty offer was made, it was increased from 250 to 300 British pounds, creating a profitable sport for many whites—including a minister of the gospel in one case. It is possible to judge just how profitable this bounty offer was by comparing it to the salary the town of Boston voted to pay schoolmaster Peleg Wiswall in 1757—120 British pounds. By today's monetary standards, a scalp back then was worth about $15,000.

ILLITERACY IN THE COLONIAL SOUTH (1744)

Southern gentlemen in the colonial South, Virginians specifically, followed the lead of their English counterparts who encouraged them to be literate but not bookish—the emphasis being on what was thoroughly practical. In other words, they were judged more by what they owned than by what they knew, more by the graciousness of their conduct than by their learning. This philosophy resulted in a scarcity of books and high illiteracy in the South. William Byrd's collection of 3,600 books by 1744, the largest outside of New England, overshadows what was typical in the South. More common were such libraries as George Washington's handful of volumes on practical husbandry. It is hard to say how many colonial Virginians could read, but in examining seventeenth-century county records, historian P. A. Bruce found that nearly half of 18,000 white male Virginians used a mark to sign their names. Undoubtedly, many of those who did so could neither read nor write more than their names. Three-quarters of the white women could not sign their names, and even more significantly, some Virginians who made marks were judges.

WINE LOOSENS PURSE STRINGS TOO (1748)

When French and Spanish privateers sacked two plantations near Philadelphia during the third colonial war, Benjamin Franklin prevailed upon his fellow townsmen to organize a municipal militia. This self-defense association wanted to elect Franklin colonel, but he declined. He did, however, travel to New York to acquire some cannon for the city's defense. At first the royal governor, George Clinton, refused to grant Franklin's request. But that evening while dining with the governor, Franklin noticed that Clinton was drinking heavily. After a few drinks Franklin again asked for cannon, and Clinton offered him six. Franklin suggested some more wine, and before the evening was over Clinton had promised Franklin eighteen guns. The canny diplomat noted, "We soon transported and mounted on our battery, where the Associators [including Franklin himself] kept a nightly guard while the war lasted."

BOUNTIES ON SQUIRRELS (1749)

Bounties on animal pests are not at all unusual in America. A major objection to settlement in New England was the prevalence of wolves, with bounties being paid for wolf skins as early as the 1630s in both Virginia and Massachusetts. The extermination efforts were successful despite occasional "counterfeiting."

Modern hunters of country animals such as the wolf or western mountain lion might be awed to know that in early America squirrels were such a pest and ate so much grain that some towns paid a bounty on them as well. Some local treasuries were apparently exhausted by these payments. The Swedish traveler Pehr Kalm reported that in the colony of Pennsylvania in 1749, 8,000 pounds were paid out for the heads (not easy to counterfeit) of black and gray squirrels at the rate of three pence a head. Some quick arithmetic would show that 600,000 were killed and turned in.

"AND CALLED IT MACARONI" (1750)

In the 1700s gentlemen devoted fully as much time to their dress as did women, using cosmetics, pomatum, perfume, and powder. In public a gentleman was expected to wear a cocked hat, ruffled shirt, embroidered frock coat, knee breeches, silk hose, and pumps with silver or gold buckles. John Hancock, the well-known patriot, cut a dashing figure in a lavender jacket and lilac-colored breeches with frills of lace on his cuffs and shirt front, becoming known throughout Massachusetts as a Macaroni. This was the name given foppish Englishmen with brightly colored silk garments, wasp waists, diamond buckles, two watches, silk stockings (usually red), a diminutive hat, a cane, a sword, and vast amounts of lace, braid, and ruffles. Gold snuff boxes were another necessity, for the image was not complete without the periodic taking of snuff and the accompanying dainty sneeze.

COLONIAL TEA DRINKING (1750)

From such accounts as the Boston Tea Party, many of us have the impression that tea was an ancient and honored English drink. Such is not the case. It did not come into use in England until around the middle of the seventeenth century, along with coffee. It took even longer for the custom to reach the Colonies and become widespread. Lack of knowledge as to how these beverages should be prepared and served probably hindered their adoption in the Colonies. Many housewives in their ignorance served the tea leaves with sugar or syrup after throwing away the water in which they had been boiled. This new drink from China was not accepted by all. Some called it a "damned weed," a "detestable weed," a "base exotick," a "rank poison farfetched and dear brought," a "base and unworthy Indian drink." Various ill effects were attributed to it—tooth decay and even loss of mental faculties.

Coffee drinking entered the Colonies at about the same time as tea, and the same ignorance was shown concerning its preparation. Many women boiled the whole beans in water, ate the beans, and drank the liquid. Coffee, incidentally, replaced tea as the national drink as a result of the break with England during the American Revolution when it became unpatriotic to drink tea. Just before the Revolution, Americans were more noted as tea drinkers than their English cousins.

"TO HELL, MADAM!" (1750)

One of the most distinguished and interesting families in early Virginia was the Custis family of Arlington. Irascible John Custis, who disliked his wife so much that he proclaimed the fact in his epitaph, once drove his carriage into the Chesapeake. When his lady asked him where he was going, he bellowed, "To Hell, Madam!" "Drive on," she said coolly. "Any place is better than Arlington."

WILL THE REAL "COVERED WAGON" STAND UP? (1750)

When we hear the term "covered wagon," the picture that comes to mind is the familiar long-bodied wagon with high, wide wheels and white canvas top. The body of the wagon was rounded like a boat to keep freight from shifting on hills, painted bright blue with a red running gear, and normally drawn by oxen or mules. There were many kinds of covered wagons, but the one described here was the Conestoga, invented and produced by Pennsylvania Germans in the Conestoga Valley around 1750. Conestoga caravans were the freight trains of the late 1700s and early 1800s.

Although they are usually pictured as the wagons of the western pioneers, they were not that popular because of their great weight and size. They were fine on the better-traveled roads in the east, but the pioneers moving west through unknown country and over mountains preferred to use lighter and more easily pulled wagons. *The Prairie Traveler,* a handbook for overland expeditions written in the nineteenth century, states that "spring wagons made in Concord, New Hampshire . . . are said to be much superior to any others." No mention is made of the much heavier Conestoga.

THE AUGUSTA WHITE HOUSE (1750)

The Augusta White House, said to be the oldest house in Augusta, Georgia, was built in 1750. It is a two-story frame dwelling on upper Broad Street used during the American Revolution as the headquarters of one of the Tory commanders. During the war, which saw violent atrocities and reprisals by both Tories and rebels, the Tory commander caused thirteen patriot prisoners to be hanged in the home's staircase well—all at the same time. It is said, for those who believe in ghosts, that if you stand at the foot of the stairs and count to thirteen, a deep groan will shudder through the house.

"VISITING" THE INSANE (1752)

Want of entertainment prompted colonial Americans to turn to some unusual diversions. One of the most sadistic was visiting the madhouse, as George Ives in his *History of Penal Methods* says, to "irritate and purposefully enrage the secured patients as their descendants tease caged animals to this day; and thus reproduced for their ghastly diversion exhibitions of madness." This practice began in America with the opening of the Pennsylvania Hospital in 1752, but it stemmed from 1247 at Bedlam Hospital in London. Hospital authorities took advantage of this innate streak of cruelty in humankind by charging visitors a gate fee: 12.5 cents during Washington's administration. No record exists of receipts at the Pennsylvania Hospital, but in 1770 Bedlam grossed 400 pounds from these exhibitions. This practice died out during James Monroe's administration, although not because of legislation or restriction.

THE WORLD STOOD STILL (1752)

Try to find something that happened between September 2 and September 14, 1752, in American history. It is impossible. No one was born or died, no events occurred. Nothing! There is actually a rather simple explanation. In 1752 the British Empire and its colonies in America officially adopted the Gregorian calendar, which had been devised by Pope Gregory III in 1582. In order to compensate for errors in the old Julian calendar, it became necessary to leave eleven days out of the calendar, so it was decided that there would be no September 3 through 13. Some confusion arose in the Colonies, but nothing like that in England. People rioted against the government's decision because they thought their lives were being shortened by eleven days.

RATIONS FOR BRADDOCK'S OFFICERS (1755)

Ben Franklin assumed the job of gathering wagons and pack horses for Maj. Gen. Edward Braddock's army in 1755, doing an admirable job of hiring 150 wagons and 1,500 pack horses. He also had to see that their loss was made up when the English army was wiped out by the French and Indians in western Pennsylvania. Of great interest, however, were the twenty pack horses loaded with gifts of food for the British officers, the inventory on one horse offering a good indication of the provisions for which an officer in 1755 was grateful:
- Six pounds loaf-sugar
- Two dozen bottles old Madeira
- Six pounds muscovado sugar

- Two gallons Jamaica spirits
- One pound green tea
- One bottle flour of mustard
- One pound bohea tea
- Two well-cured hams
- Six pounds ground coffee
- Half a dozen cured tongues
- Six pounds rice
- Biscuits
- Six pounds raisins
- Half a pound pepper
- Twenty pounds butter
- One quart white vinegar
- One Gloucester cheese

DEAD SOLDIERS TAKE REVENGE (1757)

One of the bloodiest massacres to take place on North American soil occurred at Fort William Henry in 1757. Besieged by a large force of French and Indians, the British garrison surrendered to the French upon the promise of conduct to safety. As the two thousand prisoners were leaving the fort, many of them women and children, the 1,800 Indian allies of the French fell upon the unarmed and helpless captives, butchering more than a hundred and carrying off hundreds as prisoners to be later tortured or eaten. After the massacre was halted, some of the Indians still lusted for blood and scalps. When they discovered some fresh graves in the English camp, they dug them up and scalped them. Unknown to the Indians, the dead had contracted smallpox. The Indians carried the disease back to their villages, where that fall and winter it carried out its deadly work. Almost the entire Potawatomi nation was wiped out, the English dead thus avenging the butchering of their comrades-in-arms.

FRANKLIN'S STRONG-WILLED WIFE (1757)

During the many years Benjamin Franklin spent in England (1757–75) as a representative of both Pennsylvania and the united Colonies, he grew attached to that island with its "sensible, virtuous and elegant Minds." He seriously considered moving there permanently and would have had he been able to "persuade the good Woman to cross the Seas." As the question of American rights became ever greater an issue with the Mother Country, however, his admiration for England decreased. Nevertheless, he carried on an extensive correspondence with many of those "elegant Minds" to the day he died. If his wife had been less strong willed, America's First Citizen might be unknown to most Americans today.

NOT-SO-SECRET VOTING (1758)

The so-called "secret," or Australian ballot, imported into this country late in the nineteenth century was long overdue. Paper ballots were introduced into Massachusetts as early as 1634, but there was little secrecy in most colonial elections. The most common election method was to have voters approach election officials one at a time and openly announce their choice of candidates, only to be greeted by cheers or boos from opposing factions. At the same time, betting odds were openly changed or new wagers laid. It was also the custom for the candidates to be present and personally thank each voter for the vote cast in his favor. When Washington's military duties kept him away from an election in 1758, his friend James Wood sat at the voting place and thanked each voter for the votes cast for the absent colonel.

COLONIAL MILITARY LOGISTICS (1758)

Living in an age of huge transport planes and helicopters makes it difficult to appreciate the hardships involved in providing for an army in frontier America. A British supply officer left us an estimate made in 1758 for supplying an army of 20,000 for only one month at Lake George, north of Albany. His estimate vividly dramatizes the problem. It required three weeks of good weather to move the necessary 5,760 barrels of pork, beef, and bread, each barrel being handled five times on the trip. To move these supplies required 800 wagons, 1,000 bateaux, and 1,000 ox carts. This move provided only for the food and did not take into account the usual military supplies such as cannon, powder, shot, clothing, and many other items needed for an army in the field. Certainly the average campaign lasted longer than one month. A careful reading of colonial history shows that far more armies were defeated by lack of provisions than by enemy action.

"ARMY WOMEN" (1759)

The well-known Molly Pitcher who helped man a cannon at the Battle of Monmouth was not at all unique, in the sense of women associating with fighting men in the field. This was an ancient tradition in European armies. For years British regulations had allowed as many as four to six women (drawing regular rations) per company to accompany armies in the field, acting as both laundresses and nurses. Many of these women were the wives or sweethearts of the soldiers, whereas many others came along to provide "morale." After the defeat of Gen. Edward Braddock in the French and Indian War, the victors found the bodies of six women among the slain. Some of the credit for the defeat of Gen. John Burgoyne in 1777 must be given to the women in Gentleman Johnny's Army. Their large number, with all their baggage, children, and nurses so slowed the British advance into New York that the Americans were given extra time to raise their forces. The British garrison at Quebec during the long, cold winter of 1759–60 included 569 women, or one for every thirteen soldiers.

EARLIEST SUBMARINE WARFARE (1759)

The Turtle of Revolutionary War fame, although far more sophisticated, was not the first submarine to be used in warfare. During the British attack on Quebec in 1759, three French sailors made use of an extremely crude submersible boat. Its inventor is unknown, as are the details of the boat itself. All we know is that it was about nine feet long, propelled just under the surface by the crew swimming with their heads and shoulders inside the craft, and designed to blow any ship to which it was attached. In its first and only known use, it was attached to a British warship. The crew swam to safety, but the fuse apparently got wet and went out, which made it about as successful as the *Turtle*.

WASHINGTON: PHYSICAL DESCRIPTION (1759)

A fellow member of the House of Burgesses, George Mercer, described George Washington as follows:

"He may be described as being straight as an Indian, measuring 6 feet 2 inches in his stockings, and weighing 175 lbs. when he took his seat in the House of Burgesses in 1759. His frame is padded with well developed muscles, indicating great strength. His bones and joints are large as are his hands and feet. He is wide shouldered but has not a deep or round chest; is neat waisted, but is broad across the hips, and has rather long legs and arms. His head is well shaped, though not large, but is gracefully poised on a superb neck. A large and straight rather than a prominent nose;

blue grey penetrating eyes which are widely separated and overhung by a heavy brow. His face is long rather than broad, with high round cheek bones, and terminates in a good firm chin. He has a clear rather colorless pale skin which burns with the sun. A pleasing and benevolent tho a commanding countenance, dark brown hair which he wears in a cue. His mouth is large and generally firmly closed, but which from time to time discloses some defective teeth. His features are regular and placid with all the muscles of his face under perfect control, tho flexible and expressive of deep feeling when moved by emotion. In conversation he looks you full in the face, is deliberate, deferential and engaging. His demeanor at all times composed and dignified. His movements and gestures are graceful, his walk majestic, and he is a splendid horseman."

THE POTATO IN EARLY AMERICA (1763)

Contrary to popular belief, potatoes were known to the early New Englanders, but they were rare. Strangely enough, early Americans had much the same fear of potatoes as they had of water. Growing them was rare enough that it was recorded when a farmer at Handley, Massachusetts, grew a large crop of eight bushels in 1763. Many people commonly believed that anyone who ate them every day could not live seven years. Potatoes left in the fields were carefully burned so that they would not poison cattle and horses. When a few hardy souls did eat them, they cooked them with butter, sugar, and grape juice, mixed them with dates, lemons, and mace, and then seasoned them with cinnamon, nutmeg, and pepper. Finally, this concoction was covered with a sugar frosting. Maybe they weren't so hardy after all.

TARRING AND FEATHERING (1769)

Tarring and feathering, which is strongly associated with the American Revolution, actually didn't get its start in America until 1769. In that year a mob in Boston used this Old World punishment against an informer who reported on the activities of some smugglers. After that it was used fairly consistently against tax collectors and other agents of the king. Even Gov. Thomas Hutchinson, exiled from Massachusetts, was received by King George III with the words, "I see they threatened to pitch and feather you." Hutchinson replied, "Tarr and feather, may it please your Majesty."

One of the verses in "Yankee Doodle," sung by British soldiers in Boston in 1775, carried a threat to tar and feather John Hancock. In an event immortalized by John Greenleaf Whittier, the women of Marblehead tarred and feathered "Old Floyd Ireson with his hart heart" for leaving some fellow townsmen to drown at sea. Ireson was carried in a cart, but the normal procedure after the tar and feathers were applied was to carry the victim about town, or out of it, on a rail. The latter form of social control was also introduced in Boston about 1675 when John Langworthy was ridden out of town on a rail for serving as a carpenter without first serving his apprenticeship.

THE BOSTON MASSACRE (1770)

Many interesting and commonly unknown events surround the so-called Boston Massacre. For example, Crispus Attucks, the African-American martyr, was actually part Native American and part white and, like many others in the mob, was a well-known waterfront tough who was not wielding a cudgel for the first time on March 5, 1770. The British soldiers on trial for murder were defended by none other than well-known patriot John Adams. The jury, with not a single Bostonian on it, acquitted all but two of the soldiers, who were found guilty of manslaughter and branded on the thumbs. The Massachusetts Historical Society in 1887 opposed the erection of a monument to the martyrs because the schoolbook version of the unprovoked attack by the British was not objective history.

THE SUCCESSFUL "FAILURE" (1770)

Between the Boston Massacre in 1770 and the Boston Tea Party in 1773, one man was more responsible than any other person in keeping the embers of revolution alive—Samuel Adams, cousin of America's second president. Sam lived in a run-down house on Purchase Street and dressed in shabby clothes with buttons missing, but he knew everybody in Boston and apparently was well liked. He willingly served in any job his fellow Bostonians wanted him to: he was the worst, but most popular, tax collector Boston ever had. Personally he was a failure in his private business life but an outstanding success in what he felt counted most—fomenting revolution. He talked revolution endlessly, spoke at countless meetings, and wrote letters to the *Independent Advertiser* and *Boston Gazette* under pen names such as Puritan, Populus, Determinatus, or Bostonian.

After the Tea Party, George III offered a pardon to every American patriot under arms "excepting John Hancock and Samuel Adams." This must have pleased the old patriot.

QUACKS LIKE LOCUSTS (1770)

The vast majority of doctors in early America were either self-trained or served as apprentices to others. In the 1770s only 5 percent of medical practitioners held the degree of medical doctor. Many Americans lived almost as much in fear of the doctor as of the disease. "Our American practitioners are so rash and officious," said Dr. William Douglass of Boston in 1721, "that the saying in Ecclesiasticus may with much propriety be applied to them: 'He that sinneth before his Maker let him fall into the hands of the physician.'"

"Quacks," lamented a New Yorker in 1757, "abound like locusts in Egypt." Thomas Jefferson once said that whenever he saw three or more doctors gathered, he looked up to see if there were any buzzards waiting for the kill. Praise was directed at some physicians, however. It was said of Dr. Samuel Fuller of Plymouth that thanks to his practice of depleting his patients of large amounts of blood, he "did a great cure for Captain Littleworth. He cured him of a disease called a wife."

IT HARDLY PAID TO LEARN (1771)

If you are thirty-six years of age or older, you have good reason not to long for the "good old days" of two centuries ago, for an American's life expectancy in the 1770s was less than thirty-five years. And while you are reading this bit of information, consider something else: you probably wouldn't have been able to read this two hundred years ago because the average person couldn't read well. Only the comparatively wealthy sent their boys to school beyond the age of ten, and most families didn't send girls at all. As late as 1829 even the president of the United States, Andrew Jackson, could scarcely write. Life in colonial America was hard and short, and spending long years acquiring a formal education just wasn't too appealing, even when the rare opportunities were available.

THE "FIRST CONSTITUTION" (1772)

Four years before the Declaration of Independence was signed, there was a free and independent community in America—the first in the New

World—but the British didn't seem too upset about it. In May 1772 the settlers in western North Carolina and the mountains of Tennessee organized a civil government and drew up the "Articles of the Watauga Association," the first written constitution adopted by an association of American citizens. It set up a representative assembly of thirteen men and a judicial and executive committee of five men, the first five being John Sevier, James Robertson, Charles Robertson, Zachariah Isbess, and John Carter. Interestingly enough, these people who formed their government as protection against thieves and outlaws furnished the first governors of Tennessee, Kentucky, Missouri, and Arkansas. Watauga was the first, but not the last, independent republic in what is now the United States. Vermont, Texas, and California all became self-proclaimed republics at one time.

EDICT OF THE KING OF PRUSSIA (1772)

In an effort to swing British public opinion to the American cause, Benjamin Franklin resorted to several "hoaxes" while serving in England before the Revolution. The most famous was the edict of the King of Prussia, which was an announcement that appeared in several English newspapers around 1772. The notice claimed that the king, whose ancestors had settled England many years before, still claimed the right to make laws governing that country. The notice also listed the things "his colonists in England" had the right to do, such as sending iron ore to Prussia to be smelted and beaver skins to be made into hats, allowing them to buy back the finished products. The intelligent English readers quickly caught on, but the gullible waited fearfully for Frederick to appear across the channel with his army to enforce his demands.

FRANKLIN'S HUMOR IN ENGLAND (1772)

Benjamin Franklin was sent to England previous to the outbreak of hostilities with the hope of smoothing out some of the difficulties between the mother country and her Colonies. Whereas other men might have had occasion to resort to anger at times, Franklin effectively used the humor for which Americans in general were to become so well known. When one influential Englishman attacked what he heard was an American plan for setting up bootleg whale and cod fisheries on the Great Lakes, Franklin publicly admitted that this was a serious matter, although the Great Lakes were fresh water. "Cod, when attacked by their enemies, fly into any water where they can be safest. Whales pursue them wherever they fly. The grand leap of a whale up Niagara Falls is esteemed one of the finest spectacles in nature." History didn't record what must have been the reply, if any, of a very embarrassed Englishman.

STANDING MUTE! (1772)

It is a well-known aspect of American justice that standing mute when asked to plead guilty or not guilty in a present-day court is taken as a plea of not guilty. Previous to 1772, however, a person accused in a felony case (murder, robbery, and other serious crimes) was forced to plead, under torture if necessary. In the earliest colonial days, the accused was put into solitary confinement and fed bread one day and the "coarsest" water (taken from "the next sink or puddle to the place of execution") the next day until he made his plea or died of starvation. Later on, as evidenced in the well-known Cory case in Salem in 1692, "pressing" was used to force a plea. In this case, the prisoner was stretched, sometimes over a stake, and weights were placed on him until he died or agreed to make a plea. All such tortures ended in 1772 when Parliament decreed, in a law applicable to the Colonies, that standing mute would be taken as a plea of guilty.

ONLY WALLED CITY
IN THE UNITED STATES (1772)

The history of the American Southwest is a bloody history—to a large degree resulting from the bloodlust of the Apaches, to whom man hunting was both a pastime and a business. Upon their entry into what is now Arizona, the Spaniards made great headway in converting the peaceful Papago, and together the Catholic Spanish and their Native American charges were the object of attacks by the Apaches. Thus, to protect both the Spaniards and the Papagos, Padre Garces enclosed the entire pueblo of Tucson in 1772 with a high adobe wall, giving Tucson the distinction of being the only walled city in American history. Contrary to what one may see on television, Indians seldom attacked fortified places, preferring the much safer and saner tactic of catching their enemies in the open, where the Indians were not at such a disadvantage.

COLONIAL DANCE MARATHONS (1773)

In contrast to the North, where dancing was frequently prohibited by law, the most popular amusement in the South for white people was dancing. A contemporary writing in 1773 describes a ball given by Squire Richard Lee in Virginia, which lasted from Monday morning until Thursday night. When his seventy guests were finally so tired out that they could dance no longer, their host insisted that they stay and rest up until they were able to go on with the dance. The records don't say whether they did.

By the time of the Revolution, dancing had become quite popular throughout the country. George Washington was especially fond of dancing and is reported to have "danced upwards of three hours without once sitting down" with Gen. Nathaniel Greene's wife. What he danced to is not recorded, but dances of the time included "High Betty Martin," "Rolling Hornpipe," "Orange Tree," "Springfield, The President," "The Lady's Choice," "Miss Foster's Delight," and "Leather the Strap."

A WOMAN SPY (1773)

A woman spy in the American Revolution was unusual enough, but what made Patience Lovell Wright of Bordentown, New Jersey, even more notable was that she was a Quaker, who were normally pacifists. Equally curious was her profession, a maker of wax figures, which she displayed in New York City and later in London, where she went to live just before the American Revolution. The king and queen of England, who came to know her through her work, allowed her to address them Quaker-fashion by their first names, George and Charlotte. When war loomed between the mother country and the Colonies, Mrs. Wright lectured the king on his colonial policies, and their relationship deteriorated. She nevertheless remained a favorite in London society, and when the war began, she successfully smuggled military and diplomatic information to Benjamin Franklin.

TABLE MANNERS (1773)

In a small book of etiquette for children, circulated in the Colonies just before the Revolution, we find these rules for the behavior of children at the table:

"Never sit down at the table till asked, and after the blessing. Ask for nothing: tarry till it be offered thee. Speak not. Bite not thy bread but break it. Take salt only with a clean knife. Dip not the meat in the same. Hold not thy knife upright but sloping, and lay it down at right hand of plate with blade on plate. Look not earnestly at any other that is eating. When moderately satisfied leave the table. Sing not, hum not, wiggle not. Spit no where in the room but in the corner. . . . Eat not too fast nor with Greedy Behavior. Eat not vastly, but moderately. Make not a noise with thy tongue, Mouth, Lips, or Breath in Thy Eating and Drinking. Smell not of thy Meat; nor put it to thy Nose."

"'TWAS THE 13TH OF DECEMBER IN '74" (1774)

Schoolbooks tell us that Paul Revere's warning to Lexington and Concord brought out the militia for the opening battle of the Revolutionary War. Somehow they have forgotten to mention Fort William and Mary in Portsmouth, New Hampshire. Hearing that the British intended to strengthen the fort, John Sullivan, with a group of his New Hampshire militia, marched on the fort and demanded its surrender the previous December. When the British commander fired upon them with four-pounders and muskets, the Americans stormed the fort, capturing the captain and his garrison of five invalid soldiers. Suffering no casualties, Sullivan's men carried off ninety-seven barrels of powder, 1,500 muskets, and several pieces of artillery. King George's fury over this action by the Americans led to his orders to secure all other colonial munitions, resulting in Lexington and Concord.

Paul Revere's image shouldn't suffer too much, however, should the "Battle of William and Mary" take precedence over Lexington. He was also the messenger who brought the news of British intentions to John Sullivan, and his ride was a good fifty miles longer than the one the following April.

IN THE LORD'S SERVICE (1775)

Ministers, about the time of the American Revolution, made precious little money for the amount of labor they gave the Lord and his people. Even those holding a position of authority could hardly afford to have a family. The Episcopal Conference granted the Right Rev. Samuel Seabury, bishop of Connecticut, a salary of sixty-four dollars a year, and even then he had to collect the money himself from his congregations. For this he traveled no less than 6,000 miles through the back country for the eleven years he served. This was mild work compared to Bishop Asbury of the Methodists, who traveled 270,000 miles during his long service, ordaining 4,000 ministers and presiding over 220 conferences. The itinerant preacher Peter Cartright must hold some kind of record, however, serving more than fifty years, preaching 14,000 sermons, baptizing 12,000 people, and conducting more than 550 funerals. The Reverend Cartright, incidentally, is credited with developing the camp meeting.

MINUTEMEN: 1181 (1775)

The self-armed minutemen and volunteer militia are considered by many to be a unique early American creation prompted by dangers on an ever-present frontier. That frontier conditions necessitated a colonial militia is true, but that it was a unique New World invention is not true. The farmers who took up their muskets and met the British on the common at Lexington were simply the culmination of a revival of the medieval Assize of Arms (1181), in which their mother country of England had built up a militia hundreds of years before.

Professional armies in the seventeenth and eighteenth centuries made the English militia more or less a joke, but for four hundred years every able-bodied English freeman, self-armed and trained under local officers, stood ready on a minute's notice to guard England against all enemies. Little did the founders of the system dream how effectively it would be used against the English themselves. The effectiveness of the citizen army was demonstrated as early as 1675 during King Philip's War. On the night of September 23, an alarm at a town thirty miles out of Boston brought 1,200 militiamen under arms within an hour. Exactly a hundred years later on April 19, an alarm at another town a few miles out of Boston turned out 3,600 militiamen.

THE COMIC OPERA AT THE BRIDGE (1775)

Only the diplomacy of a Salem clergyman permitted Lexington to become the opening battle of the War for Independence. It might easily have been Salem instead. Two months before the action at Lexington and Concord, Gen. Thomas Gage sent a similar detachment to Salem on a similar assignment—to seize war supplies deposited there by the rebels. As at Lexington, the Salem militia was warned of the approach of the

British and was ready for them, but in this instance the detachment was stopped by a raised drawbridge—the American militia drawn up opposite the stream.

The intervention of a Salem clergyman prevented a serious encounter, actually turning the event into a comic opera. Because saving face was important to the British commander, Col. Alexander Leslie agreed that if the bridge was lowered, he would march over it to prove his point but would then immediately turn around and march back over it to Marblehead and return to Boston. Upon reaching Marblehead, Leslie found the militia out in force, but when the rebels saw the British returning without the captured supplies, they fell in behind the British troops and accompanied them down to the docks to the tune of the British fifers. Two months later it was not to be so funny.

A FIGHTING SENIOR CITIZEN (1775)

In the flight along the Lexington-Concord road on April 19, 1775, the British regulars met some tough opponents, but probably none tougher than Sam Whittemore. Sam prepared himself carefully with a musket, a brace of pistols, and a saber. Then, bidding his wife good-bye, set out to meet the Redcoats. He was eighty years old at the time.

When a flanking party sent out by the British approached the stone wall where Sam was stationed, he rose and dropped two of the regulars, possibly hitting a third. But he didn't get away unscathed. A British musket ball shot away half his face, and he fell as the regulars vaulted over the wall. Angered by the elusive Americans, the regulars bayoneted the fallen old man again and again before moving on, somewhat appeased. But somehow, with his face half gone and his body riddled with t hirteen bayonet wounds, Sam Whittemore survived and lived to be almost a hundred. Smiling a crooked smile, Sam always insisted that he wouldn't hesitate to live that day all over again.

RICHARD DERBY: AN UNSUNG HERO (1775)

The man responsible for one of the earliest and most devastating propaganda defeats suffered by the British government in the Revolution was a Salem merchant whose name is known to probably fewer than one American school child in a thousand. He was Richard Derby, commissioned by Dr. Joseph Warren, chairman of the Provincial Congress, to speed the news of the British defeat at Lexington and Concord to London. This he did in one of his own light, but fast, schooners, the *Quero*, beating Gen. Thomas Gage's version of the battle by at least two weeks. Hiding his vessel at the Isle of Wight after a speedy crossing of only four weeks, Derby spread the American version of the "Bloody Butchery by the British Troops" to every newspaper and American sympathizer in London while successfully eluding all British attempts to track him down. Official word from the British commander in America two weeks later and all government attempts thereafter could not undo the propaganda victory brought about by Dr. Warren's Committee of Safety and the merchant Richard Derby. When Gage's report did arrive on a cargo ship, it began with what was probably the understatement of the century: "I have now nothing to trouble your lordship with, but of an affair that happened here on the 19th instant."

IN WHOSE NAME DID YOU SAY? (1775)

When the Green Mountain leader, Ethan Allen, pounded on a door and roused a sleeping and half-dressed English officer to demand the surrender of Fort Ticonderoga in 1775, did he really make his demand "in the name of the Great Jehovah and the Continental Congress"? He said he did when he wrote about it later, but some of his biographers doubt it. Having carefully researched the incident, they insist that what he really said was much more like, "Come out of there, you damned old rat!"

Historian Christopher Ward says the British officer had about as much respect for the Continental Congress as Allen had for the Great Jehovah. Whatever the case, the capture of the fort furnished the American army with tons of badly needed war supplies, including nine tons of musket balls alone. Interestingly, when Congress heard of the capture, they ordered that an exact inventory be taken of all the supplies "in order that they may be safely returned" upon the restoration of harmony between the Colonies and the mother country. Most of the shot, powder, and cannon balls were in fact returned—just not as Congress intended.

THE "BOUNTY COATS" (1775)

The Continental Army encircling Boston in the summer of 1775 found itself in need of many things, not the least of which were coats for the soldiers. To alleviate this shortage, the Provincial Congress put out an order for 13,000 warm coats for the coming fall and winter season. There being no factory, hundreds of patriotic women went to work with their wool wheels and looms, and the order was filled. So prized were such coats that the Congress decided to use them as inducement for enlistment, and one of the homespun coats was given to each volunteer who enlisted for eight months service. The coats were so dear that the heirs of the men killed at the Battle of Bunker Hill, rather than receiving their coats, received a sum of money instead. Historians today still refer to those men who enlisted for the coat bounty as the "coat roll," and at that time the British referred to Washington's army as the "homespun"—a term the Americans seemed to adopt with pride.

FIRST NAVAL BATTLE OF THE REVOLUTION (1775)

The Battle of Bunker Hill has overshadowed in history an interesting American victory that preceded it by five days. On June 12, 1775, the first naval battle of the Revolutionary War took place in the harbor of Machias, Maine. The captain of the British schooner, the *Margaretta,* lying at anchor in the harbor, had ordered the residents of the town to take down a liberty pole they had erected. Instead, a group of citizens confiscated a lumber sloop, sailed out to the *Margaretta,* and in a hand-to-hand battle captured the ship with all its cannon and crew. They then marched the sullen and disgraced crew overland to Massachusetts, where they turned them over to Gen. George Washington. The Americans lost four in the encounter in which the British schooner, armed with twenty-four cannon, was pitted against thirty-five farmers armed with old muskets, pitchforks, and axes.

JOHN ADAMS SHAKES UP HANCOCK (1775)

The nomination of George Washington as commander of the American army at Cambridge during the meeting of the Second Continental Congress in June 1775 throws an interesting and revealing sidelight upon John Hancock. John Adams, who nominated Washington, reveals this in his diary. As Adams started his nomination speech, Washington, whose name had not yet been mentioned, "from his usual modesty, darted into the library-room." But Hancock, who had an ambition to be appointed commander in chief and expected his fellow Bostonians to nominate him, listened to Adams with "visible pleasure." Adams concluded, "When I came to describe Washington for the Commander, I never remarked a more sudden and striking change of countenance [in Hancock]. Mortification and resentment were expressed as forcibly as his face could exhibit them. Mr. Samuel Adams [another Bostonian] seconded the motion, and that did not soften the President's physiognomy [facial features] at all."

WAR IS DISTRESSING! (1775)

Like his father and older cousin Sam, young John Quincy Adams also had a connection with the American Revolution, though to a far lesser degree. Born in Braintree, Massachusetts, in 1767, he witnessed, with his mother Abigail, the Battle of Bunker Hill from the top of Penn's Hill near the family farm. The spot is marked so that today's visitors may know the place.

It was after this battle that his mother wrote to his father in Philadelphia. "Dear Friend, Dr. [Joseph] Warren is no more, but fell gloriously fighting for his country." She added, "The constant roar of the cannon is so distressing that we cannot Eat, Drink, or Sleep." Without a doubt it was somewhat distressing for those untrained farmers crouching behind the earthworks on Bunker Hill also.

REVOLUTIONARY WAR SURGERY (1775)

Surgery in the 1770s was simple and crude and can be summed up by a look at the typical surgical instruments of the time. There were bullet probes, bullet extractors, forceps, catheters, lancets, amputating and trepanning sets, surgical knives, retractors or surgical hooks, tourniquets, syringes, crow-bill tooth extractors, and, of course, needles, thread, and scissors. The lancet, used for bleeding, received the greatest use because it was approved for almost any ailment. For pleurisy, twelve ounces of blood were drawn from the jugular vein while the patient was ordered to breathe deeply and cough. If pains did not diminish within twenty-four hours, the patient was bled again.

The normal treatment for rheumatism was ten ounces of blood drained from the afflicted area. Amputation knives and saws saw much use, being the normal treatment for massive infection, gangrene, and limbs whose bones had been shattered by bullets. In the Revolution, a soldier going into battle had a 98 percent chance of escaping death. His odds dropped to 75 percent if he entered a hospital. Needless to say, many soldiers suffered in silence rather than seek medical help, knowing that even multiple fractures normally resulted in amputation.

"EXTRAORDINARY OUTPOURING OF HUMAN ABILITY" (1775)

"I have not heard, nor I suppose is there, a rational explanation for the fact that this small country, possessed of a very limited population, living under harsh circumstances, produced so many, many brilliant and extraordinary figures who set the tone of national life, and who really represent the most extraordinary outpouring of human ability devoted to government than any time since the days of Greece. And any touch we may have in our lives with that period attracts us all."

So said President John F. Kennedy on the publication of the first four of the proposed ninety volumes of correspondence of the first three Adamses. It was also Kennedy who, upon the occasion of a White House dinner for several distinguished persons, remarked that the event brought together the greatest amount of intellect seen in the White House since Thomas Jefferson had dined there alone.

REBEL PUNISHMENT (1775)

Little thought is normally given to what punishment might have been in store for the patriots in the American Revolution who were, of course, traitors and rebels to their king. Legal punishment for the rebel was "that he be hanged by the neck and then cut down alive; that his entrails be taken out and burned while he is yet alive; that his head be cut off; that his body be divided into four parts; that his head and quarters be at the king's disposal."

There is no evidence that this sentence was ever carried out on any participants of the American Revolution. There is little doubt, however, that those patriots who signed the Declaration of Independence and pledged their lives as well as their fortunes and sacred honor knew exactly the risk they were taking.

WASHINGTON UNFIT FOR COMMAND (1775)

That George Washington did not seek or even desire the task of commander in chief of the American army is historical fact. He felt that he was totally inadequate for the job, and considering his record up to that point in 1775, he was technically correct. Not well-known is a conversation he had with fellow Virginian Patrick Henry immediately after his election, as reported by Dr. Benjamin Rush. He protested that he lacked the training for such an important command (he knew he was being considered but didn't think it likely that he would be chosen), assuring Henry, "Remember, Mr. Henry, what I now tell you: from the day I enter upon the command of the American armies, I will date my fall, and the ruin of my reputation."

In January 1776 he still wasn't happy about his nomination. He wrote to a colleague that month: "I have often thought how much happier I should have been if . . . I had taken my musket on my shoulder and entered the ranks, or, if I could have justified the measure to posterity and my own conscience, had retired to the back country, and lived in a wigwam."

PAUL REVERE CAPTURED (1775)

"The Midnight Ride of Paul Revere" has immortalized forever the young silversmith from Boston, but the poem doesn't tell the whole story. Riding the same night on the same errand but by a slightly different route was young Billy Dawes. After leaving Lexington, Revere and Dawes met Dr. Samuel Prescott on his way back to Concord after a date with a Lexington girl. This was a fortunate meeting, for Dawes and Revere were both captured by a British patrol, leaving Prescott alone to warn the residents of Concord—the ultimate objective of the British. Revere was released, but his horse was kept and ridden by a British officer for the rest of the war. (Actually, Revere had borrowed it from Deacon Larkin in Charleston that same night.) Later in the morning Revere went to Buckman's Tavern on the Lexington Green to get John Hancock's trunk just as the first shots were being fired on the green. Not realizing the significance of the moment, Revere picked up Hancock's trunk and walked away.

THE HESSIAN COST TO ENGLAND (1775)

King George III, unable to raise enough English troops to suppress the American rebellion, approached several small European states that were in the habit of renting out mercenaries. In 1775 Landgrave Frederick II of

Hesse-Kasses made a deal with King George to let him have 22,000 men. The soldiers were paid the same as British soldiers, but Landgrave received seven pounds for each man plus a bonus of 2,200 pounds. For each man killed he received the amount of the levy money again (three wounded counting as one killed). By mid-1777 more than two-thirds of the 21,000 men England had stationed in America were Hessians. Of the almost 30,000 Hessians who eventually served, more than 12,000 never returned to Europe. Five thousand of them, encouraged by generous offers to desert, eventually settled in America, most of them in Pennsylvania. Gen. George Armstrong Custer, later of Indian-fighting fame, was the great-grandson of a Hessian named Kuster, paroled at Saratoga.

"TOOTH-SHAKEN" (1775)

Women in colonial days were advised to marry young, for when a woman reached the age of thirty, not only was her beauty gone but so were most of her teeth as well. One of the first hazards of a move to America was the loss of teeth. As John Jesselyn, an early English traveler, said, "The Women are pitifully Tooth-shaken"—a phenomenon Benjamin Franklin attributed to the custom of eating hot soup and frozen apples. As a cure for a toothache, Jesselyn suggested rubbing the mandible with "Brimstone and Gunpowder compounded with butter." Usually the offending tooth was pulled, and since there were no dentists, the barber or local blacksmith did the honors. If false teeth were desired, peg teeth were made, usually of gold or bone, and were screwed into the jawbone. Occasionally, as in the case of General Washington during the Revolution, peg teeth were carved of wood and pushed into the cavities left from pulled teeth. In Washington's case, his jaws were deformed by his malfitting teeth.

GEORGE WAS NO STOIC! (1775)

George Washington made a superficial study of Stoic philosophy and even considered himself a stoic, which he was to a certain extent, but his well-known hot temper often betrayed him. His fierce outbursts on the battlefields of both Long Island and Monmouth are a matter of record. Not as well known is an incident at his headquarters at Cambridge soon after taking command of the American army. Working in his study at the Craigie House, he became so exasperated at the squabbling of drunken soldiers in the front yard that, forgetting the dignity he should maintain as a general, he rushed outside, "laid out" a few of the brawlers with his own fists, and then returned to his study, much relieved. The young men on his staff were terrified of Washington when he was roused to anger. Tobias Lear, Washington's private secretary, claimed that the most dreadful experience in his life was hearing the general swear.

FOR ROOM, BOARD, AND TOBACCO MONEY (1775)

Ebenezer Wild, in his Revolutionary War journal, refers to a form of punishment for capital crimes, such as robbery, which kept the army in a state of suspense. The doomed men were marched to the place of execution to the strains of the "Dead March," each one with his coffin carried before him. The men in ranks were then paraded, with the guilty men in front where they could be viewed by all. The death sentence was read in a loud voice, and the graves were dug. With a coffin beside them, each man was made to kneel beside the grave while the firing squad received orders to load, take aim, and—at this critical moment, a messenger might appear with a reprieve that was read aloud. This last act was omitted often enough to strain the nerves of everyone present by leaving the result in doubt until the last moment.

The British army, which depended to a large degree on "pressed" men (conscripted by force) to fill their ranks, was even more harsh in its discipline than the Americans. On the very eve of the Revolution, Bostonians often witnessed British soldiers being flogged to death for desertion. That Revolutionary War hero Daniel Morgan bore on his back the scars of 750 lashes of a British whip for striking one of His Majesty's officers during the French and Indian War.

THE REVOLUTION AND SLAVERY (1775)

Samuel Johnson, famed for his English dictionary, was not the least bit friendly to the American cause during the Revolution. In 1775 he published a pamphlet titled "Taxation No Tyranny," in which he proposed a fantastic solution to the problem of American discontent. He suggested that British soldiers free all American slaves, arm them, and set them up as masters over the white colonists, causing them to be more grateful and honest than their master—and thus more loyal to the king. He asked, perhaps with much reason, "How is it that we hear the loudest yelps for liberty among the drivers of negroes?" Johnson advanced two other proposals, though he did not really expect them to be taken seriously. He proposed the return of Canada to the French, feeling that a near enemy would drive the colonists back into the arms of the mother country. It probably would have. His other proposal was to arm the Indians, "teach them discipline and encourage them now and then to plunder a plantation. Security and leisure are the parents of sedition."

MUTILATED MUSKET BALLS (1776)

In 1776 British Gen. Sir William Howe complained to Washington: "My Aide de Camp charged with the Delivering of this Letter will present to you a Ball cut and fixed to the Ends of a Nail, taken from a Number of the same Kind, found in the Encampments quitted by your Troops on the 15th Instant. I do not make any comments upon such unwarrantable and malicious Practices, being well assured the Contrivance has not come to your Knowledge."

Actually, General Howe's men were adding to the lethality of musket balls by slitting them or adding nails—although it's possible he didn't know about it. Several such musket balls were found in a former British camp at Inwood, New York, when it was excavated years later.With medical practices as crude as they were, such mutilation really wasn't necessary—the surgeon's knife usually finished what the musket ball had started.

AN "HONOR" HE COULD
HAVE DONE WITHOUT (1776)

Plots against George Washington's life during the Revolution were not necessarily unique, but the result of one such plot was. One of Washington's guards, Thomas Hickey, plotted with others to capture the American general (after poisoning and stabbing him) and deliver him to Sir William Howe. The plot was uncovered while the American army was passing through New York City in 1776. Hickey was tried, convicted, and formally executed on June 27 of that year near the Bowery Lane before an assembled audience of 20,000 troops and civilians. He had the distinction of being the first soldier executed in the history of the American army. This was not the first military execution in America, however. In 1676 an Indian named Quanpen was found guilty of participating in King Philip's War against the colonists and ordered shot following a Rhode Island court martial trial.

REVOLUTION WON BY A CARD GAME? (1776)

Washington's brilliant victory over the Hessians at Trenton the day after Christmas in 1776 might easily be accredited to a card game being played by Col. Johann Gottlieb Rall, the Hessian commander. He received a note from a Tory spy warning him of the approaching American army but stuffed the note into his pocket unread because he was dealing the cards at the time. Thus, when Washington hit Trenton, it came as a complete surprise to the enemy, enabling Washington to kill or capture practically the entire Hessian army while no Americans were killed and only four wounded. This victory, Washington's first over the enemy in open field, was a tremendous boost to sagging American spirits and undoubtedly prevented the complete demoralization and collapse of the American Revolutionary cause. One authority quotes Rall as stating just before he died of wounds received in the battle that if he had read the message, victory would not have been Washington's. Considering the condition of the small, ragged American army, he could very well have been right.

NAME OF THE UNITED STATES (1776)

The name "United States" sounds so natural that it may come as a slight shock to learn that rival names competed for the official designation of the country. Just when "United States" was first used is lost to history (Thomas Paine has received credit for it), but we do know that the first recorded use of it came from the pen of Thomas Jefferson in the Declaration of Independence: "We therefore, the Representatives of the United States of America." The chief rival name goes back to 1775 while Boston was under siege. The Revolutionary poet, Philip Freneau, wrote in his "American Liberty":

> What madness, heaven, has made
> Britannia frown:
> Who plans or schemes to pull Columbia
> down?

Columbia—an easy, poetic, graceful name adopted from Columbus—remained a possible rival until 1819 when a South American country adopted it. Other rival names were "Fredonia," proposed shortly after

1800 by Dr. Charles Mitchell—a coupling of the English word "freedom" with a Latin ending. In Arizona, however, it is said to have come from "free" and the Spanish "doña," meaning "free woman"—so called by the polygamous Mormons. Other less seriously considered names were "Appalachia" or "Alleghania," proposed by Washington Irving, and later "Usona," a combination of the first letter of the United States of America.

ROGERS: DUBIOUS HERO (1776)

Kenneth Roberts made a hero of Maj. Robert Rogers and his Rangers in *Northwest Passage,* but more serious historians tend to belittle the importance of the ancestral founder of the Green Berets, or Rangers, as they were known during the French and Indian War. Whatever his true ranking among American heroes, Rogers had a chance to be more but threw it away during the Revolution. Whereas men under him, such as John Stark and Israel Putnam, became shining lights on our pages of history, Rogers courted both sides when the war came. Washington, impatient and suspicious, imprisoned him for spying. After he escaped, he raised Tories to fight against his former comrades, but his command was crushed by Washington at White Plains, and England removed all his authority. Rogers eventually fled to England, where he died in a London flophouse at the age of sixty-eight.

WASHINGTON WOULDN'T BURN (1776)

According to Nathaniel Greene, the American army did little to defend New York City in 1776. Because so much of the city belonged to the Tories, its defense wasn't worth the risk. As a matter of fact, soon after the Howe brothers took over the city in 1776, nearly a thousand Tories pledged their allegiance to the king.

Soon after British occupation began, some of these Tories on Staten Island attempted to illustrate their loyalty by burning Generals Washington, Lee, and Putnam in effigy after tarring and feathering the figures. A sudden and violent rainstorm prevented them from tarring the last figure, that of General Washington. Some British troops in the area did manage at this point to set fire to the effigies, and all of them burned except that of Washington. This lone figure of the American commander, untarred and unburned, caused a superstitious fear among the Hessian troops, who took the whole event as an evil omen. So it proved to be.

WASHINGTON'S TABLE MANNERS (1776)

During Washington's brief occupation of New York in 1776, a plot against him and the patriot cause was uncovered that resulted in at least one execution of one of his own guard. Many rumors circulated of plans to poison the commander–in–chief, one version of which crept into a New York City school textbook in 1886. It gave a verbatim account of Washington discovering poison in a plate of peas: "Fixing his eyes upon the guilty man he put a spoonful of peas on his plate, and asked him, 'Shall I eat of these?' 'I don't know,' stammered the man, turning deadly pale. Washington took some on his knife, and again asked, 'Shall I eat of these?' The man could not say a word, but raised his hand as if to prevent it." The text of this somehow made its way into the newspapers, and national indignation erupted—not because it was a fabrication but because of the reference to Washington using a knife with which to eat his peas. Seven important newspapers thundered that America's schoolchildren were being taught that the father of their country had no table manners.

TOM PAINE'S FORESIGHT (1776)

As chief propagandist for the American cause in the War for Independence, Thomas Paine's *Common Sense* and other Revolutionary writings have come to blot out his views on other subjects. As a writer and editor of the *Pennsylvania Magazine,* Paine denounced slavery, the custom of dueling, cruelty to animals, and hereditary titles. In various articles he advocated women's rights, old-age pensions (he could have used this himself in his later years), rational divorce laws (he separated from his second wife), national and international copyright laws (in later years he designed the first iron suspension bridge and experimented with steam power), international federation, and republican equality.

WOMEN'S LIB (1776)

The most often overlooked patriots in American history have been women—and usually simply because they were women. One not completely overlooked, but not given the full credit due her either, is Abigail Adams, wife of the nation's second president. Her biographer, Janet

Whitney, refers to her as America's first emancipated woman. Just how emancipated and how much of a prophetess becomes evident in reading her many letters written during the War for Independence. One of them, addressed to her husband in Philadelphia soon after the British evacuation of Boston, indicates not only her early promotion of American independence but also of women's rights. "I long to hear that you have declared independence. But remember," she adds, "all men would be tyrants if they could. If particular care and attention is not paid to the ladies, we are determined to start a rebellion and will not hold ourselves bound by any laws in which we have no voice or representation." Is it any wonder that when her husband became president she was often referred to as "Mrs. President" and sometimes "The Empress."

THE AMERICAN EAGLE (1776)

Much controversy has revolved around the choice of the eagle as America's national emblem. It first appeared as an American emblem on a Massachusetts copper cent coined in 1776. Charles Thomson, secretary of Congress when it was placed on the Great Seal, specified that the eagle should be the distinctive American bald eagle. This was certainly not the first time, however, that an eagle was chosen as a national emblem, and this is probably where the controversy arises. Xenophen tells us that eagles were on Persian ensigns, and they certainly were used by ancient Romans and Greeks. In 1804 Napoleon adopted he eagle as an ensign for his victorious armies, and in heraldic form it was adopted by Germany, Austria, Prussia, and France. Even the Russians used the double-headed eagle. It has been recorded in several histories that Benjamin Franklin suggested a beautiful and native American bird, the turkey. The word *turkey*, incidentally, comes from the Hebrew word *tukki*, meaning peacock.

Franklin described the bald eagle as a "bird of bad moral character, like those among men who live by sharpening and robbing. . . . The turkey is a much more respectable bird, and withal a true original Native of America."

REVOLUTIONARY WAR RATIONS (1776)

During the American Revolution, food rations were normally issued directly to an individual rather than to a company mess. Everybody remembers learning of the starving soldiers at Valley Forge, but early in the war, when rations were available, the soldiers ate well. The first American army around Boston, for example, was supposed to issue individual soldiers the following daily ration:

1. "One pound of bread."
2. "Half a pound of beef and half a pound of pork; and if pork cannot be had, one pound and a quarter of beef; and one day in seven they shall have one pound and one quarter of salt fish, instead of one day's allowance of meat."
3. "One pint of milk, or if milk cannot be had, one gill of rice."
4. "One quart of good spruce or malt beer."
5. "One gill of peas or beans, or other sauce equivalent."
6. "Six ounces of good butter per week."
7. "One pound of good common soap for six men per week."
8. "Half a pint of vinegar per week per man, if it can be had."

BOW AND ARROWS? REALLY, BEN! (1776)

Amazingly, one of the greatest shortages the patriot army faced at the beginning of the Revolution was weaponry. According to General Washington, writing in February 1776, 2,000 men in camp lacked guns. One month later, Col. Rudolphus Ritzema's regiment possessed in all ninety-seven firelocks and only seven bayonets. In the same month the Declaration of Independence was signed, one-fourth of the army had no arms. That same summer, in calling up the militia, the New York Congress ordered each man to report to duty with a shovel, spade, pickax, or a scythe, straightened and made fast to a pole.

The weapon shortage was so serious that Benjamin Franklin suggested early in the war that the Continental Army be supplied with bows and arrows. He listed the advantages they had over muskets: they were cheaper and quicker to produce, they wouldn't be affected by rain, they had greater killing power, they were easier to acquire than gunpowder, and they could be fired at a more rapid rate. In addition, arrows in flight would have a profound psychological effect on the enemy. Makes a lot of sense, doesn't it? Except the Indians never seemed to win.

FIRE-CAKE AND WATER (1777)

The suffering of American troops at Valley Forge is probably the best known aspect of American history, but actual comprehension of such suffering is seldom reached. Lafayette wrote, "The unfortunate soldiers were in want of everything . . . their feet and legs froze until they became black and it was often necessary to amputate them." The most moving description, however, is found in the journal of Albigence Waldo, a Connecticut surgeon:

"There comes a soldier, his bare feet are seen thro' his worn-out shoes, his legs nearly naked from the tattered remains of an only pair of stockings, his Breeches not sufficient to cover his nakedness, his Shirt hanging in Strings, his hair dishevell'd, his face meager; his whole appearance pictures a person forsaken and discouraged. He comes and crys with an air of wretchedness and despair, I am Sick, my feet lame, my legs are sore, my body covered with this tormenting Itch [a common camp disease]."

The men lacked everything—clothing, food, water, shelter, and fuel. The wonder is that anyone stayed with the army. "Fire-cake [flour and water paste baked in thick cakes on hot stones] and water for breakfast! Fire-cake and water for dinner! Fire-cake and water for supper! The Lord send that our Commissary for Purchases may have to live on Fire-cake and water!"

ARNOLD: IN MEMORY OF A LEG (1777)

The most imposing monument on the Saratoga Battlefield is one 150 feet tall, erected in 1877 to the memory of the American officers responsible for the victory there. In each of the monument's four sides is a niche containing statues of Gens. Horatio Gates, Philip John Schuyler, and Daniel Morgan. One side is empty and is known as the "Arnold Niche." If Benedict Arnold had not later committed treason, it would have contained his statue in recognition of his great contribution to the battle.

The most interesting monument, however, is a small one at Bemis Heights, erected at the spot where Arnold was wounded in the leg. The monument, with a carving of a leg in bas-relief and an inscription to a brilliant soldier, nowhere contains Arnold's name. It is, in effect, a monument only to his leg, which was wounded in the cause of freedom.

"AND THEIR SIZE!" (1777)

The bitterness of a conquered foe is an expected thing in warfare, but it is certainly not evident in a description of the victorious Americans penned by one of Gen. John Burgoyne's men at Saratoga:

"Not one of them was properly uniformed, but each man had on the clothes in which he goes to the field, to church or to the tavern. But they stood like soldiers, erect, with a military bearing which was subject to little criticism. . . . Nature had formed all the fellows who stood in rank and file, so slender, so handsome, so sinewy, that it was a pleasure to look at them and we were all surprised at the sight of such a finely built people. And their size!"

He also noted the large number "between their fiftieth and sixtieth year," who at this age had apparently "followed the calfskin [drum] for the first time." And yet, "it is no joke to oppose them. . . . They can cold-bloodedly draw a bead on anyone." He was also apparently pleased that "there was not a man among them who showed the slightest sign of mockery, malicious delight, hate or any other insult; it seemed rather as if they wished to do us honor."

MASSACRE AT PAOLI (1777)

In the Revolution, as in any other war, battle casualty figures don't tell the whole story. Sometimes it wasn't even a battle that brought death to many soldiers, as was the case on the night of September 21, 1777, at Paoli, Pennsylvania. Tory spies led British soldiers to a detached force of sleeping American patriots during General Howe's advance on Philadelphia. Rushing in with bayonets fixed, the British repeatedly stabbed the sleeping and stunned Americans, killing or wounding about three hundred patriots while losing only a handful of their own men.

Gen. "Mad Anthony" Wayne, the American commander on that tragic night, must have had good reason to live up to his name, but even more so a year later. In the fall of 1778 the same British commander of Paoli fame, Gen. Charles Grey, fell upon another one of Gen. Wayne's detachments at Old Tappan, New York, and once again surprising them while asleep and refusing quarter, bayoneted forty-eight American troops. Forty others were spared but only through the intervention of one of Grey's captains who was more of a humanitarian.

"SILVER BALLS" (1777)

As General Burgoyne advanced down the Champlain Valley in the summer of 1777, the Americans under Generals Philip John Schuyler and Arthur St. Clair retreated before him. The military is always ripe ground for rumors, and there were plenty of them that summer among the patriot troops who wondered why their officers didn't put up more of a fight.

When Fort Ticonderoga was abandoned without a fight, the rumor mills worked overtime, promoting the belief that St. Clair and Schuyler were not only incompetent but also traitorous. One of the most fascinating stories to come out of the war concerned the so-called treason of these two officers. The story, which prompted a plague of desertions, had Burgoyne "buying" the American generals by firing "silver balls" into Fort Ticonderoga, which St. Clair promptly gathered up and sent to Schuyler. The rumors came to a sudden end when Burgoyne surrendered his entire army a little farther south at Saratoga.

DUPING A BRITISH GENERAL (1777)

Many students of American history have been curious about why Gen. William Howe, with his superior forces, kept his army in Philadelphia during the winter of 1777–78 without once attempting to crush the ragged and outnumbered American army at nearby Valley Forge. The truth is that Washington and an aide, Maj. John Clark, sent an agent to Howe with an offer to supply him with secret papers from the American commander's files. When Howe bit at this deception, Washington himself composed some fake returns concerning his army's strength. When Howe received the "stolen" papers in Washington's own handwriting, he believed them and kept his army safely in Philadelphia the entire winter.

A REVOLUTIONARY "GIANT" (1777)

When Peter Francisco joined the Continental Army at the age of sixteen, he was six feet six inches tall, weighed 260 pounds, and was noted for his great strength. An ordinary sword was too small for this giant, so Washington ordered a special five-foot broadsword made for him. Like Paul Bunyan, the truth is obscured by many legends about this brave young giant. Participating in battles such as Brandywine, Stony Point, Camden, and Yorktown, Francisco became the campfire talk of the entire Continental Army. At Camden he was said to have saved a small 1,100-pound cannon by lifting it on his back and walking off with it. At Guildford Courthouse he is credited with slaying eleven British soldiers in a frenzy so great that one guardsman's body was split in half. Francisco's charges ended when he blacked out from pain and loss of blood resulting from bayonet thrusts. After recovering from his wounds, and on his way to rejoin the army, he encountered nine of Col. Banastre Tarleton's troopers. Attacking them single-handedly, he dispatched four of them before the other five broke and ran, leaving him with their horses. Many other legends attest to the strength and bravery of this simple soldier, whose body rests today in Richmond under a tombstone bearing the epitaph, "A soldier of Revolutionary fame."

WASHINGTON'S RAGE AT MONMOUTH (1777)

Coming upon the American army in full retreat at the Battle of Monmouth Court House, with Gen. Charles Lee leading the retreat, Washington's temper flared and he swore "till the leaves shook on the trees," according to Gen. Charles Scott, who witnessed the scene. "Charming! Delightful! Never have I enjoyed such swearing before or since. Sir, on that memorable day he swore like an angel from heaven!" To the angry questions of Washington, Lee could only stammer, "Sir? Sir?" In a rage, Washington called Lee "a damned poltroon" and then personally turned the troops to face the British attack that had not even commenced at this point. Both sides held their positions in this costly battle, but during the night the British retreated. Washington's anger may have been justified because some historians believe that as early as this battle, General Lee was actively cooperating with the enemy.

"COWBOYS" AND "SKINNERS" (1778)

One of the most prominent Tory families in the Colonies was the de Lanceys, one of whom, James, organized a Tory troop of sixty light-horse soldiers, all from Westchester County, New York. Riding, plundering, and burning were their primary objectives, and because cows were a major source of their plunder, James and his men were called "cowboys." There was another group in the same area at this time that sparks disagreement among historians. Known as the "skinners," some historians claim that they were the cowboys' rebel counterparts, whereas other authorities claim that their loyalty jumped from one side to the other as occasion demanded. There is even disagreement over the name. One authority suggested they were named after Gen. Cortland Skinner's brigade of New Jersey volunteers; yet another historian, North Callahan, claimed that their nickname was derived from "their fondness for clothing which they badly needed, and which they often 'skinned' right off the victims." Members of the latter group lived an extremely dangerous life from 1778 to 1783 because both sides suspected them and often hung or shot them whenever they caught them.

NO THANKS FOR CLARK (1778)

George Rogers Clark and his deeds for his country are remembered and appreciated in modern America, but he received little recognition or thanks while he lived. What did he do? He simply guaranteed his country's claim to a fabulous chunk of territory at the Peace Treaty of 1783. With a small band of men, suffering incredible privations, he won and held onto the territory north of the Ohio River, the breadbasket of the United States that included the cities of Cincinnati, Cleveland, Detroit, Chicago—and he founded Louisville. Finally, unremembered and unhonored, he died in poverty, begging drinks from his friends.

Years later the city of Louisville decided to honor its founder but didn't know exactly where his body was. It dug where he was believed buried and discovered several skeletons. Searchers finally found one without a leg (Clark had lost a leg as an old man to paralysis) and moved it to a tomb, still not quite certain they were honoring the right remains. But Clark was used to that sort of thing.

"NEGRO BY NAME" (1778)

Militia rolls of each of the thirteen Colonies show a smattering of African-Americans, but the black soldier was more likely to be found in the Continental line. By 1778 the army was well sprinkled with black troops, totaling 755 on August 24 of that year, most of them from New England. As a matter of fact, a Pennsylvania soldier writing to his wife from Ticonderoga in 1776 described the New England troops as "the strangest mixture of Negroes, Indians, and whites, with old men and mere children, which together with a nasty lousy appearance make a most shocking spectacle." A year later, Gen. Philip John Schuyler complained of the New England soldiers at Saratoga. One-third of "the few that had been sent" were boys, old men, or Negroes, and the latter "disgrace our arms." From the North or the South, the typical black soldier was a private, and more so than white privates he tended to lack identity. He often carried no specific name but was carried on the rolls as "Negro by Name" or "Negro Name unknown" or "A Negro Man."

The most knowledgeable authority on the subject, Benjamin Quarles, says the most accurate figure for the number of blacks who served in the patriot army was 5,000. This does not include the thousands who hoped to gain freedom by joining his Majesty's forces—a vain attempt, sadly enough.

A WOMAN WARRIOR (1778)

It is amazing that Hollywood or TV has not latched onto the story of Deborah Sampson. At age twenty-two, this Plymouth, Massachusetts, woman, disguised as a man, enlisted in the Continental Army only to immediately get drunk and have her gender discovered. She tried again and succeeded as Private Robert Shurtleff. She not only shared army life with her male companions, her gender undiscovered, but she also took part in several battles. Twice wounded, she retired alone to the woods until her wounds healed. Finally, at the Battle of Yorktown, her luck ran out. Down with a fever, she underwent a routine examination by an army doctor, who discovered her true gender. With her army days ended, she received a purse of money from her commander in chief, an honorable discharge, and a land grant from Congress. Back in Massachusetts, she married Benjamin Gannett, by whom she had three children. She became a traveling lecturer, and to the end of her days she carried a British musket ball in her body.

U.S. FLAG RECOGNIZED (1778)

An American hero most closely associated with the first stars and stripes was John Paul Jones. Coincidentally, he was appointed by Congress to command the *Ranger* on the same day as the Flag Resolution was adopted in 1777. The following year, on February 14, he induced the admiral of the French fleet in Quiberon Bay to exchange salutes, thus gaining the first formal recognition of the new American flag by a foreign power.

Two months later off the coast of England, the *Ranger* emerged victorious in a battle with the British sloop *Drake,* marking the first time the Stars and Stripes was to wave in victory over a defeated enemy. Exactly what this first Stars and Stripes looked like, we don't know. We do know that the *Bonhomme Richard,* which Jones sailed in the following year when he defeated the *Serapis,* carried a flag with three horizontal rows of stars arranged four, five, four, along with thirteen stripes—five of them red, four of them white, and four of them blue with no special arrangement.

WASHINGTON'S VIEWS ON DUELING (1778)

It is probably on the subject of dueling that the character of George Washington comes into most marked contrast with that of the seventh president of the United States, Andrew Jackson. Jackson's fondness for dueling was well known, whereas history appears silent as to Washington's contact with the so-called "gentlemen's sport." However, a letter by one of his contemporaries is most revealing. Shortly after the Battle of Monmouth, where the American commander had berated Gen. Charles Lee for his lack of courage, some of Washington's friends feared that Lee, as fond of dueling as "Old Hickory" would be fifty years later, would challenge his commander. Washington's friend George Mason did not share this fear, however, as he expressed in a letter to Edmund Randolph a month later:

"Indulge no such apprehensions, for he (Lee) too well knows the sentiments of General Washington on the subject of dueling. From his earliest manhood, I have heard him express his contempt of the man who sends and the man who accepts a challenge, for he regards such acts as no proof of moral courage, and the practice he abhors as a relic of old barbarisms, repugnant alike to sound morality and Christian enlightenment."

PART TWO

INDEPENDENCE
AND CIVIL WAR
(1779–1885)

FIRST ST. PAT'S PARADE (1779)

According to an article in the old *New York Mercury,* the St. Patrick's Day Parade in New York City was actually started by the British army of occupation in 1779. New Yorkers had been holding an annual St. Patrick's Day breakfast for many years, but in 1779 George Augustus Francis Rawdon rounded up four hundred Irish soldiers from His Majesty's army to march in a parade to a tavern in the Bowery for their breakfast. Thus the parade tradition started.

The article goes on to say, however, that after eating breakfast, "great numbers" of the Irish paraders went to see General Washington. This so incensed Lord Rawdon that he offered a bounty of ten guineas per head for these deserters. Desertion to the American cause became common later in the war, but at this point the American "cause" was a losing cause and desertion in "great numbers" sounds illogical.

"NOT WORTH A CONTINENTAL" (1779)

A "continental" was money issued by Congress, as opposed to paper money authorized by each of the thirteen Colonies. Because of the lack of specie in the Colonies, continental currency quickly depreciated in value with no gold or silver to back it. By 1779 in Philadelphia a suit of clothes cost $1,600; a hat $400; a pair of shoes $125; a handkerchief $100; flour $95 per 100 pounds; and fish hooks 50 cents apiece. The well-known John Witherspoon paid $1,000 for a coat that didn't fit. By 1781 the ratio between specie and continental currency was 1 to 75. Thomas Paine paid $300 for a pair of woolen stockings, and Jefferson paid $355 for three quarts of brandy. In Boston flour sold for $1,575 a barrel, and Samuel Adams paid $2,000 for a hat and a suit of clothes. Another man the same day paid $1,500 to have his coat patched, and a quartermaster paid 60 pounds for having a team of horses shod and 15,000 pounds for half a ton of bar iron. The rapid rate of inflation is evident from the records of a Philadelphia wholesaler who sold a barrel of beef in January 1779 for 16 pounds. In December of that same year the price was up to 242 pounds.

A NATURAL DEATH (1780)

Violent death was such a common occurrence on the American frontier that a person dying a natural death often became a novelty to those around him. Such was the case with a young man in Kentucky, cited by the historian W. H. Bogart:

"An old lady who had been in the forts (in Kentucky) was describing to Dr. Brown the scenes she had witnessed in those times of peril and adventure; and, among other things, remarked that during the first two years of her residence in Kentucky, the most comely sight she beheld was seeing a young man dying in his bed a natural death. She had been familiar with blood, and carnage and death, but in all these cases the sufferers were the victims of the Indian tomahawk and scalping knife; and that on an occasion when a young man was taken sick and died, after the usual manner of nature, she said that the rest of the women sat up all night, gazing upon him as an object of beauty."

"LYNCH LAW" (1780)

During the American Revolution, a Virginian living in the Shenandoah Valley led a group of patriots against Tories and outlaws, circumventing the normal channels of justice by merely tying the culprits to the nearest tree and flogging them.

This form of social control became so effective that it developed into a traditional method of execution, especially in the South and against the blacks. The leader and originator of this type of frontier justice was

Charles Lynch Jr. Such extralegal "justice" was administered by both Tories and rebels during the Revolution.

Statistical information on lynchings was not kept until 1882, but data compiled at the Tuskegee Institute indicate that between 1882 and 1936 there were 4,672 persons lynched in the United States; of this number, 3,383 were African-Americans.

If Lynch Law was not already a firmly embedded term in American history, it would be assured of immortality by the name of a city—Lynchburg, Virginia, named after John Lynch, brother of Charles Jr.

CAUGHT WITH PANTS DOWN (1780)

Battles are lost for many seemingly insignificant or ironic reasons, but the prize must go to the Battle of Camden, fought in South Carolina in 1780 between American troops under Gen. Horatio Gates and Gen. Charles Cornwallis's army. Gates, an inept and overrated commander, marched on Camden with insufficient and undersupplied troops. The Americans, without rations, had been eating green peaches for weeks, and when they demanded a rum ration, Gates had a bright idea: he would substitute bran and molasses for rum. The combination of green peaches and molasses took care of the American army before the British even had time to attack, and when they did they literally caught the Americans with their pants down. The British might have won under any conditions, but with a totally incompetent commander, coupled with green peaches and molasses, the Continentals were in no condition to stand up and fight.

DARK DAY IN NEW ENGLAND (1780)

About 9 A.M. on May 19, 1780, an unusual darkness enveloped New England, bringing terror to the inhabitants who felt that the Day of Judgment was at hand, it being "as dark as it commonly is at one hour after sunset." The more scientific-minded citizens believed, and probably rightly so, that the darkness was caused by smoke from fires on the frontier. The masses, however, believed that the unnatural gloom was a direct fulfillment of Bible prophecy. It happened that the Connecticut Legislature was in session, and sharing the general terror, moved an adjournment. At this moment an old Puritan legislator, Davenport Stanford, said if it was the last day, he wished to be found at his post and therefore moved that candles be brought so that the legislature could proceed with business.

Gen. Robert E. Lee often referred to the moral of this incident during the dark days of the Civil War nearly one hundred years later. It apparently sustained him.

A FEMALE "PAUL REVERE" (1780)

Paul Revere, whose total ride covered no more than twelve miles on that April night in 1775, will be forever remembered by Americans. A North Carolina woman, the mother of nine, rode five times that distance on the same kind of mission, but few have ever heard of her. Her name was Jane Thomas, and when she overheard the Tories speak of a surprise attack on a rebel force at Cedar Springs, she mounted a horse and rode for two days to warn sixty patriots, including two of her sons. She reached the small patriotic force in time for them to make preparations for the coming attack. The attack soon came under cover of darkness, and the rebels who had left their fires burning were waiting in ambush. The 150 Tories were overwhelmingly defeated, thanks to the courage of Mrs. Thomas, wife of an American colonel.

"THEY DIDN'T KNOW THE RULES" (1781)

It is commonly assumed that a massacre simply cannot be condoned by rules of civilized warfare, but this is not true. Rules of European warfare in the eighteenth century permitted massacres of defenders if they insisted on defending untenable places. There is one instance of this barbaric rule being carried out in the American Revolution by a British detachment under Benedict Arnold at New London, Connecticut, in 1781. Six hundred regulars under Arnold attacked unfinished Fort Griswold on the Thames River, defended by 158 American militia. Within forty minutes, the British lost 192 men. When Arnold's men finally took the fort, they ignored appeals for mercy and, angered by what they considered an unnecessary loss of British lives, proceeded to massacre nearly the whole garrison. An eyewitness reported that the American commander, Col. William Ledyard, was impaled with the sword he offered to a British officer. This atrocious act has been denied by some historians, but the facts are that only twenty-six of the American garrison escaped unhurt, and Arnold's name caused his former countrymen to spit at the mention of it.

FIRST PRESIDENT OF THE UNITED STATES— REALLY? (1781)

A small but vocal group of scholars actively campaigned in the 1960s and 1970s for general acceptance of their contention that the first president of the United States was not George Washington but rather a relatively unknown politician named John Hanson. He was elected chairman of the Confederation Congress under the Articles of Confederation in 1781 and as such was often addressed as "President of the United States," although there was no executive office as such. In 1971 the group started excavating a site not too distant from Mount Vernon, hoping to uncover the burial of Mr. Hanson, believing that a successful find would generate acceptance of their proposed goal—recognition of John Hanson as the first president of the United States.

If this recognition is ever granted, which is highly doubtful, George Washington would not be the second president but the ninth. The Confederation Congress sat for eight years, 1781–88, and each year a new chairman was elected by the body. Thus, there would be eight presidents of the United States before Washington took over as first president under the Constitution.

JEFFERSON FORCED TO SERVE (1782)

Many present-day "reluctant" politicians would like the public to think they are being "forced" to run for a particular office, but Thomas Jefferson literally was forced to hold an office he neither sought nor wanted. After retiring as governor of Virginia under a cloud of censure in 1782, the people of Albermarle County elected him to the House of Burgesses. Stung with what he considered public ingratitude over his treatment as governor, he sent his refusal to House Speaker John Tyler, who replied that under the Constitution his resignation could not be accepted. After being threatened "to give attendance without incuring Censure of being seized," Jefferson finally accepted his post of honor.

Ironically, Jefferson's decision to retire at this point in his life (he was not yet forty) prompted more widespread criticism than he had previously suffered as governor. It is even more ironic that such a thin-skinned public servant would find himself eighteen years later running for the most critically assailed office in the land—the presidency.

THE PURPLE HEART (1782)

The military award of the Purple Heart—given to any soldier wounded in war today—is almost as common as the good-conduct ribbon. This was not always so. The Purple Heart Badge of Military Merit was established by general order of George Washington on August 7, 1782, for "not only instances of unusual gallantry, but also of extraordinary fidelity and essential Service." Surviving records indicate that this honor badge was granted to only three men before it was discontinued as a military award in 1783 and then revived in 1932 as a decoration for wounds. The first two Purple Hearts were awarded by Washington to two Connecticut soldiers, Sgts. William Brown and Elijah Churchill, for gallantry in battle. The third and final award, made in June 1783, went to a little-known hero of the Revolution, Sgt. Daniel Bissell, also of Connecticut, who operated as a spy behind British lines. At Washington's request, allowing himself to be listed as a deserter in the American army and to fall into disgrace among his closest friends and family, Bissell operated effectively, unable to reveal his true patriotism until the war's end.

EVEN A TRAITOR DOESN'T DESERVE THAT! (1782)

He never lived to see the end of the war in which he fought with such dubious distinction. On October 2, 1782, one year after Yorktown, Gen. Charles Lee died in Philadelphia, bitter to the end for the court-martial and reprimand he had received after the Battle of Monmouth. This still-suspected traitor willed that he not be buried "in any church or church-yard, or within a mile of any Presbyterian or Anabaptist meetinghouse. For since I have resided in this country I have had so much bad company when living that I do not choose to continue it when dead." He was nevertheless buried with full military honors in an Anglican churchyard where, as Postmaster General Ebenezer Hazard described his grave, "No stone marks his head. Indeed, those who saw his open grave can scarcely mark this site, as it is continually trodden by persons going into and coming out of church." To poor General Lee, this must have been greater punishment than his court-martial.

LAST "SHOT" OF THE REVOLUTION (1783)

The last "shot," or more accurately, blow, of the American Revolution was struck by a woman. As the British were evacuating New York City in November 1783, Gen. William Cunningham, commander of British prisoners in that area, was headed for the battery to board his ship. Passing the home of Mrs. Day on Murray Street, he spied a flag on a liberty pole and apparently decided it would be a great souvenir to take back to England. When he attempted to lower the flag, however, Mrs. Day came rushing out of the house swinging a broom. At the end of the encounter, Mrs. Day had her flag and General Cunningham was retreating with a bloody nose. It was a rather inglorious end to an inglorious war for the British.

Militarily, perhaps, there was no last shot. The frontier war against the Indians, encouraged by their former British allies, continued until Gen. "Mad Anthony" Wayne's victory at Fallen Timbers in 1794. But as far as the settled East and the Continental Army were concerned, the war ended when the last British troops marched down to their waiting barges on the New York waterfront, and the last "shot" was fired by Mrs. Day.

AMERICA'S FIRST MILLIONAIRE (1784)

The first millionaire in the United States was a Salem merchant whose lofty and pilastered mansion was one of the houses that made Salem noted throughout the Western world for its architectural glory. In 1784 Elias Hasket ("King") Derby, already rich from privateering, was sending his merchant ships around the world and piling up an even greater fortune. When he died in 1799, he was worth more than a million dollars, the greatest American fortune of the day. His financial success could easily have been attributed to his farsightedness but not to his eyes themselves, one of which was brown and the other blue. In 125 voyages only one of his ships was lost, and at one time profits on a single voyage ran as high as $100,000.

WASHINGTON'S STYLE OF DRESS (1785)

We do not lack for descriptions of George Washington, but one of the more interesting descriptions comes from a Boston printer who saw Washington immediately after the Revolution. He was apparently quite fashion conscious.

"He wore a pea-green coat, white vest, nankeen small clothes, white silk stockings, and pumps fastened with silver buckles which covered at least half the foot from instep to toe. His small clothes were tied at the knees with ribbon of the same colour in double bows, the ends reaching down to the ankles. His hair in front was well loaded with pomatum, frizzled or craped and powdered. Behind his natural hair was augmented by the addition of a large queue called vulgarly a false tail which, enrolled in some yards of black ribbons, hung half way down his back."

Before you question George's manhood, it should be noted that this dress was not at all unusual for men. An English traveler in America in 1740 reported that both men and women dressed as brightly every day as courtiers in England at a coronation.

WASHINGTON'S VIEWS ON SLAVERY (1785)

It is a well-known fact that Washington owned slaves, but his personal opinions of slavery are not well publicized. One view came out on a May evening in 1785 when Washington was entertaining two Methodist clergymen at Mount Vernon. He informed his guests that he was aware of their sentiments about freeing those in bondage. When they produced a petition for slavery emancipation, begging his signature, Washington, for whatever reason, "did not see it proper to sign." But in a letter to Robert Morris a year later, he wrote, "There is not a man living who wishes more sincerely to see a plan adopted for the gradual abolition of it." The *Writings of Washington* reveal another letter to a friend in which he determined never "to possess another slave by purchase, it being among my first wishes to see some plan adopted by which slavery may be abolished by law." Upon his death, Washington's will provided for the immediate emancipation of all of his slaves at the age of forty and the eventual freeing of all other slaves.

WASHINGTON'S SENSE OF HUMOR (1786)

A letter from George Washington to a Maryland friend concerning a Jack (male donkey) given to our first president as a gift from Ferdinand VI, king of Spain, gives us an interesting insight into Washington's sense of humor. A letter to William Frisbie Fitzhugh, dated May 15, 1786, reads:

"Dear Sir: Your favor of the 13th came to me this day. Particular attention shall be paid to the mares which your servant brought: and when my Jack is in the humour they shall derive all the benefits of his labours. At present tho' young, he follows what one day may suppose to be the example of his late Royal Master, who cannot, tho' past his grand climacteric, perform seldomer or with more majestic solemnity than he does. However I have my hopes that when he becomes a little better acquainted with Republican enjoyments he will amend his manners and fall into our custom of doing business; if the case should be otherwise, I shall have no disinclination to present his Catholic Majesty with as valuable a present as I received from him."

WHY NOT RELIGIOUS QUALIFICATIONS? (1787)

Many people today believe that the First Amendment to the Constitution guarantees freedom of religion. It does not—at least it didn't in the early days of the nation. What it did do was prohibit the establishment of a national religion, while preventing the federal government from becoming involved in state establishments of religion.

Virginia and Rhode Island were the only colonies requiring no religious qualifications either for voting or for holding office. Six colonies insisted still on some form or Protestantism, and two others were satisfied if you were a Christian. Four colonies demanded a belief in the divine inspiration of the Bible, and two were satisfied if you believed in heaven and hell. In Massachusetts, South Carolina, Connecticut, Maryland, and New Hampshire, the prevailing church was a state establishment.

As fashionable as it sometimes becomes to point out a lack of freedom in the United States, it must be noted that this country was the first place in the world where complete religious liberty was actually tried in a political state. A certain irony might be seen in this important freedom, however. Religious liberty was actively promoted in the American Colonies for the very reason that many colonists were not affiliated with any church.

BURNED AT THE STAKE (1787)

From the Manuscript Records of Duplin County Court, North Carolina, March 15, 1787:

"Whereupon the Court doth pass this Sentence . . . that the said Negro man Darby be immediately committed to the Gaol under a good

Guard and that on Tomorrow between the Hours of one and Four o'clock in the afternoon he be taken out thence and tied to a Steak on the Court House Lott and there burned to Death and to Ashes and his ashes strewed upon the Ground."

As barbaric as it sounds, burning at the stake was not unknown in America—but only for crimes such as murder and rebellion. In 1741, ten years after the Nat Turner Rebellion, a rumor spread in New York City that at least a hundred slaves were planning a rebellion with some white indentured servants. Eighteen of those suspected were hung, at least seventy were sold into the south, and thirteen others were publicly burned at the stake. Of those punished, four white persons were hanged, including two women.

TO PRAY OR NOT TO PRAY! (1787)

After several weeks of bitter wrangling at the Constitutional Convention in Philadelphia and just when tempers and jealousies threatened to doom the new constitution, Ben Franklin rose and rebuked the members for having neglected prayer, moving that daily prayers precede every day's business. An interesting debate then arose of this motion.

Alexander Hamilton and others were opposed because of possible public criticism or because the public would interpret the prayers as an indication of how bad the situation in the convention was. Roger Sherman and others felt that once the proposal was made, there would be greater public criticism if the suggestion was not adopted. Hugh Williamson observed that the reason for not having prayer was lack of funds to pay a clergyman. Several unsuccessful attempts were made to postpone the matter by adjourning before adjourning was finally accomplished. No vote on the question of prayer was ever taken.

FRANKLIN OPPOSED EXECUTIVE PAY (1787)

At the Constitutional Convention in 1787, Ben Franklin made a speech opposing any pay for the national executive. He argued, "Place before the eyes of such man a post of honor, that shall be at the same time a place of profit, and they will move heaven and earth to obtain it." He used as precedents certain public offices in Britain, among the Quakers, and Washington's salary-less service during the war. Yet, when Charles Pinckney made a proposal that the president, federal judges, and congressmen must have unencumbered estates of at least $100,000 before they could serve, Franklin took violent exception with the proposal for being undemocratic.

The $400,000 paid the president today doesn't provide nearly the incentive that the prestige of the office does. For this, and the power inherent, we do see "heaven and earth being moved" every four years.

WASHINGTON COUNTS PEAS (1788)

Did you ever wonder what our first president did in the less exciting moments of his life? Fortunately, his diary records one such day a year before he assumed the highest office his nation had to offer:

"Sunday, May 11, 1788. At home all day. Counted the number of the following articles which are contained in a pint: viz. of

The small round pease commonly called Gentleman's Pease: 3144

Those brot from York River by Majr. G. Washington: 2268

Do. those brot. from Mrs. Dangerfield's: 1375

Those given by Hezh. Fairfax: 1330

Large, and early black eye Pease: 1186

Bunch hominy Beans: 1473

"Accordingly, a bush of the above, allowing five to a hill, will plant the number of hills which follow: viz.

1st Kind 40,243

2. Ditto 29,030

3. Ditto 17,200

4th Kind 17,024

5. Ditto 15,180

6. Ditto 18,854."

"THE GREATEST MAN" (1788)

In 1774, when Patrick Henry's neighbors asked him who the greatest man at the First Continental Congress was, he replied that for wisdom and solid judgment, George Washington. Thirteen years later, at Virginia's Constitutional Ratifying Convention, he still had an unalterable regard for Washington, but he had broken with him on the Constitution. Day after day he argued against ratification of the document for fear of a dictatorship. Even news of the birth of another child did not interrupt an impassioned plea he was making on monarchy. After all, in a house where the cradle began to rock when Henry was eighteen and continued until he died at sixty-three, a birth announcement was not cause for excitement.

Henry's abilities as an orator are proverbial. At St. John's Church in Richmond in March 1775, during his famous "give me liberty or give me death" speech, Col. Edward Carrington was so moved that he stated a desire to be buried on the spot outside a window from where he was listening. Thirty-five years later his wish was carried out. At the ratifying convention in 1788, however, the spirit of Washington, then waiting for news at his home at Mount Vernon, was too much for Henry's powers of persuasion. Henry lost by ten votes, and Virginia came into the Union.

BUT NOT FIRST IN SPEAKING (1789)

William Maclay, a member of the first Senate meeting in New York in 1789, gives in his diary a firsthand impression of President Washington's first inaugural address:

"This great man was agitated and embarrassed more than ever he was by the leveled cannon or pointed musket. He trembled, and several times he could scarce make out to read, though it must be supposed he had often read it before. He put part of the fingers of his left hand into the side of what I think the tailors call the fall of the breeches, changing the paper into his right hand. After some time he then did the same with some of the fingers of his right hand. When he came to the words all the world, he made a flourish with his right hand, which left rather an ungainly impression. I sincerely, for my part, wished all set ceremony in the hands of the dancing-masters, and that this first of men had read off his address in the plainest manner, without ever taking his eyes from the paper, for I felt hurt that he was not first in everything."

WASHINGTON SICKENS ADAMS (1789)

During the first presidential election, Washington received all sixty-nine electoral votes cast—the only president to achieve this honor. In the election of 1821, James Monroe of Virginia came close, receiving 231 of the 232 votes cast. The single dissenting vote was cast by William Plumer of New Hampshire, who desired no president other than Washington to have the distinction of receiving all the electoral votes.

Plumer's feeling reflected the adulation of most Americans for Washington as a result of the war against England. Benjamin Rush summed up the people's feelings when he remarked, "We derive all the blessings of our present glorious revolution from his arm alone." A visitor to America in 1783 was shocked to hear people talk of Washington "as if the Redeemer had entered Jerusalem!" Such worship of Father Washington has not always been universal. During the early, dark days of the rebellion, Washington was the object of much criticism, especially from Congress. Even then "the superstitious veneration that is sometimes paid to General Washington" sickened John Adams, and he, along with other critics, condemned those who "were disposed to idolize an image which their own hands have molden."

IMPRISONED FOR DEBT (1789)

The financier of the American Revolution, the man most responsible for keeping the American army financially afloat during its darkest hours through personal efforts and his own credit, ironically spent three of his final years in a Philadelphia debtors' prison. During the war, Robert Morris had written, "Washington is the greatest man on earth," but during the latter's presidency he ignored Washington's advice and entered land speculation. Largely through the fault of his partner, Morris ended up in prison in 1798, where he remained until 1801. His wife, unable to afford the maintenance of a home, moved into the prison with her husband, and it was there that George and Martha visited their friends shortly before Washington died. Mrs. Morris was invited to stay at Mount Vernon, but she declined, preferring to stay in prison with her husband.

A CONTEMPORARY
DESCRIBES JOHN ADAMS (1789)

William Maclay, a caustic member of the first Senate under the new Constitution, leaves us in his diary an interesting impression of our first vice president:

"Mr. Izard and sundry gentlemen of the Senate were dissatisfied with our Vice-President. He takes on him to school the members from the chair. His grasping after titles has been observed by everybody. Mr. Izard, after describing his air, manner, deportment, and personal figure in the chair, concluded with applying the title of Rotundity to him.

"I have really often looked at him with surprise mingled with contempt when he is in the chair and no business before the Senate. Instead of that sedate, easy air which I would have him posses, he will look on one side, then on the other, then down on the knees of his breeches, then dimple his visage with the most silly kind of half smile which I cannot well express in English.

"The Scotch-Irish have a word that hits it exactly—smudging. God forgive me for the vile thought, but I cannot help thinking of a monkey just put into breeches when I saw him betray such evident marks of self-conceit."

EARLY AMERICAN MORTALITY (1790)

About 1790 Dr. Benjamin Rush of Philadelphia compiled statistics based upon his experience as a physician and reflecting the heavy mortality in early America. His studies revealed how long a group of nearly two hundred people, born the same year, lived.

Number of People	Years Lived
64	6
46	16
26	26
16	36
10	46
6	56
3	66
1	76

Much of the mortality rate is accounted for by the inability of the medical profession to control epidemics. In 1793 when the yellow fever epidemic hit Philadelphia, nearly 10 percent of the population died during the course of the summer and fall. To appreciate the meaning of such figures, imagine a similar epidemic hitting the same city today. A death rate of 10 percent would bring about 150,000 deaths.

I LOVE YOU TOO, GEORGE (1790)

Shortly before his death in 1790 at the age of eighty-four, Benjamin Franklin received a letter from President Washington:

"If the united wishes of a free people, joined with the earnest prayers of every friend to science and humanity, could relieve the body from pain and infirmities, you could claim an exemption on this score. If to be venerated for benevolence, to be admired for talent, if to be esteemed for patriotism, if to be beloved for philanthropy, can gratify the human mind, you must have the pleasing consolation to know that you have not lived in vain. As long as I retain my memory you will be thought of with respect, veneration and affection by, dear Sir, your sincere friend and obedient humble servant, G. Washington."

When, a short time later, Franklin died and Jefferson asked the president to follow the French government's example with a three-day period of national mourning, Washington refused, regretfully. He did not wish to set a precedent that he felt might later prove embarrassing.

A BOB-TAIL POLITICIAN (1790)

Gov. William Branch Giles of Virginia once sent a note to Patrick Henry, demanding satisfaction for what he considered an offensive statement by the well-known patriot:

"Sir, I understand that you have called me a 'bob-tail' politician. I wish to know if it be true; and if true, your meaning. William B. Giles."

To which Henry replied, "Sir, I do not recollect having called you a bob-tailed politician at any time, but think it probably I have. Not recollecting the time or occasion, I can't say what I did mean, but if you will tell me what you think I meant, I will say whether you are correct or not. Very respectfully, Patrick Henry."

One of those unfortunate lapses in history's bookkeeping has deprived us of the reply Governor Giles sent Henry—if he ever did.

NOTHING LEFT TO INVENT (1790)

The U.S. Patent Office, which today grants tens of thousands of patents each year, got its start with the first Congress under the Constitution in 1790. In that year it enacted the first patent law as a result of receiving so many petitions from inventors asking for a monopoly for their discoveries. Some of these first petitioners and their inventions were John Fitch, applying steam to navigation; E. Cruse, a steam engine for pumping water; S. Briggs, a machine for making nails; L. Harbaugh, threshing and reaping machines; C. Colles, a machine to count the revolutions of a wheel; and J. Macpherson, a lightning rod. The first administrator of our patent system was himself an inventor, a man who had invented a hemp beater, a moldboard plow, a pedometer, a sundial, a leather buggy top, and a swivel chair—although he never took a patent out on any of these inventions. His name was Thomas Jefferson.

Only three patents were issued the first year, the first one to Samuel Hopkins of Vermont on July 31, 1790, for a process of making potash and pearl ashes. By 1833 the head of the patent office wished to resign because "everything seems to have been done"—about nine thousand patents had been issued as of that date. Since then the patent office has issued about three million more.

THE PERFECT HOST (1790)

Thomas Jefferson once wrote of his home near Charlottesville, Virginia, "All my wishes end where I hope my days will end, at Monticello." He designed this unique home himself and spent twenty-five years building it. From its hilltop vantage point, Jefferson often observed through a telescope the construction of the nearby University of Virginia, for which he was also responsible. Then, as now, Monticello was a popular place to visit. In fact, it was so popular that Jefferson became practically destitute trying to feed and entertain visitors who felt Monticello was a public shrine even while Jefferson was yet alive. His steward once complained, "I have often sent a wagon load of hay up to the stable and the next morning there would not be enough to make a bird's nest. I have killed a fine beef and it would all be eaten in a day or two."

After Jefferson's death his daughter was forced to sell Monticello to pay his debts, which amounted to $107,000.

A FRONTIER "FIGHT"? (1790)

Frontiersmen were masters of subtle humor and understatement. One of the most beautiful examples of this occurs in an early frontier court record. One man charged with assault and battery left us this statement:

"I told him he lied; he told me I lied. I spit in his face; he spit in my face. I slapped him in the face; he slapped me in the face. I kicked him; he kicked me. I tripped him up; he tripped me up. I struck him and knocked him down; he got up and knocked me down. I then got mad; he got mad. And we was just a-going to fight when the saloon keeper got betwixt us."

In this particular case, the squire or justice of the peace fined both men a dollar each, which certainly seemed the fair thing to do.

PRISON LIFE (1790)

Early jails weren't used for rehabilitation; they were used for punishment. The experience of Stephen Burroughs of New Hampshire illustrates this. This college-educated criminal, although obviously guilty of many crimes, suffered as no present-day prisoner would be forced to.

Iron bands were welded around each leg and his waist, which were in turn bolted to the floor and his wrists placed in irons. Then, practically unable to move, he was placed in an unheated cell in the wintertime, with little clothing, only a little straw under him, and given nothing to eat until a relative left two dollars for food. Thirty-two days later, through the intervention of an uncle, he was relieved of his bonds, but by then he was described as "emaciated almost to a skeleton, with uncut beard, uncombed hair, a sore on his leg from which he never recovered, and he had more the appearance of a savage beast of the forest than anything appertaining to the human species." Shortly after this he escaped, was recaptured, and sentenced to one hundred lashes with a cat-o'-nine-tails. According to a witness, he was "punished with great severity, the flesh flying off at every stroke." It took him three months to recover from his whipping.

FIRST STARS AND STRIPES AROUND THE WORLD (1790)

Capt. Robert Gray is usually remembered for his discovery of the Columbia River and naming it after his ship in 1792. It was on his previous voyage, however, that the *Columbia* became the first American ship to circumnavigate the world after a voyage of 42,000 miles, carrying with it the Stars and Stripes. The voyage, for purposes of trade, put the ship on the Northwest coast, where it traded with Indians for a load of sea otter skins. The *Columbia* then went to China for a load of tea and then back to Boston. This history-making trip took three years, beginning two days after the U.S. Constitution was completed and ending during Washington's first full year in office. The birth of the United States as a world maritime power thus occurred simultaneously with the birth of the United States itself.

BLOODLETTING (1790)

Bloodletting was one of the basic treatments of early American medicine, used whenever a doctor was unsure of the trouble, or even when he was sure. There were two normal methods of drawing blood: opening a vein and running about a pint into a specially designed metal cup, or applying leeches. The number of leeches depended upon the seriousness of the sickness. Doctors paid small boys for bringing them swamp leeches, which would then be carried by the physician in a jar as part of his medical equipment. Many historians believe that Washington's death can be attributed, at least partly, to this practice of leeching, which so weakened him that it made death certain.

Because bleeding required so little skill, the first surgeons (inferior to physicians) who dealt only with superficial external problems were often assigned this task. Because barbers had the necessary equipment, they more often than not were "barber chirurgeons." In fact, the two arts were not separated in England until 1745. Even today, the barber pole with its white spiral bandage over red is a reminder of earlier, bloodier days.

JEFFERSON THE INVENTOR (1790)

Thomas Jefferson, known for his statesmanship, was as much the inventive American as was Benjamin Franklin. At Monticello, Jefferson designed a weather vane that transmitted its message to the porch roof. He also invented a clock, weighted by cannonballs arranged in such a manner as to tell the day of the week, that could be read both indoors and out. His own bed was fitted in a wall between his study and his bedroom to provide a natural breezeway. Twin doors were rigged so that both opened when one was pushed. Ladders folded up, chairs swiveled, music stands folded into boxes, and dumbwaiters simultaneously raised and lowered bottles from the cellar. Jefferson also invented a folding chair, a pedometer (to measure his walks), a letter-copying machine, a hemp machine, a two-wheeled carriage, and a plow with an advanced moldboard that was awarded a gold medal in France.

Significantly, Jefferson cared nothing about being remembered for these things. He wished his epitaph to note only his authorship of the Declaration of Independence and the Bill for Religious Freedom in Virginia, and his fathering of the University of Virginia.

A HUMILIATING DEFEAT (1791)

The Continental Army suffered many serious and embarrassing defeats during the Revolutionary War but never one as complete or humiliating as that suffered by the army eight years after the war ended—and not by a professionally trained army at that!

In 1791 Gen. Arthur St. Clair took 1,500 effective and trained fighting men (along with 200 wives) into the Northwest Territory against Chief Little Turtle and his Miami Confederacy. Although warned by Washington against a surprise attack similar to the one that had destroyed Gen. Josiah Harmer's army the year before, the experienced St. Clair allowed his army to be surprised on the morning of November 4 by Little Turtle and 1,400 Indian warriors. When the survivors of St. Clair's badly mauled force reached the safety of Ft. Jefferson twenty-nine miles away later that same day, they were minus 687 of their number, including 38 officers and 56 wives. Counting an additional 242 wounded, of whom a large number later died, this became the worst mauling the U.S. Army ever experienced, in relation to the numbers engaged—a humbling encounter at the hands of the Miami chief known to his own people as Michikiniqua, a name even West Pointers might find difficult to recognize.

AMERICA'S FIRST CREMATION (1792)

Various Indian tribes in America cremated their dead, but the first recorded cremation of a white person in this country occurred in 1792 near Charlestown, South Carolina. The object of the unusual event was Henry Laurens, South Carolina merchant, planter, statesman, and one-time president of the Continental Congress—and the only American ever imprisoned in the Tower of London. But that is another story.

Laurens had a horror of being buried alive, brought about when an infant daughter, pronounced dead from smallpox, revived while being prepared for burial. To prevent this from happening to himself, his will enjoined his son "as an indispensable duty that, as soon as he conveniently can after my decease, he cause my body to be wrapped in twelve yards of tow cloth, and burnt until it is entirely consumed, and then collecting my ashes, deposit them wherever he may see proper." This wish was carried out on the family estate near Charleston soon after Laurens's death.

THANKS FOR THE WAR, ELI (1793)

One of the greatest ironies in history involves Eli Whitney and the invention of the cotton gin. A native of Connecticut and a graduate of Yale, he was visiting some friends on a plantation near Savannah,

Georgia, in 1793. He watched slaves at work separating the cottonseed from the lint cotton and discovered to his amazement that it took one slave working all day for two to three months to clean one bale of cotton. Whitney had no way of knowing that because this made cotton growing unprofitable, its days were numbered, and slavery on a large scale was doomed with it. Feeling sorry for the slaves assigned this task, he designed and built in less than a week the first cotton gin, the design principles of which have not been improved upon since. As a result of his invention, cotton production rose at a fantastic rate, and the institution of slavery increased with it. Having no name for his invention, he applied the word *gin,* a contraction of the word *engine.* As successful as the gin was, Whitney's invention brought him nothing but debt and lawsuits against patent infringers. In gratitude for what the gin did for the economy of the South, South Carolina gave Whitney $50,000 years later, which he used to pay off some of his debts.

JUST DON'T TAX MY WHISKEY! (1794)

The uprising of the farmers in Western Pennsylvania in 1794—angered over several federal policies but specifically the excise tax on their chief transportable product, whiskey—is an event well known to American history students. Circumstantial evidence at this late date in history now tends to suggest that the whole misunderstanding that resulted in the insurrection was promoted by Alexander Hamilton in order to strengthen his political power over the Federalists. If true, this is one of those rare instances in which a government purposely promoted an insurrection in order to indicate strength by putting it down.

To quell this first rebellion against the U.S. government under the Constitution, the government turned to Gen. "Light Horse Harry" Lee, who did so with speed and efficiency at the head of 15,000 troops. Ironically, only sixty-seven years later his own son would lead the greatest rebellion this continent has ever seen—Gen. Robert E. Lee.

BUT IT'S SUPPOSED TO BE THERE! (1794)

Much of what people knew about the interior of North America for a full two centuries after the first settlement at Jamestown was based on conjecture. Concepts of the land west of the Appalachians up until the Lewis and Clark Expedition in 1804 were so distorted that even

Jefferson's plans for future western states makes little sense on a modern map. According to Morse's New Map of North America, "from the latest and best Authorities" in 1794, the southern tip of the Rocky Mountains was placed north of Lake Superior. Although seen and mapped as early as 1775 by Bruno de Hezeta, the Columbia River was not included on Morse's map, nor were the Sierra Nevada Mountains. As late as 1690, 113 years after Sir Francis Drake's coasting the California shoreline, the future golden state was considered an island totally separated from mainland North America. Maps of the time showed a lake just north of Florida as large as Lake Ontario.

One of the most interesting examples of distorted geography concerns the Buenaventura River, a river that never existed. This river, which was presumed to connect the Great Salt Lake and the Pacific Ocean, was regularly placed on maps because most people believed that such a river should be there. Men like John C. Fremont were still searching for this imaginary river as late as the 1840s.

POOR LITTLE JIMMY! (1794)

Slightly built (barely a hundred pounds), James Madison was a figure of respect among his fellow statesmen in Philadelphia, but he was never a man to impress the ladies. One pretty sixteen-year-old, Catharine Floyd, summarily turned down his suit, signing her letter with a seal of rye dough. A widow in New York also held out against him. Not to be deterred, the forty-three-year-old Madison resolved to try once more in 1794, but this time with the help of his friend Aaron Burr. The object of his advances was Dorothea (Dolley) Payne Todd, nineteen years his junior. Dolley was a Quaker widow with one son. When she heard of Madison's intentions she panicked, asking a close girlfriend to be around the first time Madison called on her. Madison persevered, however, and four months later, at the home of Mrs. George Steptoe Washington (Dolley's sister and George Washington's niece), the couple was wed.

"SOME PEACE PIPE!" (1794)

On his twenty-eighth birthday, young John Quincy Adams described in his diary the reception for a delegation of Chikasaw Indians at which President Washington played host, not only giving a speech but also smoking and passing around a pipe of peace. Adams questioned whether this was truly a

Native American custom because "these Indians seemed to be quite amused by it, and . . . looked as if they were submitting to a process in compliance with our custom. Some of them, I thought, smiled . . . as if the ceremony struck them not only as new, but also as ridiculous." Adams was wrong; it was an Indian custom. What the Indians were undoubtedly smiling about was the pipe. Not having an authentic Indian pipe, a large East Indian pipe was substituted, having a leather tube for a stem "twelve or fifteen feet in length."

MOUNT VERNON (1795)

More than a million visitors pass through the rooms of Mount Vernon each year, seemingly in response to Washington's own invitation, "I have no objection to any sober or orderly person's gratifying their curiosity in viewing the buildings, gardens, & ca. about Mount Vernon." He thought that the estate, which he inherited from his half-brother, Lawrence, was "more pleasantly situated" than any other "estate in United America."

Mount Vernon's safety was believed in jeopardy for several days in 1814 as a British squadron approached it on its way up the Potomac to Washington. There was reason enough for the fear—the British burned Washington a few hours later—but at Mount Vernon the squadron merely slowed down, fired a salute in Washington's honor, and then moved on.

The federal government is purchasing or gaining control of all land on both sides of the Potomac within view of Mount Vernon with the object of excluding all industry, homes, and so forth, and restoring the area to its original beauty—the way Washington enjoyed it when he lived there.

THE POISON PLOW (1797)

In 1797 Charles Newbold, an American, invented a plow made entirely of iron and in a shape that was a vast improvement over the crude wooden plows then in use. Although easier to use and more effective in operation, it did not catch on. Farmers would have nothing to do with it, believing that the iron poisoned the soil even though the iron came out of the soil. Wood, they argued, was natural to the soil.

Newbold, who expected great success, faded from sight in disappointment and poverty. The fear of an iron plow lasted at least twenty years. Then, in 1819, an improved iron plow invented by Jethro Wood, a New York farmer, quickly caught on. Why? The new theory: strong iron, strong soil, fine crops.

JOHN ADAMS AND "FRIENDS" (1797)

President John Adams's strong characteristics of personal courage, integrity, wisdom, and patriotism are well known and need little elaboration, but his weaknesses tell us much about his other side. Personal vanity was probably his weakest point, but his hot temper made enemies of many people, including just about every prominent American of his time. He started Washington on his rise to fame by getting him elected commander in chief, but he later came to be openly jealous of him. He had been a friend of Jefferson, but he came to despise his "democratical" thinking: "There never was a democracy that didn't commit suicide."

But Adams reserved his worst feelings for the leader of his party— Alexander Hamilton. Several times Hamilton schemed to undermine Adams before and after his election to the presidency, so it was probably with some justification that Adams referred to Hamilton as "the bastard brat of a Scotch pedlar."

DUELING FOR PRESIDENT (1797)

Most Americans are familiar with Alexander Hamilton's fatal duel with Aaron Burr, but less commonly known is an "almost duel" in which the two were involved earlier. In 1797, when Hamilton believed his integrity was being questioned by James Monroe over an incident that had occurred several years previously, he sent an assistant to Monroe with the following note: "The result to my mind is that you have been and are actuated by motives towards me malignant and dishonorable." Although not wishing to duel, Monroe stated his readiness to accept a challenge. Hamilton's assistant thereupon delivered what amounted to a challenge, and Monroe named his friend Aaron Burr to act for him. Interestingly enough, Burr resolved the matter without a duel by simply not delivering Monroe's final communication. Ironically, Hamilton lived to fight his fatal duel with Burr seven years later, whereas Monroe lived to become president of the United States, a position to which both Hamilton and Burr had aspired.

EYE GOUGING (1798)

The term "violent Americans" might well be justified, especially when we consider the necessity of certain laws that were enacted in the Northwest (Ohio) Territory in May 1798. One law starts out, "Whosoever

. . . shall voluntarily, maliciously, and on purpose pull out or put out an eye while fighting or otherwise . . ." It then sets the penalty at imprisonment or a fine up to $1,000.

Such a law was designed to modify the brutal frontier fighting called "rough and tumble," in which kicking in the crotch, groin, or belly, throttling, biting off ears or noses, breaking backs or limbs, tearing out corners of mouths, and eye gouging were normally considered permissible. Maj. Eluries Beatty of Louisville, Kentucky, in 1791 described one frontier fighter who "was so [dexterous] in these matters, that he had, in his time, taken out five eyes, bit off two or three noses and ears and spit them in their faces."

Of course, there were just causes for such mutilations, as a Virginian described them in 1773: "One has called him a thick-Scull or a Buckskin, or a Scotchman, perhaps one has mislaid the other's hat . . . or offered him a dram without wiping the mouth of the bottle."

DUELING CHALLENGE DECLINED (1799)

Judge John Breckinridge, whose father, John C., was vice president under James Buchanan, was challenged to a duel by a British officer in the late 1790s but declined with this letter:

"Sir, I have two objections to this duel matter, the one is lest I should hurt you; the other lest you should hurt me. I do not see any good it would do me to put a bullet through any part of your body. I could make no use of you when dead for any culinary purpose, as I could a rabbit or turkey . . . for though your flesh might be delicate and tender, yet it wants that firmness and consistency which takes and retains salt. At any rate, it would not be fit for long sea voyages. You might make a good barbeque, it is true, being of the nature of a raccoon or an opossum, but people are not in the habit of barbequing anything human now. As to your hide, it is not worth taking off, being little better than that of a two-year-old colt. As to myself, I do not much like to stand in the way of anything that is harmful. I am under the apprehension you might hit me. That being the case, I think it most advisable to stay at a distance. If you want to try your pistols, take some object—a tree or a barn door—about my dimensions, and if you hit that, send me word. I shall then acknowledge that if I had been in the same place you would have killed me in a duel. I have the honor to be, Sir, Your hmbl. & obdt. Servant, John Breckinridge."

HENRY HELPS SAVE THE UNION (1799)

In 1799, shortly before his death, George Washington saw his beloved government on the verge of collapse with states passing nullification acts and the country torn from within. The center of the strife was his beloved state of Virginia. With elections approaching, he appealed to Patrick Henry, the arch foe of federalism, to run for public office and put his influence behind the central government to prevent the breakup of the Union. Although sick and infirm, Henry responded to his friend's plea. In his campaign he warned that no state is above the central government or can pass upon the validity of federal laws. His eloquence and prestige averted the destruction of the young republic, and he was elected to the Virginia House of Representatives. But before the assembly sat, with his most important work finished, Patrick Henry died—as did George Washington, the old patriot who had summoned him to it.

WASHINGTON'S DEATH (1799)

The beginning of the end for America's first president occurred on December 12, 1799, when the sixty-seven-year-old recently retired president made a lengthy horseback tour of Mount Vernon through snow, sleet, cold, and windy rains. The following day he had a sore throat, and the day after that he was seriously ill, unable to talk and scarcely able to breathe. Doctors applied leeches four times, at the same time applying wheat bran to his legs and feet, feeding him molasses and butter, forcing him to inhale fumes of sage tea and vinegar, and giving him calomel and tartar emetic— all to no avail. With the end obviously approaching, Washington whispered to his aide, Tobias Lear, "I am just going. Have me decently buried and do not let my body be put into a vault in less than two days after I am dead." Washington looked at Lear and said, "Do you understand?" "Yes, sir," Lear replied. The president's last words were, "'Tis well." A little after 10 P.M., after taking his own pulse, Washington died.

THE NAME WASHINGTON (1799)

It is appropriate that George Washington is the only American president to have had a state named after him. By the same token, it is perhaps inappropriate that seven of our states are named for European monarchs: Maryland, Virginia, West Virginia, North Carolina, South Carolina, Georgia, and Louisiana.

In addition to having a state named after him, America's first president leads all other Americans, and perhaps all other men in history, in having his name attached to places. George Stewart, the authority on place names, claims that America has honored Washington's name with 33 counties, 121 cities and towns, 257 townships, 10 lakes, 8 streams, and 7 mountains. This authority doesn't begin to count all the streets, schools, monuments, forts, parks, and so on that carry Washington's name.

ARNOLD'S DEATH (1801)

Benedict Arnold's last years and days were spent in exile in London, with even fewer friends than he had in the country he betrayed. His friendless state was emphasized by the *London Morning Post,* commenting on his death on June 14, 1801: "Poor General Arnold has departed this world without notice—a sorry reflection for other turncoats." These same thoughts must have been on his mind just before he died. According to the account of his wife, Peggy, his last words were, "Let me die in my old uniform"—referring to his Continental uniform of a major general. "God forgive me for ever putting on any other." Most historians consider this story highly unlikely, as they do her diagnosis of his death. Although doctors diagnosed Arnold's death as dropsy brought on by gout, his wife claimed that her husband "literally fell sacrifice" to a "perturbed mind."

THE COURT BEFORE MARSHALL (1801)

The most sought-after political office in the United States today, next to the presidency, is the Supreme Court—a lifetime position with prestige and financial reward. Such was not the case the first dozen years of the nation's highest court. Prominent men like Robert H. Harrison, Charles C. Pinckney, Edward Rutledge, Alexander Hamilton, and Patrick Henry turned down appointments to the court. Two of the first chief justices resigned for "better positions," and a third became senile in office. So obscure was their infrequent meetings that for many years historians had difficulty in placing their actual meeting places. When the first Capitol building was designed, no one remembered to put in a room for the Supreme Court.

For the first three years, justices met only to adjourn, although they did travel circuit. As a matter of fact, they spent so much time traveling that the horrible conditions of travel in those times made physical ability a necessary qualification for life on the bench. John Marshall himself broke a collarbone in a carriage mishap. Gouvenor Morris once remarked that the major requisite for the job was not legal learning (Marshall had less than two months of such learning) but the "agility of a postboy."

THAT DIRTY LITTLE PAINE! (1801)

As president, Jefferson looked after his friends, but there was a limit beyond which he wouldn't go, even for them. He rescued the unstable and eccentric Thomas Paine from squalor and disgrace in France and brought him home. The well-known author of *Common Sense* was facing possible imprisonment in France because he dared suggest that Jefferson's inaugural address was superior to the words of Napoleon. Jefferson enjoyed being with Paine and often entertained him in the White House, but he refused to appoint him to public office. This refusal had nothing to do with Paine's abilities but with his stubborn refusal to wash, according to some historians. Whatever the case, historians always seem to touch upon the issue of Paine's cleanliness. Even his admiring biographer, W. E. Woodward, seems to protest too much. Referring to Paine as a guest at the executive mansion, he states, "He was always clean-shaven, neatly dressed, his face washed, his hair combed and brushed." As late as the twentieth century, however, that epitome of Americanism, Teddy Roosevelt, still referred to Paine, perhaps erroneously so, as "that dirty little atheist."

A FRONTIER "SAINT" (1801)

Born in Massachusetts in 1774, John Chapman was first sighted on the frontier while floating down the Ohio River on two canoes lashed together and filled with rotting apples. Normally he filled his well-known bags of apple seeds from cider presses and traveled hundreds of miles throughout the frontier wilderness planting and pruning his orchards, charging a "fipenny bit" for an apple sapling—as often as not taking a promissory note and never collecting. Johnny Appleseed, as he came to be called, was, to say the least, eccentric. He was always the dreamy type, but a kick in the head by a horse early in his career didn't help any and might explain why he always wore a cooking pan for a hat.

Being a religious mystic and a Swedenborgian missionary, he quoted scripture to anyone who would listen. This and his Jain-like kindness to all forms of life earned him a reputation as a frontier saint. For forty-five years, beginning in 1801, he consecrated himself to the single mission of bringing seeds from Pennsylvania, including flower seed, and planting them deep in the forests so they would be ready for use when the settlers arrived. Descendants of his trees survive by the thousands today from Pennsylvania to Fort Wayne, Indiana.

JEFFERSON THE REBEL (1801)

It is surprising that more young revolutionaries have not adopted Thomas Jefferson as their idol, in view of his ideas on revolution. "A little rebellion now and then is a good thing, and as necessary in the political world as storm in the physicals," he once said. He remarked another time that "the tree of liberty must be refreshed from time to time with the blood of patriots and tyrants." It is difficult to imagine that great statesman exclaiming, "God forbid that we should ever be twenty years without . . . a rebellion!" Perhaps it was merely the hot blood of youth and inexperience talking, for when he ascended to real authority, president of the United States, his inaugural address records these words: "Americans need . . . a wise and frugal government which shall restrain men from injuring one another." Time does temper, even in such men as Jefferson.

"ROLLING, SHOUTING, AND JERKING" (1801)

Religion on the American frontier was as unsophisticated as was everything else in the lives of the people. Traveling preachers held huge camp meetings, and with their fire and brimstone talks, they worked the masses into a frenzy of rolling, shouting, and jerking. In 1801, at a meeting of 25,000 people in Bourbon County, Kentucky, 3,000 fainted and 500 others jerked and barked in chorus. One Methodist preacher who rode circuit in Virginia in 1807 wrote this in his diary:

"June 15th . . . I preached and almost killed myself. A gracious time. Brother W. and L. Isbell had the powerfullest time shouting and rolling on the floor.

"Wed. 19th . . . I saw a young woman who had the jerks two years and was very wicked (her parents were Baptists). She said she wished I might go to hell.

"22nd . . . young woman who only the week before wished I Might go to hell . . . had the most powerful manifestations I ever saw. She leaped from the floor and jumped and shouted and jerked all night and until I left the next day at ten o'clock. I hardly think, besides many others, I ever saw the like before."

EITHER WAY, HAMILTON WON (1802)

Most students of American history look to the John Peter Zenger case of 1735 as the establishment of the principle of freedom of the press in America. Actually, the almost identical issue of libel and press freedom had to be fought over again sixty-seven years later. Paradoxically, the second case involved a case of libel against that great standard bearer of freedom, President Thomas Jefferson, by Harry Croswell, an editor in Hudson, New York. Croswell was accused of libeling Jefferson in an article in his paper, the *Wasp,* and his case was defended by the great Alexander Hamilton. As in the Zenger case, Hamilton argued that the fact of publication was not the issue but rather the truthfulness of the article. This case resulted in the liberalizing of libel laws in 1805 and thus achieved the freedom-of-press victory usually credited to the Zenger case. By coincidence, the defending lawyer in the Zenger case was also named Hamilton, Andrew Hamilton.

PUBLIC GRATITUDE TO BOONE (1802)

As the young Republic moved toward a new century, peace and prosperity moved across the former "dark and bloody ground" south of the Ohio. Daniel Boone had opened a huge green empire for the bursting young giant of a country; in his honor Kentucky named a county after him. Almost immediately, however, sheriffs sold 10,000 acres of his land for taxes. Much of Boone's work, such as the cutting of the Wilderness Road, had been paid for in land, but legal rights for it were declared worthless. Land speculators with their lawyers and sheriffs moved onto Boone's former large holdings, laying claim to even the land under the Boone cabin. When he had nothing left, someone robbed him of $50,000 entrusted to him by neighbors for the purpose of purchasing valid titles to land. It took twenty years of hard labor—farming, surveying, trapping—to pay it back. Then almost seventy years old, Boone and his wife, Rebecca, were poorer than when they had opened the land a quarter of a century before. So, giving up nothing, Boone moved west to Missouri. Twenty-five years later, Kentucky demanded his return. Now dead, he could not object, and four white horses drew his remains to a flower-strewn grave at the state capitol, where speeches of praise were made to a man who could no longer hear them.

BUT IT IS RAINING! (1803)

Chief Justice John Marshall was known to take an occasional drink. Nevertheless, he became extremely concerned about judges drinking to excess—so concerned, in fact, that he and members of the Supreme Court shunned all drink except in rainy weather. Upon receiving notification of the Louisiana Purchase, however, judges permitted drinks for themselves by ruling that it was raining somewhere, though it was perfectly dry at the time in Washington.

"DETECTING CONSPIRACIES" (1807)

In 1807 Aaron Burr was indicted for treason and brought to trial in Virginia for activities that are to this day a question of controversy and uncertainty. Although he was acquitted, it is historical fact that he was involved to some extent in a conspiracy against the United States. It is also a fact, though much less known, that this same man helped organize the Secret Service for the United States during the Revolutionary War. Paradoxically, in a special order by Gen. George Washington on July 4, 1778, he was made head of that department for detecting and defeating conspiracies. So turn the wheels of fate and history.

THESE BONES ARE NO ASSET! (1809)

The man who Andrew Jackson dared to say "needs no monument made by hands; he has erected a monument in the hearts of all lovers of liberty" found mostly "monuments" of hate and abuse during his later years by the very people for whom he had fought, written, and suffered during the War for Independence. Going to France in 1787 to participate in the French Revolution, he barely escaped the guillotine, avoiding it and prison through the intercession of James Monroe. While in Europe he wrote *The Age of Reason,* which was critical of the Old Testament but was not "the atheist's Bible," as has often been said. Thomas Paine was actually a pious deist, believing in both God and heaven.

He returned to America and settled in New York state in 1802. There the old man lived for only seven years, receiving incredible abuse, hatred, and neglect, and living in poverty and ill health. His adopted countrymen

did not remember *Common Sense*—only the "atheistic" *Age of Reason.*
New York denied him the right to vote on the grounds that he was not
an American citizen. As an indication of the depth of hatred felt for the
misrepresented old man, when he died in 1809 at the age of seventy-two,
he was denied burial in a Quaker cemetery and was buried instead on a
corner of his farm in New York. His body was later secretly dug up and
taken to England for a proposed monument. During a controversy over
possession of the remains, a court declared his bones no asset, and they
disappeared.

A YEAR TO REMEMBER (1811)

Many years are remembered for some natural phenomenon that
occurred at the time, but the year 1811 seemed to have several, at least
in the Ohio-Mississippi Valleys. In the spring of that year, vast flooding
struck the two river valleys, followed by widespread epidemics. Then, vast
numbers of squirrels started an insane migration from north to south
with thousands of them drowning in the Ohio River. In September both
an eclipse and a comet caused further widespread uneasiness. On the elev-
enth of that same month, the *New Orleans,* the first successful steamboat
launched on inland waters, started its voyage from Pittsburgh to New
Orleans. As it neared the mouth of the Ohio River, the worst earthquake
in the history of the Mississippi Valley struck. Terror-stricken settlers,
linking the quake to the churning river steamer, fled its approach, and
Indians were sure the monster was a portent of more evil to come. (They
might have been right, for the following year brought not only equally
severe quakes but also war with England.) The most extensive recorded
change in American topography took place as the result of the 1811 earthquake. Thirty thousand square miles sank in depth from five to fifteen
feet, while an equal area was raised the same amount, and the mighty
"father of waters" actually changed its course in several places.

THE "DOWAGER QUEEN" (1812)

Dolley (as she spelled her name) Madison left behind her a legacy
as the most popular White House hostess and First Lady of all time. In
addition to her own term as First Lady, she acted for two terms as official
hostess at the White House for widower Thomas Jefferson. Not even the
burning of Washington and the White House during her husband's term

quenched her high spirits and gracious ways. When Henry Clay said, "Everybody loves Mrs. Madison," she replied, "Mrs. Madison loves everybody!" After her husband's death in 1836, Dolley the "Dowager Queen" returned to Washington to be wooed by the greats—from President John Tyler to Samuel F. B. Morse, who invited her to reply to the first telegraph message, "What hath God wrought." Her reply: "Message from Mrs. Madison. She sends her love to Mrs. Wethered." Although she was in such financial straits in her later years that Daniel Webster regularly dropped off baskets of groceries to help out, she was always included in the capital's great events until she reached the age of eighty-one, voluntarily retiring from the limelight.

IT WAS A GREAT BUSINESS! (1812)

As during the Revolution, a major method for carrying the war to the enemy in the second war with England was through privateers. When the war began, the British navy had the most powerful fleet in the world: more than eight hundred ships in commission compared to only eighteen American ships fit for sea duty. Thus it was that privateers were sought— and they were extremely effective. At the end of the first seven months of war, Lloyds of London announced the loss of five hundred merchant ships to American privateers, sending both prices and insurance rates sky high in Great Britain. Flour rose to $58 per barrel, and to send goods to Nova Scotia, insurance rates cost the shipper more than one-third the cost of the entire cargo.

The success of the American privateer is illustrated by the story of the *Rossie,* a fast Baltimore schooner with fifteen guns and 125 men. Within a ninety-day period in 1812, she seized four ships, eight brigs, three schooners, and three sloops valued at $1.5 million. This amounted to a captured enemy vessel every five days, returning with twice as many prisoners as there were men in the crew.

PROTESTING THE WAR OF 1812 (1812)

Resistance to the War of 1812 was proportionately greater in this country than any war the United States has ever engaged in, with the possible exception of the War for Independence. Exactly one week after war was declared, Gov. Caleb Strong of Massachusetts declared a public fast in view of the war "against the nation from which we are descended." That same day the Massachusetts House of Representatives asserted that "there be no volunteers except for defensive war." On July 2, only two weeks after the declaration, the Connecticut governor refused to supply militia to the federal government, and the following month the state assembly condemned the war. New Hampshire followed with veiled threats of disunion, threats the New Englanders continued through the war.

In addition to the outright opposition to the war, there were undisguised and well-organized enterprises to supply the British army in Canada and the British navy off the coast with American goods or provisions. Even the blockading British squadron off Sandy Hook was provisioned by New York merchants.

BATTLES OR MASSACRES? (1813)

"We fight battles, they conduct massacres" is an adage that aptly applies to the white history of Indian wars in the United States. It is most dramatically illustrated in the historical versions of the Great Swamp Fight in King Philip's War in 1675 and the Fort Mims Massacre during the War of 1812. The names themselves suggest the double standard of terminology and interpretation.

In 1813 a force of about one thousand Creek Indians attacked a frontier fort north of Mobile, Alabama. Finding the gate open, they entered, and a desperate battle took place in which more than five hundred white men, women, and children were killed. This has come to be known as the Fort Mims "Massacre." In 1675 the situation was reversed when approximately one thousand New England soldiers attacked a Narragansett fort in what is now Rhode Island. Again there was a desperate battle, in the process of which more than seven hundred Indian men, women, and children were killed by the whites. This has come down in history as the Great Swamp Fight.

BURNING THE WHITE HOUSE (1814)

When British troops, meeting little opposition, marched on Washington in 1814, they found a dinner for forty people waiting to be served at the White House. Helping themselves to the steaming food, they proceeded to ransack the executive mansion. The British admiral, Sir George Cockburn, took a hat belonging to President James Madison and a chair cushion belonging to Dolley as his personal souvenirs and then ordered the building to be burned. Fifty British soldiers surrounded the White House and, upon an order, hurled burning balls of pitch through the windows. Overseeing the burning of much of the rest of Washington, including the uncompleted Capitol, the admiral rode about the city making vulgar jokes about the cushion dangling from his saddle.

The British government and press were both critical of Admiral Cockburn and the British supreme commander, Gen. Robert Ross, for burning the American Capitol—"acts of an uncivilized people," they called it. But the British military justified it by saying that it was in revenge for the American burning of a public building at York (now Toronto) the year before.

MRS. PICKERSGILL'S FLAGS (1814)

Whether Betsy Ross made the first Stars and Stripes may be open to dispute, but it is highly doubtful that any adult American doesn't recognize her name. How many would recognize the name of Mary Young Pickersgill? It was Mrs. Pickersgill, also a widow, and living at 844 East Pratt Street in Baltimore, who was commissioned in the summer of 1814 to make a flag for a local fort. How long it took her to complete the 30-by-42-foot flag is not known, but she apparently completed it in time for the attack on Baltimore. This was the flag Francis Scott Key saw waving over Fort McHenry on the morning of September 14 that inspired him to write "The Star Spangled Banner." The battered remains of this colossal banner, for which the widow was paid $405.90, hangs today in the Smithsonian in Washington. The words Key wrote were put to the tune of "Anecreon in Heaven," a popular song at English drinking clubs; the flag that inspired it, because of its immense size, was sewn together on the floor of Clagett's brewery malt house in Baltimore.

"WANTED: AN ARMY!" (1814)

On August 24, 1814, at Bladensburg, Maryland, only five miles from the nation's capital, 6,000 American militia tried to stop 4,500 British regulars. The militia, driven in panic before Lord Wellington's best troops, caused the battle to become known in history as the "Bladensburg Races." In fact, the rout, which opened Washington to occupation and burning, was so complete that American officers for days afterward were putting ads in local newspapers notifying their lost men where to report. Maj.

Gen. Robert Ross, who commanded the victorious army that routed the civilian soldiers and later burned the city of Washington, was killed a few days later near Baltimore. Great Britain, however, knows how to honor its heroes. After death he was granted the title "Ross of Bladensburg" and granted a family coat of arms. To young America's embarrassment, the Ross coat of arms consists of the Stars and Stripes floating from a broken flagstaff, the emblem of defeat.

He Didn't Like Ministers (1814)

One of the most unique characters in American history was Stephen Girard, a wheeling-dealing, hardheaded, cold-blooded miser who made few friends and many enemies as he was accumulating his fortune in the "city of brotherly love." When the yellow fever epidemic struck Philadelphia in 1793, however, he not only gave freely to buy medicines, train nurses, and provide health care, but he also entered homes to care for the sick. His enemies suggested that he was a victim of coprophilia, impelling him to handle filth and disease. Although history books seldom mention it, he was the prime financial support of the unpopular War of 1812, subscribing in 1814 for 95 percent of the total war loan, amounting to about five million dollars. His fortune at the time of his death was the largest yet seen in America, roughly 7.5 million dollars, most of which he left to public charity.

Girard's most interesting donation was for the founding of a school for white male orphans (Girard College), which took $5,260,000 and came with the provision that religious professionals not be permitted on the grounds and that a twenty-foot wall be built around the school to keep them out.

The Rewards of Battle (1815)

The Battle of New Orleans brought quite different fortunes to the opposing commanders. Gen. Andrew Jackson, whose command of pirates, "free men of color," Choctaw Indians, his own backwoodsmen, and regular troops dealt such a decisive defeat to the British that he became the greatest national figure of his day. "I cannot believe," wrote Henry Clay, "that the killing of 2,500 Englishmen at New Orleans qualifies a person for the various, difficult, and complicated duties of the chief magistracy," but Jackson was propelled into the White House for two terms nevertheless.

The opposing commander at New Orleans, Gen. Edward Pakenham, was not the first choice of his government for the job, but he was burning to distinguish himself. His desire for fame, which probably contributed to his foolhardy attack on entrenched infantry, came from the fact that his brother-in-law was none other than Lord Wellington, the greatest English soldier of that generation. Pakenham was never to know that same fame. Fatally wounded on the field of battle that day, his body was sent home to England in a cask of rum.

A PRISON MASSACRE (1815)

The War of 1812 officially ended with the Peace of Ghent in December 1814, but as late as April of the following year, England still held more than five thousand prisoners at the Dartmoor military prison. Anger over the continued confinement, strict discipline, and bad food brought about a near riot on April 6, 1815. British soldiers, called to quell the disturbance, were jeered and stoned by the prisoners until, without orders, they fired into the prison crowd. Then, losing their heads, they continued to fire indiscriminately into the prisoners struggling to escape the massacre. The few officers present (most were at dinner) and the hospital surgeon eventually stopped the slaughter but not before more than sixty were shot, seven of whom died immediately. A joint American-British investigating commission exonerated the commander. The soldiers were blamed but not prosecuted. The British government did provide for the families of those killed and gave pensions to those disabled.

STEPHEN DECATUR (1815)

For a second time within a generation, the young American Republic was forced to take action against Mediterranean pirates who were capturing ships and men, and exacting tribute from many nations, including the United States. Upon the termination of the War of 1812, Stephen Decatur was sent to the trouble spot with a squadron to end the humiliating treatment. Within forty days Decatur had brought Algiers, Tunis, and Tripoli to their knees, and at the mouth of the cannon, forced them to sign treaties indemnifying the United States for past losses and giving up all future bribes or tribute. To lesson the humiliation, the Dey's officials in Algiers begged Decatur to continue a token tribute of gunpowder. The reply, "If you insist on receiving powder as tribute, you must expect to receive BALLS with it," was warning enough. North African pirates bothered no more American ships.

Decatur came through many pitched battles in two wars against the North Africans and against the British in the War of 1812 only to be killed by a fellow American naval officer. In 1820 he died in a duel with Comm. James Barron, whom he had opposed for reinstatement into the navy because Barron had sat out the War of 1812 in Europe. Decatur's sense of patriotism forced him to oppose Barron; his sense of honor forced him to accept a needless duel.

OLD PAUL REVERE (1818)

Henry Wadsworth Longfellow made it extremely difficult to picture Paul Revere in any other role than that of the midnight rider. That he lived to be eighty-three and participated in many other historical events tends to be lost in the mists of history. But not only did Paul Revere furnish much of the material for the building and sheathing of the *USS Constitution* ("Old Ironsides") and live to see it outfight the French, the Algerians, and the English in the second war with England, but at the age of eighty, he led 150 "Mechanics of the town of Boston" in formally tendering their services to help in the building of more forts in Boston Harbor.

Except for old John Adams, Revere was the last of the Revolutionary patriot leaders when he died in 1818, just a week before Congress passed an act granting pensions to needy Revolutionary War veterans. Revere, however, was not needy and certainly not forgotten—Longfellow made sure of that.

A MOST SIMPLE INVENTION (1818)

The common tin can, manufactured today by the millions, did not come into being until 1818, when it was invented by Peter Durant. For many years thereafter, canned food was a novelty—popular with few, distrusted by many, and expensive to all. The Civil War did much to make tin cans popular when the North supplied its troops with canned foods. The canned-food industry as we know it today, however, did not get its start until 1885 when a machine for making cans automatically and cheaply was put into production in Baltimore. The term "can" comes from the word *canister*—a shell filled with gunpowder and lead balls.

Because of the similarity between these military projectiles and the bright tin food containers, the word can was coined.

SNAIL WATER (1818)

The cause of most illnesses in early America was unknown, and the remedies used were primitive and at times outrageous. One of the most common preparations was snail water, which was made by pounding snails and earthworms in a mortar. This resulting mixture was boiled in ale with various garden herbs, bottled, and then used as a tonic, often daily. Abigail Adams reported that she used this drink in such a manner from the time she was a small girl. Apparently it did her no harm—she died of typhoid fever in 1818 at the age of seventy-four. Her husband, John, lived on another eight years and, come to think of it, he never drank that horrible concoction.

EARLY OIL POLLUTION (1818)

Pollution, oil and otherwise, is not new to the United States. One of the earliest reports of a serious case of pollution occurred in Kentucky in 1818. At that time oil (petroleum) had no known use and was referred to as "Devil's Tar" by the man responsible for the 1818 mishap, Martin Beatty. His drillers, searching for brine for his salt works, struck oil with a five-inch auger at 536 feet. Unable to plug the oil well with sand, Beatty allowed it to flow into the Cumberland River, where it covered the surface for a distance of thirty-five miles. Because it was ignored, it caused an enormous fire that destroyed trees along the banks of the river and the salt works itself.

At this time oil had no commercial value, so the flowing well was merely considered a curiosity. It wasn't until 1855 that oil developed a value, and then it was bottled and sold for medicinal purposes. We can imagine the medicinal value of the Cumberland River oil flow to the marine life in that river.

TAKE ANOTHER BATH? (1820)

By the mid-1700s some of the more elaborate homes in Philadelphia had bathhouses, but these were the exceptions. As late as 1820 no home in Quincy, Massachusetts, a rather respectable town, had a bathroom. Even John Adams, in referring to the cold temperatures in the northern clime, pointed out that "there is no inducement . . . to waste any unnecessary time in washing." A fairly typical colonial attitude toward bathing is recorded in the diary of a Philadelphia Quaker named Elizabeth Drinker. Writing in 1799 of a shower she had installed in her backyard for therapeutic use, she reported that she "bore it better than I expected, not having been wett all over at once, for twenty eight years past." This distaste for water was not uniquely American. Samuel Pepys wrote of his surprise in the late 1600s when his wife not only took a bath but also said she might do it again soon.

MASTERS AND SLAVES (1820)

The fondness of some white planters in the antebellum South for their female slaves is proverbial for its prevalence and tragic consequences. A sister of President James Madison once said, "We southern ladies are complimented with name of wives; but we are only the mistresses of seraglios." Another planter's wife voiced the same bitterness when she complained that a planter's wife was only "the chief slave of the harem." Examples of related tragedies include the case of the Louisiana planter who, when he died, left three daughters of a quadroon mistress, all well educated and raised as his own children. Louisiana authorities, to settle the estate, sold them as prostitutes despite the pleading of an uncle from New Hampshire. Another case involves a Georgia congressman who raised a family by a slave woman, acknowledging his children and allowing them to call him "papa." They were all sold at public auction during his lifetime. Many masters saw their children work under the whip, and young masters sold their own brothers and sisters. One of the more coldhearted cases is of a young husband who, upon learning that his beautiful Cuban wife was formerly a slave, felt betrayed and sold her to a slave dealer.

THAT WAS LOVE (1820)

Rachel Donelson (Jackson) was recovering from an unpleasant marriage to Capt. Lewis Robards when Andrew Jackson married her in 1791. Unfortunately, her divorce from Robards had been delayed, unknown to the Jackson couple, and they were forced to marry again in 1793, a humiliating experience to both of them and one that Jackson's enemies never let him forget. Due to the divorce delay and Rachel's habit of smoking pipes and cigars, Jackson, who loved his wife dearly, felt compelled to defend her honor on several occasions—even to the point of dueling and killing Charles Dickinson in 1806. When his beloved Rachel died in 1828, he could not believe she was gone. He ordered blankets kept ready for hours after her death in hopes that she would revive. For the next seventeen years of his life, the general kept her portrait where it would be the first object he would see each morning.

JACKSON'S "CHILDREN" (1820)

Andrew and Rachel Jackson had no biological children of their own, but they raised several children. Among those they loved as their own was an adopted son, Andrew Jackson Jr.; an orphan of an old war companion, Andrew Jackson Hutchings; and a nephew who later in life was nominated for the vice presidency with Millard Fillmore, Andrew Jackson Donelson. In addition to these three, Jackson took into his home a Creek Indian orphan, Lyncoya. When only one year old, Lyncoya was taken from the breast of his dead mother and brought to Jackson's tent after the Battle of Tallushatches. There the general kept him alive with brown sugar, water, and bread crumbs. Despite his ruthlessness toward Indians, Jackson reserved a favorite niche in his heart for Lyncoya. He raised the boy and later apprenticed him to a saddle maker, only to be grieved when the Indian youth died, probably of tuberculosis.

A NE'ER-DO-WELL MAKES GOOD (1821)

He called himself George Guess, the half-breed son of a ne'er-do-well who left the boy's mother before the child was born. He grew up with and was accepted by the Cherokees, although he was considered a dreamer. His dreaming led him on many a search for a way to put the Cherokee language on paper just like the English language—"talking leaves," as writing was called by his friends, who considered him crazy. Undaunted, he continued his quest from his late thirties into his fifties. Finally, in 1821, he finished his work—an alphabet of eighty-five characters with six musical sounds, the vowels; plus twelve dividing sounds, the consonants. Quickly the Cherokees learned this written language, and within one year of the founding of the first Native American newspaper in North America, the *Cherokee Phoenix,* three-quarters of the Cherokee nation could not only read but also write the alphabet. It was said that this was only the sixth time in recorded history that a completely new written language had been devised, and the first time in the history of the world that one person had devised a new syllabary. Because of this accomplishment, George Guess (Gist) is honored with a statute in the nation's capital. But his greatest monument has been preserved in the name given to the great redwood trees—the mighty Sequoia, his Indian name.

CONGRESS WAS EXCITING BACK THEN (1824)

One of the most brilliant minds in the history of Congress was John Randolph of Roanoke, who served for thirty years in that body. Some of the most remembered and most often quoted wit and biting sarcasm ever uttered in the House of Representatives came from his tongue:

- "That most delicious of all privileges—spending other people's money."
- "Clay's eye is on the Presidency; and my eye is on him." (They fought a duel in which neither was wounded.)
- "Never were abilities so much below mediocrity so well rewarded; no, not when Caligula's horse was made Consul." (On the appointment of Richard Rush to secretary of the treasury.)
- "Asking one of the States to surrender part of her sovereignty is like asking a lady to surrender part of her chastity."
- "He rowed to his object with muffled oars." (Of Martin Van Buren.)
- "An English noble has but one son. All the rest are bastards."

J. Q. ADAMS, THE SWIMMER (1825)

Anyone falling into the Potomac River today is advised to get a tetanus shot because of the pollution. Only a century and a half ago, this same river was the daily swimming pool of our sixth president. Each warm morning between four and six, John Quincy Adams would slip down to the river from the White House, strip on the bank, and jump in for a brief swim (he was an excellent swimmer). Coming out, he would stroll back to the executive mansion to read his Bible, write in his massive diary, or read the papers before breakfast.

It was on one of these early morning swims that a lady reporter, who had been trying in vain to corner him for an interview, found him. She immediately sat down on his clothes, forcing him to remain in the water until the interview was granted and completed.

JEFFERSON, ADAMS, AND THE FOURTH OF JULY (1826)

Thomas Jefferson and John Adams, members of the committee that drafted the Declaration of Independence, continued a correspondence throughout their lives, though they were estranged for a while. As a matter of fact, as John Adams lay dying at his home in Quincy, Massachusetts, his last thoughts were of his friend from Monticello: "Thomas Jefferson survives." Unknown to him, his old friend had died a few hours earlier that same day. Jefferson's last moments were recorded by his physician, Doctor Dunglison: "Seeing me staying at his beside, (he) exclaimed, 'Ah, Doctor, are you still there?' in a voice, however, that was husky and indistinct. He then asked, 'Is it the Fourth?' to which I replied, 'It will soon be.' These were the last words I heard him utter. . . . About one o'clock [the next day] he ceased to exist."

The day? July 4, 1826, the fiftieth anniversary of the signing of the Declaration of Independence—the document to which both men had contributed mightily. Their deaths on that day were viewed by millions as a sign of the supernatural. As the *National Intelligencer* put it, "It is one of those events which have no example on record, as a beauteous moral must forever stand alone on the page of history."

THE LONG CLIMB (1827)

In a public shrine in Greeneville, Tennessee, stands a weatherworn tailor shop, reminding visitors of a poverty-stricken youth. To help support his widowed mother, a young man became a tailor's apprentice at the age of fourteen and eventually went into business himself in 1827, the same year he married Miss Eliza McCardle. Until he met her, the young tailor was practically illiterate. His wife read to him while he worked, and at night she taught him to write. Becoming interested in politics, he ran for and was elected alderman. Thus he began a long, slow climb, becoming the mayor of Greeneville, a state legislator, then a state senator, and finally a congressman. In 1853 he was elected governor of Tennessee, and four years later he was elected to the U.S. Senate. In 1861, when Tennessee broke from the

Union, he alone of all the Southern senators remained in his seat and loyal to the Union. This act propelled him into the vice presidency in 1864, and upon Lincoln's assassination, the former illiterate tailor from Tennessee, Andrew Johnson, became president of the United States.

SHE WAS A TROLLOP (1827)

The definition of a trollop is fairy common knowledge. According to Webster, it is "a slovenly woman, slattern, a loose woman." The term has come down to us from a Mrs. Frances Trollope, who was not a loose woman at all but was so despised by millions of Americans that the name became the ultimate insult.

Mrs. Trollope was an Englishwoman who came to the United States in 1827 to found a department store in Cincinnati, Ohio. There she failed completely, and everything she owned was taken from her to pay off her debts. In 1831 she returned to her native country, bitter over her experiences and with a manuscript of her American travels. When her book, *Domestic Manners of the Americans,* was released in 1832, it contained an insulting blow-by-blow description of the crudeness of American democracy. Feelings created by this best-selling English book reached such a peak that many responsible people in both England and America feared an international incident. It took many years for this war of pen and tongue to blow over, and when it did it left behind as part of the American vocabulary the word *trollop,* an eternal monument of contempt for a critic of American democracy.

KING ANDREW THE FIRST (1828)

Andrew Jackson, the first president of the common people, was not the happy choice of all the people by any means. His frontier reputation and lack of formal education horrified the genteel. John Quincy Adams moaned when Harvard conferred a doctorate of laws on a "barbarian who could . . . hardly spell his own name." Justice Joseph Story of the Supreme Court, distressed by the jam of people that nearly wrecked the White House, felt that "the reign of King 'Mob' seemed triumphant."

Henry Clay, Daniel Webster, and other Whig leaders in Congress proclaimed themselves defenders of popular liberties against the usurpation of President Jackson. Many cartoonists of the day depicted Jackson as King Andrew I. But Jackson probably received his most criticism when he dismissed his entire cabinet because of a woman. His secretary of war had married a beautiful woman with a questionable background, Peggy O'Neale Timberlake. When the other cabinet wives gave her a hard time and their husbands wouldn't or couldn't stop them, Jackson dismissed them all.

PRESIDENT JACKSON: "AN OUTRAGE" (1829)

The man who assumed the highest office in the land in 1829 couldn't have presented a sharper contrast to the man who preceded him. As a young boy, John Quincy Adams had been secretary and interpreter for the U.S. minister to Russia. At that same age Andy Jackson scratched out a memorandum in his notebook that most vividly illustrates the difference between the two: "How to feed a cock before you him fight Take and give him some Pickle Beaf Cut fine." Jackson became more cultured and literate, but even years later, when Harvard College was to confer a doctor of laws upon President Jackson, Adams was horrified. He asked Harvard whether there was some way to stop such an outrage. From the university's president came the reply, "None." He said, "As the people have twice decided that this man knows law enough to be their ruler it is not for Harvard College to maintain that they are mistaken."

HOUSTON GIVES UP CIVILIZATION (1829)

Sam Houston of Texas fame led anything but a boring life. In 1829, after only twelve weeks of marriage, Houston left his new bride (or she left him; historians are uncertain which), resigned as governor of Tennessee, and fled to Indian country in Oklahoma. There he joined a tribe of Cherokees with whom he had spent time in his younger days. The Raven, as they called him, lived as an Indian, getting drunk with them and even refusing to speak English. For four years he lived with the Cherokees, part of the time as an effective leader of his adopted people and part of the time as a tribal misfit. Twice, dressed in Indian buckskins and a blanket, he traveled to Washington, D.C., to represent his people. During his second visit, his old friend Andrew Jackson persuaded him to give up his Indian ways and return to white society.

"A PERFECT PEOPLE" (1830)

The American Plains Indians have been described in many different ways by many different writers, but perhaps the most revealing and interesting description comes from George Catlin, a gifted artist who traveled the Great Plains from 1830 to 1836, observing, painting, and living with more than forty different tribes. He summed up his observations in his *Last Rambles amongst the Indians of the Rocky Mountains and the Andes,* published in London in 1868:

"I love a people who have always made me welcome to the best they had . . . who are honest without laws, who have no jails and no poorhouse . . . who never take the name of God in vain . . . who worship God without a Bible, and I believe that God loves them also . . . who are free from religious animosities . . . who have never raised a hand against me, or stolen my property, where there was no law to punish either . . . who never fought a battle with white man except on their own ground . . . and oh! how I love a people who don't live for the love of money."

EARLY DENTISTRY (1830)

Before 1830 all dentists, such as they were, were untrained itinerants, very often tinkers, who, being handy men in general, could pull a tooth at the home of the patient or at a crossroads store. Many of these tinkers prepared themselves in a rather unusual way for pulling out teeth. As they jogged along the road between the farms or hamlets, they developed extraordinary strength in the index finger and thumb of the right hand by constantly tugging away at a nail driven deeply into a block of wood. In the early days of dentistry, the only anesthetic available was alcohol. Tooth brushing was considered merely a cosmetic measure for the vain and finicky. Some false teeth were available, usually made of some kind of animal ivory. George Washington had a well-known set made of hippopotamus bone, but better remembered are the wooden teeth he is said to have whittled for himself during the Revolutionary War.

AN INCREDIBLE "CURE" (1832)

Americans have been notorious for falling for quack remedies, but probably no remedy has been more outlandish than the "cure" for gout, rheumatism, cramps, and infirmities of the sinews and joints recommended by Doctor Richard Carter on the trans-Appalachian frontier:

"Take a young fat dog and kill him, scald and clean him as you would a pig, then extract his guts through a hole previously made in his side and substitute in the place thereof, two handfuls of nettles, two ounces of brimstone, one dozen hen eggs, four ounces of turpentine, a handful of tansy, a pint of red fishing worms, and about three quarters pound of tobacco cut up fine; mix all these ingredients well together before depositing in the dog's belly, and then sew up the whole, then roast him well before a hot fire, save the oil, anoint the joints and weak parts before the fire as hot as you can bear it, being careful not to get wet or expose yourself to damp or night air, or even heating yourself or in fact, should you not expose yourself in any way." Incredibly enough, many patients attempted this "cure."

WASHINGTON TAKES A BACK SEAT (1833)

Philip Hone, a wealthy New York merchant and acute observer of the scene of his day, left an interesting view of President Andrew Jackson:

"June 13

"The President is certainly the most popular man we have ever known. Washington was not so much so. His acts were popular because all descriptions of men were ready to acknowledge him the 'Father of his Country.' But he was superior to the homage of the populace, too dignified, too grave for their liking, and men could not approach him with familiarity.

"Here is a man who suits them exactly. He has a kind expression for each—the same to all, no doubt, but each thinks it intended for himself. His manners are certainly good, and he makes the most of them. He is a gourmet of adulation, and by the assistance of the populace has persuaded himself that no man ever lived in the country to whom the country was so much indebted.

"Talk of him as a second Washington! It won't do now; Washington was only the first Jackson."

WHEN JACKSON LOST HIS HEAD (1834)

The *USS Constitution,* popularly known as "Old Ironsides," has been rebuilt and repaired many times in her long history. Those working on her have faithfully adhered to the original construction, except for one detail: she has carried eight or nine different figureheads. At her first major reconstruction in Charlestown in 1833–34, the yard commander decided to refit her with a figure of President Andrew Jackson, not taking into account the sentiments of the Boston Federalists. On the night of July 2, 1834, a young mariner named Samuel Dewey (cousin of George Dewey of future Manila Bay fame who would himself command "Old Ironsides" for a short time) rowed out to the ship and, under the noses of the marine guards, sawed off Andy's head and escaped with it. Despite the furor the theft aroused, Dewey was not arrested when he handed the head over to the secretary of the navy several months later. Old Hickory himself must have been losing some of his fire, for it was said that he viewed the entire exploit with amusement.

THE LIBERTY BELL: WHEN CRACKED? (1835)

It is a common impression that the Liberty Bell cracked while being rung to celebrate the Declaration of Independence, on July 4, 1776. In fact, it wasn't rung at all that day but rather four days later at the reading of the document in the state house yard.

The crack actually occurred fifty-nine years to the day later, July 8, 1835, while tolling for the funeral of Chief Justice John Marshall. The crack was later drilled out to separate the sides and make it useable while improving sound. It was an unsuccessful experiment, and the bell has not been rung since. It has been "tapped," however, and the sound recorded for special occasions. The bell no longer hangs in the steeple but rests in Liberty Bell Center at 6th and Market Street in Philadelphia.

Although the word *liberty* appears in the biblical quotation on the bell, it did not receive the common designation Liberty Bell until it was called that in antislavery propaganda in 1839.

ATTEMPTED ASSASSINATION OF JACKSON (1835)

The first attempt on the life of a U.S. president occurred on January 30, 1835, at the Capitol. A tall stranger pointed a cap and ball pistol at Jackson, but the weapon misfired. Before the attacker could be subdued, he had lifted another pistol, which also misfired. The odds against such an occurrence are incalculable. Jackson himself went after the assailant with his walking stick. The attacker, Richard Lawrence, was committed to an insane asylum. At the time of the incident, Jackson was attending the funeral of Rep. Ransom Davis of South Carolina. It was thirty more years before another assassination attempt was made against a president. Unfortunately, John Wilkes Booth's gun did not misfire.

BURR'S FINALE (1836)

When Aaron Burr's schemes for a western empire came to nothing, and Chief Justice John Marshall brought about the acquittal of his fellow Federalist, Mr. Burr decided to seek richer ground in Europe. He spent some time there trying to interest Napoleon in paying him to overthrow the new American government. Unsuccessful in his intrigues, he finally returned to New York at the beginning of the War of 1812. From then until he died in 1836, he experienced little but grief. A daughter he loved dearly, Theodosia, disappeared on an ocean voyage, and for years he walked the Battery at the southern tip of Manhattan waiting vainly for her ship to reappear. Finally, at the age of seventy-seven, he married Betsy Bowen Jumel, a wealthy woman he had kept as a mistress for years. She shortly threw him out of the house and divorced him on grounds of infidelity. He was afraid of death, and as he lay dying, he struggled and cried out, "I won't die!" His doctor calmly assured him that he was already dying.

REPORTING CASUALTIES: THE ALAMO (1836)

Overestimating the enemy dead and underestimating your own is nothing new to military commanders, but Santa Anna apparently pulled out all stops when he reported to Gen. Jose Maria Tornel, the Mexican secretary of war and navy after the Battle of the Alamo.

Scribner's Dictionary of American History (an American source, of course, but still reliable) reports that 187 Alamo defenders were killed compared to approximately 1,500 Mexicans killed. It also reports that Santa Anna had an attacking force of 6,000–7,000. In his report to General Tornel, however, Santa Anna gave himself an attacking force, excluding recruits, of no more than 1,400. Rather than 187 enemy dead, he reported that "more than six hundred corpses of foreigners were buried in the ditches and entrenchments, and a great many who had escaped the bayonet of the infantry, fell in the vicinity under the sabers of the cavalry." Rather than 1,500 Mexicans dead, he told his commander, "We lost about seventy men killed." Such is the game of war when there are no referees around.

THE ALAMO DEAD (1836)

The story of the Alamo is one well known to all students of American history, but the part that is perhaps least known is what happened to the bodies of the brave and fallen few. Santa Anna decided on a cruel example to all revolutionists in North America who might follow their Manifest Destiny—he would burn the bodies, a tradition going back to Homer's heroes at Troy and beyond. The job of soaking the bodies with grease and oil and burning them was given to the Alcalde of San Antonio, Francisco Ruiz, who later wrote:

"Santa Anna . . . sent a company of dragoons with me to bring wood and dry branches from the neighboring forests. About three o'clock in the afternoon of March 6 we laid the wood and branches upon which a pile of dead bodies was placed, more wood was piled on them and another pile of bodies was brought, and in this manner they were all arranged in layers. Kindling wood was distributed through the pile and about five o'clock in the evening it was ignited.

"The dead Mexicans of Santa Anna were taken to the graveyard, but not having sufficient room for them, I ordered some to be thrown into the river, which was done on the same day."

THE WHITE INDIANS (1837)

One of the most unusual Indian tribes in American history was the Mandan tribe, of which there were about nine thousand in 1750, populating an area along the Missouri River in what is now North Dakota. The first white explorers to come in contact with them described their looks and ways of living as much different from other Indians. They were a light-skinned and often blue-eyed agricultural people, living in stockaded villages and cultivating corn, beans, pumpkins, squash, and tobacco. Scholars speculate that they might have been descendants of Norse people who may have visited the Minnesota area in 1362, leaving their sad story of Indian attacks on the Kensington Rune Stone and then disappearing. Unfortunately, anthropologists were never given the opportunity to explore this interesting theory. In 1764 the first of a series of smallpox epidemics struck the tribe. When Lewis and Clark visited them in 1804, the Mandans had been reduced to about 1,250 people living in two villages. In 1832 the painter George Catlin visited them. He concluded that they were the descendants of Prince Madoc, a Welch explorer of the twelfth century. Unfortunately, another smallpox epidemic struck them five years later, killing more than a thousand and leaving only thirty-one. Today not a single full-blooded Mandan lives.

A PROFITABLE FIESTA (1837)

Scalping, a custom universally associated with the American Indian, was not widespread, it is believed, until the coming of the Europeans. The whites adopted the custom, their government came to offer rewards for the taking of enemy scalps, and the practice spread rapidly across the continent. The colony of Massachusetts once offered as much as 100 pounds, and as late as 1866 an Arizona county was still offering $250 for each Apache scalp. The ultimate in tragic consequences resulting from such an inhumane practice occurred in 1837 at the Santa Rita copper mines in what is now southwestern New Mexico. At that time it was Mexican territory, and the Mexican states of Chihuahua and Sonora were paying generous bounties for Apache scalps—$100 for each adult male, $50 for each squaw, and $25 for each child. At the mines lived a large band of friendly Apaches but Apaches nevertheless. Two trappers named Johnson and Gleason, with a large party of Missouri trappers, put on a big fiesta for the Indians. When they had them bunched in the main plaza—men, women, and children—they opened fire on them pointblank with a concealed howitzer loaded with bullets, nails, chain, and so forth. The trappers then moved in with clubs, knives, and sabers to finish the slaughter. An estimated four hundred Apaches, mostly women and children, were killed.

THE UNTRUSTING OSCEOLA (1837)

In 1837 the great Seminole chief Osceola lay dying as a prisoner at Fort Moultrie after being captured under a flag of truce a few months before. Many sympathetic whites could not understand why the malaria-ridden chief was so bitter toward the whites that he even refused the help of the gentle and compassionate post surgeon, George Weedon. Toward the end of January, the still-young chief was dead, despite the administrations of an Indian medicine man. But perhaps Osceola had his reasons for not trusting the seemingly gentle white doctor. Following the Seminole's death, the white doctor cut off Osceola's head and kept it in his home as a grisly souvenir of his relationship with his almost-patient. When his young sons misbehaved, the gentle surgeon hung the trophy on their bedsteads as a reminder to be good boys.

JOHN QUINCY ADAMS AND SLAVERY (1837)

John Quincy Adams was the first president to serve in the House of Representatives after retiring from the presidency. Soon after taking his seat in that body, the abolition movement got underway. To prevent the introduction of petitions against slavery, Southern congressmen passed the gag rule, which prevented the reception of these petitions by the House, thus throttling the constitutional right of petition. Adams then began a one-man crusade against the gag rule. On February 6, 1837, he asked the House speaker for his judgment on the propriety of presenting a petition from slaves. He was immediately shouted down by cries of "Expel him! Expel him!" A full three days passed before he could again gain the floor in his own defense. He then reminded the speaker that he had only asked an opinion about presenting it, and besides, the petition itself prayed that slavery should not be abolished. Needless to say, his detractors were too embarrassed to reply.

It took Adams thirteen long years, but "Old Man Eloquent," with hands shaking, eyes watering, and a voice cracking with age, finally won—the gag rule was removed. It was recorded by a single line in his diary, "Blessed, forever blessed be the name of God."

MORMON PERSECUTION (1838)

Opposition to any minority religion is usually cloaked in a pretext of outraged righteousness. This was certainly true of many of the anti-Mormons in Missouri and Illinois in the 1830s and 1840s. Most people in the two states opposed the Mormon practice of polygamy and used it as an excuse to drive the Mormons from their fertile farms. In the Mormon War in Missouri in 1838, no less than fifteen Mormon girls were raped by the so-called "defenders" of Christianity.

Such persecutions did not end—rapes, murders, beatings, burned homes and crops, and so forth—until eight years later, when anti-Mormons drove fifteen thousand Mormons west, forcing them to vacate Nauvoo, the largest city in Illinois, in the greatest mass religious persecution this continent has ever seen.

WHY DIDN'T I THINK OF THAT? (1839)

Those infused with high regard for Yankee ingenuity are often astonished when they discover that an extremely simple invention took so long to appear. The envelope, so simple that the idea might have occurred to anybody, did not come into use until 1839. In that year a Mr. Pierson of New York City started manufacturing envelopes in a little store on Fulton Street. Until that time people folded their letters both ways, sealed them with wax, and wrote the address on the back. (Postage, incidentally, was normally paid by the person receiving the letter.)

It was another sixty long years before a "mechanism for folding and sealing envelopes" was patented and put into use in Massachusetts. When it was, it reduced the cost of envelopes from sixty cents to eight cents per thousand.

JOHN QUINCY ADAMS FREES THE SLAVES (1839)

On a warm night in July 1839, a Spanish schooner named the *Amistad* was transporting a shipload of fifty African slaves from Cuba to Principe. Led by a handsome young black man named Joseph Cinque, the African slaves seized weapons, killed the captain, set the sailors adrift, and ordered their two former owners on board the ship to steer for Africa. Two Spaniards, however, zigzagged for sixty-three days north and west, eventually arriving off Long Island. There, a U.S. navy brig boarded the *Amistad,* convoyed it to New London, and imprisoned the Africans, except for three little girls, on charges of murdering the ship's captain.

The case became a cause celebre throughout the United States, involving questions of marine law, jurisdiction, extradition, and more important to most people, the freedom of the Africans. The case ended up before the U.S. Supreme Court, where John Quincy Adams, now a congressman from Massachusetts, was so moved by the situation of the black prisoners that after thirty years out of law practice, he decided to argue the case. Weak and almost sightless at age seventy-three, he presented a nearly nine-hour argument to the court and won an acquittal for the Africans. In 1842 Cinque and his fellow crewmen made it home to Africa.

"KEEP THE BALL ROLLING, O.K." (1840)

The presidential campaign of 1840 between Martin Van Buren and William Henry Harrison produced two of our most commonly spoken slang phrases. Being from Kinderhook, New York, an Old Kinderhook Club was formed by the partisans of Van Buren in 1840. Their rallying cry was "O.K."; thus, what was O.K. was good. The backers of the opposition candidate, William Henry Harrison, a Whig, organized a spectacular feat of rolling a huge paper ball all the way from Kentucky to Baltimore, where the national convention of Whig Young Men was being held. The slogan during this campaign stunt was, "Keep the ball rolling on to Washington." Thus, from it came the expression to "get" or "keep the ball rolling!" The Whigs won with their stunts—they got their man to Washington but not for long. One month after being sworn into office, the former physician was dead of pneumonia.

HARRISON GETS UNEXPECTED HELP (1840)

During William Henry Harrison's campaign for the presidency in 1840, his opponents accused him of cowardice at the Battle of the Thames in 1813. As a result of these campaign slurs, Harrison received some help from a rather unexpected quarter—some old Indian enemies. Two of them who had fought with Tecumseh against Harrison made public a letter "To General Harrison's Friends" in which they referred to General Harrison as "the terror of the late tomahawkers." The two former enemies named Shaubenee and Billy Caldwell (Sauganash) expressed their astonishment at the charges, saying that they had found General Harrison "a brave warrior, and humane to his prisoners" and that he had "routed both the red men and the British." They concluded by saying that they hoped "the good white men will protect the name of General Harrison." It would be interesting if history could record what effect this letter had on the campaign.

THE STENCH OF APPLE BLOSSOMS (1840)

Series abound about how Chicago got its name. In 1837 the Illinois legislature had incorporated the small community under the name of Chicago, an anglicized Indian word supposed to mean "the smell of wild onions." Other sources, however, say it comes from a Pottawottomy Indian word, *chicagou,* meaning "stench"; others say an almost identical Chippewa idiom means "apple blossoms." Considering the location on low, wet, malarial, marshy ground, the former meaning is more logical.

Even after its name was adopted, Chicago went by more common names such as Slab Town because of the construction style of most of the early houses; just as often, it was called Mud Hole of the Prairies.

Whatever the case, neither mud, stench, or all-too-common murders held back the growth of the town. From 1840 to 1880 it was the fastest growing community in the world.

BEARDS COME AND BEARDS GO (1840)

The wearing of beards has followed an interesting pattern in American history. They were much in fashion in early America, beginning with bearded explorers like Champlain, DeSoto, Raleigh, John Smith. Then came the Pilgrims and Puritans, also bearded. But they gradually reduced the size of their beards until by 1720 American colonists were wholly free of facial hair. You will see no bearded fighting man in the portraits of the American Revolution or in any portraits of the signers of the Declaration of Independence. Even cartoonists' conception of Uncle Sam was of a tall and lanky yet smooth-shaven man. In the 1840s beards came into favor again, and by the Civil War they were universally accepted. Lincoln became the nation's first bearded president. By the turn of the century, they were on their way back out again. Woodrow Wilson was the first of a line of smooth-shaven presidents that continues to the present.

EARLY PRIZE FIGHTING (1842)

The world's first prize fight is not a matter of record, but the first fatality resulting from an organized match is. A New York merchant named Philip Hone records this event for us in his multivolume diary. The sport was banned by New York authorities, and thousands, like Hone, viewed it with disgust:

"Orderly citizens have wept for the shame which they could not prevent. . . . Two men, named Lilly (Chris Lilly, an Englishman) and McCoy, thumped and battered each other for the gratification of a brutal gang of spectators until the latter after one hundred nineteen rounds fell dead in the ring, and the other ruffian was smuggled away. . . .

"McCoy went into the battle . . . deficient in science, but a bulldog in courage. The fight lasted two hours and forty-three minutes. McCoy received one hundred square blows and was knocked down eighty-one times."

THE COSTS OF A "LITTLE WAR" (1842)

The year 1842 saw the official end of one of America's least publicized and least glamorous wars—the second Seminole War. When the little war ground to an inconclusive end, Americans counted the cost and discovered that, as with many "little wars," it hadn't been a little war at all. The nation had lost two thousand men, half as many as in the War for Independence and approximately the same number as in the War of 1812 or in the Mexican War, which was yet to come. The war had cost $60 million, more than half of what eight years of war against England had cost in the Revolution and two-thirds of what the War of 1812 had cost. The Mexican War would cost about the same.

HIS DAD WAS NO HELP (1842)

There never has been an actual mutiny on board a U.S. navy ship, although some have been nipped in the bud. One mutiny was allegedly nipped on December 1, 1842, when three men were hung from the main yardarm of the U.S. brig-of-war *Somers* without benefit of a trial or being allowed to testify in their own defense. Official inquiry later cleared the captain, Alexander Mackenzie, but historical evidence suggests that the captain acted hysterically and partly from personal motives. The only real evidence was against midshipman Philip Spencer, an unstable youth of eighteen who romanticized a great deal about mutiny and piracy. The entire event might still have been lost to history except for two interesting facts. Midshipman Spencer's father was the U.S. secretary of war, a fact that apparently failed to impress the ship's captain. The other interesting sidelight concerns Chi Psi fraternity, which Spencer had helped to found when he was a student at Union College in Schenectady, New York. In accord with Chi Psi tradition even today, Philip Spencer was hanged for refusing to reveal his fraternity affiliation.

"LIVER EATING" JOHNSON (1843)

John Johnson was an obscure mountain man—so obscure that he can't be found in history books. How much of his story is legend is hard to know. From what can be determined, he, like many other mountain men, married an Indian girl, an attractive Flathead known as the Swan. While off on a trapping expedition, some Crow warriors visited his cabin and killed his wife and unborn child. Finding only his family's bones upon his return, he swore an oath of vengeance against the entire Crow nation. The oath the huge red-haired trapper carried out was so terrible

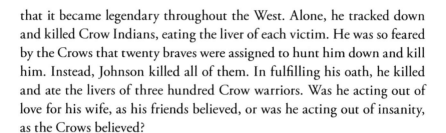

that it became legendary throughout the West. Alone, he tracked down and killed Crow Indians, eating the liver of each victim. He was so feared by the Crows that twenty braves were assigned to hunt him down and kill him. Instead, Johnson killed all of them. In fulfilling his oath, he killed and ate the livers of three hundred Crow warriors. Was he acting out of love for his wife, as his friends believed, or was he acting out of insanity, as the Crows believed?

JACKSON'S FINE RETURNED (1844)

In January 1815 one of the most incredible victories in American military history was won at the mouth of the Mississippi. Gen. Andrew Jackson destroyed a British army, saving New Orleans and possibly all of the Louisiana Purchase from British control. Historical evidence shows, contrary to school textbook versions, that the Battle of New Orleans was not an unnecessary battle at all but that the British were ready to assume and maintain control of the entire territory with the capture of New Orleans, the Treaty of Ghent notwithstanding. As important as Jackson's victory was, therefore, it was apparently not appreciated by all Americans.

On March 31, 1815, a U.S. District Court judge at New Orleans fined Andrew Jackson $1,000 for contempt in declaring martial law during the defense of the city against the British. Twenty-nine years later the U.S. House of Representatives voted 158 to 28 to return the fine to Jackson with interest at 6 percent.

THE FIRST TUESDAY AFTER THE FIRST MONDAY (1845)

In 1845 Congress passed an act that designated the first Tuesday after the first Monday in November of every even-numbered year as General Election Day. As a result, the date has since varied between November 2 and November 8.

The day was fixed in such a manner in order to eliminate the possibility of an election day falling on the first day of November, a day often inconvenient to merchants balancing their books for the month. Monday was also found objectionable because before the building of good roads, voters often took more than a day to reach polling places. In addition, a Monday election day would have necessitated many voters leaving their homes on Sunday, the day of rest. So why couldn't Congress have said "the second Tuesday"? It just wouldn't have sounded like a congressional act, would it?

CAPTAIN PIERCE FAINTS IN BATTLE (1845)

In a cavalry charge near Vera Cruz, Mexico, during the Mexican-American War, Capt. F. Pierce fainted and fell off his horse. This rather unsoldierlike incident was, unfortunately, used against the poor captain seven years later when he was running for public office. His friends claimed that his horse had stumbled and that the saddle horn struck Pierce in the groin, causing him to lose consciousness and fall from his horse. Whatever the facts, the event probably wouldn't have warranted the publicity except that the political campaign was for the presidency and the former army captain was Franklin Pierce, who won despite the charges, becoming, ironically, America's most obscure president. Horseback riding was obviously not the president's forte. While horseback riding in Rock Creek Park, he ran a woman down and earned the distinction of being the first American president to be involved in a criminal offense.

THE PEOPLE DIDN'T WANT A POLITICIAN (1846)

The nickname "Old Rough and Ready" resulted partly from Zachary Taylor's customary mode of dress. As a professional soldier, his sloppiness increased with rank. He had legs so short that he had to be helped onto his horse, he chewed tobacco, and he wore a straw hat and gingham coat at the time he became a general in the Mexican War. The general, who never lost a battle, dressed entirely for comfort, even to the point of sitting his horse sideways in battle. He was certainly no politician: he had never cast a vote in his life. Even so, the Whigs, who had opposed the Mexican War all along, decided to nominate its most popular hero as their candidate for president. When they mailed their nomination to him, he received the letter with ten cents postage due. Taylor refused it and sent it back unopened. But his idiosyncrasies only seemed to endear him to the common people and help propel him into the presidency, where disheveled as always, he garbed himself in a black broadcloth suit purposely cut too large.

HISTORY'S LONGEST INFANTRY MARCH (1846)

In 1846 Brigham Young and his Mormon followers who had been

driven out of Nauvoo, Illinois, were gaining their strength at Council Bluffs, Iowa, preparatory to striking westward to find a new home free from persecution. Fearing a possible alliance of Mormons and Mexicans (the war with Mexico had now begun), President James Polk called upon Young to raise a loyal battalion of five hundred men to assist in the conquest of California. This was soon accomplished, and on August 12 the Mormon Battalion left Ft. Leavenworth for California. Enduring countless hardships, including a battle with a herd of wild bulls near what is now Tombstone, Arizona, the small army arrived at its destination, San Diego, on January 29, 1847. Carving out a wagon road as they went, the Mormon soldiers covered two thousand miles through some of the world's most forbidding and dangerous wasteland in a little more than five months. The non-Mormon commander, Lt. Col. Philip St. George Cooke, congratulated his command for accomplishing what he called the greatest march of infantry in the history of the world.

SACAJAWEA'S SON (1846)

Sacajawea needs no footnotes in history, but a note of explanation about her son should be appreciated. Baptiste Charbonneau was the infant Sacajawea carried on her back on the trek westward with Lewis and Clark. This fact is usually the first and only fact that we learn about with this little nonentity. Actually, however, he does reappear in history.

In 1846 we find him with, of all people, the Mormon Battalion. Lt. Col. Philip St. George Cooke, leading the battalion from Santa Fe to California, hired several mountain men as scouts. One of them was the little-known son of Sacajawea. He was a well-traveled man, having met a visiting German prince in 1824 and returning to Europe with him. He served most of his life as an interpreter and guide among the Indians and was employed as a guide for the Mormon Battalion in 1846. He died in Oregon at age eighty, the last survivor of the Lewis and Clark Expedition.

MEASLES AND MASSACRES (1847)

In the vast westward migration in American history, we sometimes lose sight of the fact that someone had to be the first man—or woman— to make the trek. In the woman's case, there were actually two—Narcissa Whitman, wife of the missionary Marcus Whitman; and Mrs. Henry Spalding, wife of a second missionary—who crossed the continent with their husbands in 1836. At first, Indians were highly impressed with the white women, but this changed eleven years later on a dark morning in November 1847 when the Whitman mission was attacked by Cayuse Indians. Fourteen people, including the Whitmans, were killed. Forty-seven others were taken captive but later ransomed for clothing, ammunition, and tobacco. The interesting footnote to this event is the reason for the massacre: measles. A party of white immigrants brought with them an epidemic of measles that struck Indians and whites alike. With no natural immunities, half the Cayuse tribe died, whereas most of the whites recovered. The Whitmans, who were giving the same care to both Indians and whites, were suspected by the former of deliberately poisoning them to get their land. After all, wasn't it Indian custom to punish the medicine man who failed?

FIRST COMIC STRIP (1848)

There seems to be some controversy over the appearance of the first American comic strip. One source lists John Donkey, appearing in 1848, as the first. Published in Philadelphia, it was a crudely done sheet, amusing only to those of that generation.

Another source claims a more recent strip as being the first. *The Old Farmer's Almanac Sampler,* edited by Robb Sagendorph, names "Mutt and Jeff," created by Bud Fisher and appearing for the first time in 1907, as the first.

If the criteria in deciding the first strip were longevity, the honors would have to go to the latter, published continuously for half a century and making the creator both famous and rich. John Donkey, on the other hand, sixteen pages long and selling for six cents a copy, lasted for less than ten months.

AND THE MINISTER CONCURRED! (1848)

The first woman's rights convention generated a Declaration of Sentiments at Seneca Falls, New York, in 1848, but the convention only formalized what was already prevalent in the United States. One of the most common and interesting ways of asserting equality for women was through marriage contracts and ceremonies. Many young people foregoing the usual ceremony—because they felt that it degraded women—simply complied with the bare essentials of law and often drew up a statement of protest. One such couple to do this in 1855 declared that they could not sanction "voluntary obedience to such of the present laws of marriage as refuse to recognize the wife as an independent rational being, while they confer on the husband an injurious and unnatural superiority, investing him with legal powers which no honorable man would exercise. . . . We believe . . . that marriage should be an equal and permanent partnership, and so recognized by law. . . . Thus reverencing law, we enter our earnest protest against rules and customs which are unworthy of the name, since they violate justice—the essence of law."

The same *New York Tribune* article contained a letter from the officiating minister who gave a "hearty concurrence."

JOHN SUTTER'S QUEST (1848)

Most Americans remember John Sutter as the owner of the land upon which gold was discovered in 1848, prompting the massive Gold Rush to California. At the time of the discovery, Sutter lived baronial style in a large fort on the present site of Sacramento. His wealth can be assumed from his 4,000 oxen, 1,200 cows, 1,500 horses and mules, 1,200 sheep, and thousands of acres of fertile cropland. During the rush following the discovery of gold, his lands were overrun and his goods stolen. In addition, his workers left him, and he was financially ruined. He spent the remainder of his life appealing to the U.S. government for compensation—to no avail. One version of his death has him making his daily pilgrimage to the Capitol (he lived in Washington at the time) seeking redress from Congress. A young boy who was familiar with his quest rushed up to him with the false news that Congress had finally granted him compensation. The excitement of his dream fulfilled was too much for his aged heart, and he dropped dead on the Capitol steps.

JAMES MARSHALL'S REWARD (1848)

Like his partner John Sutter, James Marshall also led a life filled with tragedy after the discovery of gold on Sutter's property. The first gold seekers paid Sutter and Marshall a small fee for digging gold, but later ones ignored the two men and the right of property ownership. At this point bitterness set in. Marshall was hounded by men who thought that because he had found gold once he could do it again. They did not let him prospect in peace but followed him wherever he went and persecuted him

when he failed. Deluded into believing that he was the rightful ow
all the gold in California, he argued and fought with other miner:
cabin was burned and his property stolen, and twice he had to flee for his
life. He never married, living a lonely and unhappy life. Things looked up
when the California Legislature voted him a pension in 1872, but his luck
ran true to form when the pension was discontinued in 1878. He spent
his last years doing more digging—as a gardener near Colona, California,
where he died in 1885.

"A LOAD OF DIRTY LAUNDRY" (1849)

The extremely high price of commodities during the California Gold
Rush is common knowledge and partly understandable because of the
freight costs for bringing in merchandise. Less understandable are the
prices charged for labor. Laundries are a good example. Chinese laundries charged as much as $1.50 for washing and ironing a shirt and were
then two months behind. Irish washerwomen known as "clothing refresh-
ers" charged the same and were also as far behind. Because of the price
and delay, many men in San Francisco sent their laundry all the way to
Hawaii, where it was less expensive and they got it back just as quickly.
It is easy to imagine embarrassed ship captains having to declare their
cargoes to the harbor master in Hawaii: a load of dirty laundry.

PRESIDENT FOR ONE DAY (1849)

President James Polk's four-year term of office constitutionally ended
at noon on March 4, 1849. Since this date fell on a Sunday, president-elect
Zachary Taylor chose not to take his oath of office until Monday, March
5. Normally the vice president, in this case George Mifflin Dallas, would
have served as president for that single day. But he had resigned as president of the Senate on Friday, March 2, and so Sen. David Rice Atchison
of Missouri was elected president of the Senate pro tempore. Because of
the way many historians have interpreted Article II of the Constitution,
many insist that Atchison was president of the United States for one day.
At least the state of Missouri thought so, for legislators there appropriated
$15,000 after his death for a monument that bears witness to his presi-
dency "for one day."

SHIPS BUT NO CREWS (1849)

The effect of gold upon men has always been difficult to understand, as illustrated during the 1849 Gold Rush in California. Tales of quick riches were so prevalent that even sailors of ships docking in California, both foreign and American, deserted in large numbers for the gold fields of the interior. At one time in 1849 in San Francisco harbor, four hundred ships had been deserted by their crews. Unable to find crews to operate these ships, many of them became permanent fixtures. As late as the twentieth century, some of the buildings serving various purposes around the harbor were former ships that had been beached and converted because they had no crew to sail away.

The first photograph ever taken of San Francisco shows a panorama of the waterfront in either 1850 or 1851. Stretching across the entire picture are hundreds of deserted ships, their gray and sail-less masts making up what was known as the "forest of Yerba Buena Cove."

CLEANING UP THE YANKEE STRIP (1849)

One of the most popular routes to the gold fields of California from the East Coast was by ship to Panama, then across the isthmus by foot, mule, or on the backs of Indian porters, and then by ship again up the coast to California. Because of the number of Americans who crossed the isthmus in both directions, the route became known as the Gold Trail, or the Yankee Strip. It promised to be the road to wealth for hundreds of highwaymen. One traveler wrote in 1849 of a returning Californian just arriving on the West Coast "with a box containing twenty-two thousand dollars in gold dust, and a four pound lump in one hand." The outlaw situation in Panama became so desperate that Wells Fargo imported a Texas gunman named Randy Runnels and ordered him to restore safety on the strip by whatever means necessary. Within two nights he and his deputies had hanged seventy-eight highwaymen from the sea wall at Panama City, and within a short time they lynched hundreds of others and left their bodies swinging along the Yankee Strip as a warning. Within weeks the trail across Panama was almost as safe to walk as a street in Boston.

LINCOLN'S PATENT (1849)

An interesting and unusual side of President Abraham Lincoln emerges in a patent he applied for and received in 1849, the year he ended his first term in Congress and what he believed would probably be his last term. Almost everything had gone wrong that year: he tried his only case before the Supreme Court and lost, and he applied for an appointment in the General Land Office and was turned down. However, his patent application for an invention was accepted. The invention, of which there is a model in the Smithsonian Institution, was a device to lift ships over shoals and sandbars by means of buoyant chambers forced under the hull. But there is no record of his device, about which he was so optimistic, ever being put into practical use. One of his lesser-known inventions indicates his creative capacity. In 1840 he made a model of a wagon on which the front wheels turned instead of the whole axle—the forerunner of the tie-rod principle used on modern automobiles. It was never patented. Ironically, Lincoln was to achieve his ultimate success in the political realm, where he considered himself a failure.

MORE DEADLY THAN INDIANS (1850)

Though not nearly as exciting as renegade Indians, disease was far more deadly on the western frontier. Dr. William Allen, who traveled west on the Oregon Trail in 1859, reported that 2,000–3,000 travelers died of cholera that year. He treated seven hundred cases himself—the same number of people claimed by the disease that year between the Missouri River and Fort Laramie.

Mortality from diarrhea and such prevalent diseases as cholera, typhoid fever, and diphtheria seemed just as high even in settled towns. In the 1870s, Lawrence, Kansas, suffered a high mortality rate, with the average age of death being eighteen. Dr. N. J. Morrison reported that in one school in Kansas during that decade, fifty children came down with diphtheria, twenty-five of them dying. Disease was so common and doctors were so busy that they worked out a system of priorities: children first, then women, old men, adult men, and finally the "known hysterics."

A REAL TOWN BOOSTER! (1850)

Well-known Southern judge and Henry Clay supporter William H. Underwood of Georgia is best remembered for his caustic sense of humor. For some reason he greatly disliked the town of Marietta, Georgia. So it seemed surprising that once, while presiding in the court in Marietta, he commented, "When my time comes, I am coming to Marietta to die."

"Ah, I'm glad you think so much of our little town."

"It is not that," replied the judge. "It's because I can leave it with less regret than any other place on the face of the earth."

"UNCLE ROBIN IN HIS CABIN" (1851)

The impact of the anti-slavery book *Uncle Tom's Cabin,* published fourteen years before the Civil War, is known to most history students. But what is not so well known is the number of proslavery books it immediately engendered. Most of these defended slavery by attacking the miserable life of the Northern wage earner. One such author, William J. Grayson, in his *The Hireling and the Slave,* referred to the North's

> *Labor with hunger wages ceaseless strife*
> *And want and suffering only end with*
> *life,*
> *And then to the happy life of the slave*
> *Safe from harassing doubts and animal*
> *fears*
>
> *He dreads no famine in unfruitful years.*

A reader had to look no further than the title of a book by J. W. Page to get the message: *Uncle Robin in His Cabin in Virginia and Tom without One in Boston.*

None of the defenders of slavery, however, could match the sales of *Uncle Tom's Cabin,* which the Southern states finally had to ban. It really didn't matter, though, because eight printing presses working around the clock could not supply the demand even outside the South. Three hundred thousand copies were sold the first year.

"YOU'LL BE FREE OR DIE!" (1851)

Born a slave in Maryland in 1823, Harriet Tubman escaped to freedom and thereafter freed so many others that Southern slave owners offered $40,000 for her capture. She made nineteen secret trips deep into the South and guided more than three thousand slaves to freedom, including her own aged parents. If any of her charges wanted to change their mind about escaping, Miss Tubman would pull a pistol she always carried and say, "You'll be free or die!" They always chose freedom.

In one party of eleven slaves that she guided to Canada in 1851 was a frightened man on whose head was a $1,500 reward. He was so scared that he didn't dare speak or even look out of the train window while crossing the border from Buffalo into Canada, but once on free soil he shouted and sang so much that he couldn't be shut up. "You old fool, you!" said Miss Tubman. "You might at least have looked at Niagara Falls on the way to freedom."

JEFF DAVIS AIDS THE NORTH (1853)

For lending his support during the presidential campaign, Jefferson Davis was awarded the position of secretary of war in President Franklin Pierce's cabinet. He already had a respected position in military affairs, having served as chairman of the Senate Committee on Military Affairs in which he had actively labored for a larger army. Now as secretary of war only eight years before that army would be used against his native South, Davis did everything in his power to improve it as an effective fighting force. He undertook to reform and enlarge the Military Academy at West Point. He enlarged the army itself, modernized its equipment, increased coastal and frontier defenses, made advancement in the military dependent upon merit rather than on seniority or party, reorganized the Signal Corps, imported camels as army beasts of burden in the Southwest, and conducted extensive surveys of the West as a preliminary to the building of the transcontinental railroad. There must have been many times during Davis's reign as president of the Confederacy that he wished he had not done such a thorough job.

A STRANGE INDIAN POLICY (1853)

How do you fight people who won't fight back? This was a problem the Ute Indians faced with the Mormons in Utah Territory in 1853. Believing it was cheaper to feed and in almost any way pacify the Indians than to start wars that might bring the U.S. Army into Utah, Brigham Young gave orders to his religious followers to avoid at all costs retaliation against Indian attacks. Normally the Indians were peaceful, but when the Mormons forbade them to sell captive Indian children to slave traders from New Mexico, the Utes struck furiously at Mormon settlements. When news of the Utes flaunting freshly taken Mormon scalps reached him, Young still refused to be moved to retaliation. Instead he sent Wakara, the principal chief of the Utes, "tobacco for you to smoke in the mountains when you get lonesome. You are a fool for fighting your best friends." Against this strange white policy, the Utes had no defense, and by the end of 1853 the one-sided war sputtered out for lack of fuel. Lest it be misunderstood, the Mormons were not pacifists but merely hardheaded realists.

THE "COW" WARS (1854)

The great wars between the whites and the Plains Indians began with a butchered cow. Until August 17, 1854, there had only been minor incidents of begging, pilfering, and occasionally an isolated killing by Indians along the western wagon trails but no major incidents. On that day, however, the real wars began. Some Miniconjou Sioux killed a cow belonging to a Mormon immigrant, who immediately appealed to the military. A young lieutenant, John Grattan, marched out of Laramie with twenty-nine troopers, a drunken interpreter—as one story goes—and two cannons. No one knows for sure what happened after they made contact with the Sioux, but tempers flared, fighting erupted, and the entire troop was wiped out. The army responded, naturally enough, with more troops and a pitched battle on the North Platte, and the Indian wars had begun.

"LORD HELP THE FISH!" (1854)

Sam Houston was a man pursued and driven by wild and bizarre urges, never knowing exactly what he wanted. In the 1840s, encouraged by his wife, Margaret, and minister friends, he became interested in religion. He started attending church, but for some time he refused the sacrament of the Lord's Supper, claiming he was spiritually unprepared. Finally in November 1854, Sam's search for religion came to an end in what was almost a national event, at least in clerical circles.

When Houston was immersed in the chilly waters of Rocky Creek by a Baptist minister, a nationally read church periodical noted: "The announcement of General Houston's immersion has excited the wonder and surprise of many who have supposed that he was 'past praying for' but it is no marvel to us . . . three thousand and fifty clergymen have been praying for him." When a friend remarked, "Well, General, I hear your sins were washed away," Houston replied, "I hope so, but if they were all washed away, the Lord help the fish down below."

AMERICAN SAFARI (1855)

Just as Americans would participate in safaris in Africa, Europeans had conducted hunting expeditions earlier in America. One such excursion was led by Sir George Gore of Ireland in 1855–56 through Colorado and Wyoming. To transport himself and his personal hunting equipment, which included seventy-five sporting rifles, fifteen shotguns, dozens of pistols and fishing rods, special tents, brass bedstead, tables, and so forth, he required 112 horses, 40 men, 6 wagons, 21 two-wheeled carts, and even the personal services of Jim Bridgers. At the conclusion of his hunting trip, he boasted to an American Indian agent at Fort Union that that spring alone he had killed "one hundred five Bears, two thousand Buffalo Elk and Deer sixteen hundred."

In reporting this incident later, Alfred Vaughn, the agent, commented on the anger of the Indians "who have been loud in their complaints," but that nothing could be done to stop the slaughter.

CAMELS IN ARIZONA (1855)

The U.S. War Department spent money on many unusual experiments in its history, but the most unusual was approved by Congress in 1855 with an appropriation of $30,000. Having acquired the arid Southwest from Mexico as a result of war, Jefferson Davis, as secretary of war, decided that an ideal work and pack animal for desert country would logically be the camel. Thus, seven-six camels were brought to Texas from Asia and Egypt, along with Arab drivers, to teach Americans how to handle these alien beasts. After being used for a short time as mail and pack animals, they were sold or turned loose—not because they were unfit for the work but primarily because the Americans couldn't get used to them. During the Civil War, a San Francisco merchant imported more camels that eventually ended up in British Columbia. No further importations took place in the United States, and the entire experiment was considered a failure. For years afterward wild camels wandered the West, mostly in Arizona. Ironically, archaeologists have discovered that prehistoric camels once roamed this same territory thousands of years ago.

"BEECHER BIBLES" (1856)

Early in the controversy over slavery in Kansas, Henry Ward Beecher gave a speech in New Haven in which he said that for the slaveholders in

Kansas, a Sharps rifle was a greater moral argument than a Bible. Before the meeting at which he was speaking had adjourned, money was raised to equip an entire company of free-state immigrants in Kansas with new breech-loading rifles. About nine hundred of these "Beecher Bibles" came to be used by the Free State Party in the Kansas Border War, giving their owners some superiority throughout the conflict. This long-range and highly accurate rifle, invented by Christian Sharps in 1850, was the same rifle used by John Brown at Harper's Ferry, and at least 80,000 of them were used by the North during the Civil War—though they were not adopted by the U.S. Army.

PRESIDENTIAL ACCESS (1857)

An anonymous citizen describing Washington, D.C., just before Lincoln's first presidential term said the following about the ease of meeting the president:

"Every citizen in the United States who visits Washington considers he has a claim to visit the Chief Magistrate of the Union; and he is accordingly presented to him, and after shaking hands and conversing for a few minutes, retires, delighted with the suavity of the President, and elevated in his own estimation. It is easier to gain an interview with the President of the United States than with the most insignificant, petty noble in a monarchy."

Sometimes it was too easy. President Ulysses S. Grant once strolled into a washroom on a train to shave. Beside him stood a salesman who apparently hadn't been making too many sales. To make conversation with the unknown bewhiskered gentleman, the salesman began to blame the recession on "that idiot in the White House." Grant, not known for his tact, thereupon proceeded to chew the salesman out like a drill sergeant would a recruit. Apparently the salesman didn't mind too much, for he subsequently bragged to his friends about being chewed out by the president of the United States.

DRED SCOTT AFTER THE CASE (1857)

Few Americans have not heard of the Dred Scott case in which the Supreme Court in 1857, with Roger Taney presiding, ruled that blacks were property and not citizens of the United States and thus could not sue. Additional rulings on this matter made it a landmark case, but beyond these rudimentary facts, few know what happened to the principal involved, the slave Dred Scott. Ironically, after the court ruled that he was still a slave, his owner freed him, and he worked the rest of his life as a "good-natured porter" at a hotel in St. Louis. A certain amount of irony came from the criticism Chief Justice Taney received from Northern abolitionists, for personally he hated slavery and liberated his own slaves. As a Catholic he often waited in line with blacks at the confessional door.

SOUTHERN KNIGHTS AND TOURNAMENTS (1857)

The South entered the Civil War with what many have thought was an unjustified confidence in the outcome. One possible reason for this may have been a militant and romantic vogue that swept the South from Virginia to Texas in the 1840s and '50s, giving Southern men supreme confidence in their martial talents. These were the "ring tournaments" in which competing "knights" in costume—with names such as "Ali Pascha," "Rob Roy," or "The Knight of Avon" or "of Avenel" or "of the Lancel" or "of McIvor"—and on mounted horses tilted at rings in much the same manner as did legendary figures of medieval days. The tournaments had all the trappings of the Middle Ages with poets reciting to the masses and with "Queens of Beauty" traipsing with their maids.

At an 1857 tournament held on the plantation of a son of Chief Justice John Marshall, the show was stolen by an uninvited Indian who made a perfect pass at the ring at full speed, bounded over a high stone wall at the end of the field, and disappeared. This could have been an omen for the "invincible" Southern horsemen who were put to the supreme test four years later.

DIXIE LAND (1859)

Southerners who feel a strong emotional attachment to the word *Dixie* might be interested in the origin of the word. Truth is always obscured by the passage of time, but one of the most prominent theories revolves around the song "Dixie," originally titled "I Wish I Was in Dixie's Land," written and composed by Daniel E. Emmett, a Northerner who introduced it at Mechanics Hall in New York City in 1859. The tune may have been based on a song by slaves who lamented that their master had found his plantation unprofitable and had sold his slaves to a planter in South Carolina. The song tells of their desire to return to the land of their former master, a Dutch tobacco planter named Dixye, who tried to raise tobacco unsuccessfully in Harlem, New Amsterdam (New York). Another version has Dixye himself taking his slaves south when slavery was outlawed in New York. Still another theory concerns the $10 bank notes printed in French Louisiana with the word *Dix* on them. Eventually Louisiana came to be known as Dix's Land, and eventually the whole South came to be known as Dixie Land.

HOUSTON DRUMMING UP VOTES (1859)

R. P. Littlejohn tells the story of an incident regarding Sam Houston while he was running for governor of Texas. Scouring the countryside for votes, Houston asked to stay at a farmer's house for the night. After talking with his host and being promised his support in the coming election, the politician was shown to bed by the farmer's son, a boy who looked old enough to vote. Thinking him another prospective supporter, Houston inquired as to his age. The young man responded, "I was twenty one las' gone April, but I didn't bow me head when dad ast the blessin', so he sot me back two years, he did, an' I can't vote."

JUST LIKE BEN FRANKLIN (1859)

The democratic attitudes of American citizens have given them problems many times at court presentations in the aristocratic courts of Europe. One such occasion occurred when James Buchanan was minister to England shortly before his election to the White House. He rebelled at court dress for his presentation to Queen Victoria because he had his orders to appear "in the simple dress of an American Citizen," just like Franklin did almost a century earlier. When court officials objected to such dress, Buchanan replied that it "would not make the slightest difference to me, individually, whether I ever appeared at Court." London papers considered this an insult, one of them saying, "There is not the least reason why her Majesty should be troubled to receive the gentleman in the black coat from Yankeeland." Fortunately, a compromise was worked out that included a white waistcoat and cravat, black pants, dress boots, and a plain sword. It was the sword that apparently made him presentable, although the old bachelor always maintained that he only wore it to avoid being mistaken for a waiter.

"BLOOD IS THICKER THAN WATER" (1859)

One of America's most colorful naval officers was Josiah Tattnall, who participated in the War of 1812, the Barbary Wars with Decatur, the Mexican War, and the Civil War. He was apparently so fond of conflict that he even engaged in an unauthorized conflict in China in 1859. Standing by in charge of the American Asiatic Squadron while the British fleet was making an attack on Taku forts in China, he couldn't resist the fight and joined in on the side of the British. When asked for an explanation for his violation of American neutrality, he replied that "blood is thicker than water," an adage that became a part of American history. Both the American public and his government sustained his action. Only three years later, as captain of the *Merrimac* (*CSS Virginia*), he sunk her off Craney Island to prevent her from falling into Union hands.

THE OUTRAGED HUSBAND (1859)

Gen. Dan Sickles, who lost a leg to a Confederate cannon ball at Gettysburg, is well known to any Civil War buff. Less well known are his exploits before and after the war. As a congressman in 1859, he shot and killed the Washington, D.C., district attorney, Philip Barton Key, for adultery with his wife. Key was the well-known son of Francis Scott Key, but the whole country rejoiced when the offended husband was acquitted for this "justified" killing.

Years later while Sickles was serving a government mission in Spain, his second wife left him because he was habitually unfaithful. One of his conquests was the former Queen Isabella, who it was said easily matched Dan in promiscuity. Poor Philip Key never had the chance to enjoy old age and what the "outraged husband" Dan Sickles found could go with it.

FAILURE OF PONY EXPRESS (1860)

Because its exploits so fire the imagination, the Pony Express strikes most Americans as a resounding success story. Actually, it was a failure on most accounts. The company of Russell, Majors, and Waddell started the experiment in hopes of gaining a valuable mail contract. It went to another firm. The company also hoped to show the feasibility of a central route; the outbreak of the Civil War made the selection of such a route inevitable. Eighteen months after the firm inaugurated the service, the first transcontinental telegraph line was completed, and all need for the Pony Express was eliminated. During those eighteen months of operation, costs greatly exceeded revenue, bringing virtual financial ruin to the company. It showed a net loss of $200,000, and yet, ironically, the project that was such a failure is better remembered than the famous company that sponsored it.

LINCOLN'S SELF-DESCRIPTION (1860)

Five months before receiving the nomination for president, Lincoln sketched his early life:

"I was born February 12, 1809, in Hardin County, Kentucky. My parents were both born in Virginia, of undistinguished families—second families, perhaps I should say. My mother, who died in my tenth year, was of a family of the name of Yanks. . . . My father . . . removed from Kentucky to what is Spencer County, Indiana, in my eighth year. . . . It was a wild region, with many bears and other wild animals still in the woods. There I grew up. There was some school, so called; but no qualification was ever required of a teacher, beyond readin', writin', and cipherin', to the Rule of Three. . . . Of course when I came of age I did not know much. . . . The little advance I now have upon this store of education, I have picked up from time to time under the pressure of necessity."

Of his physical appearance, Lincoln added, "I am, in height, six feet, four inches, nearly; lean in flesh, weighing, on average, one hundred and eighty pounds; dark complexion with coarse black hair and grey eyes—no other marks or brands recollected."

GRANT—THE "FAILURE" (1860)

In April 1860, Ulysses (sometimes called "Useless" as a child) S. Grant returned to his brothers' leather goods store in Galana, Illinois. He had been a failure in all he had attempted: he failed after six years of farming, he failed at selling real estate, and he couldn't even succeed as a peacetime army officer. The main reason for his failures was lack of an aggressive personality (ironic, because no general was more aggressive than Grant later proved to be). His failures and resulting poverty made him a drunkard for a while. In the 1850s he became so desperate that he attempted to sell his wife's two slaves for cash on which to live. Now he was being offered $800 a year to work for his brothers. Grant, shabby, bearded, and followed by his wife, a former St. Louis Belle named Julia Dent, and their four children, look forward to a bleak future.

Less than two years later he was a brigadier general in the U.S. Army, a national hero, and well on the road to the White House, where he would be able to afford $4,000 worth of Brussell's lace for his daughter's wedding gown.

SAM HOUSTON OPPOSES SECESSION (1861)

Many people raised their voices against secession in the South in the early months of 1861, but none was better known or held a more important position than the governor of Texas. Sam Houston had been elected governor of Texas in 1859, and for two years he had led a battle to prevent Texas from following the secession move of neighboring states, even though his life was threatened. He lost his battle, and when summoned before the secession convention to take the Confederate oath, he declined:

"In the name of my own conscience and my own manhood I refuse to take this oath. It is perhaps meet that my career should close thus. I have seen the patriots and statesmen of my youth one by one gathered to their fathers, and the government they reared rent in twain. I stand last almost of my race, stricken down because I will not yield those principles I have fought for."

Two years later he died, still withholding his allegiance from the Confederacy. His son fought for the Confederacy and was wounded at Shiloh.

THE CONFEDERACY'S RELUCTANT LEADERS (1861)

In February 1861, under a constitution guaranteeing the perpetual existence of slavery, the Confederate States of America elected its two highest executive officers. Jefferson Davis accepted the presidential office against his will—he would have preferred to command the Southern armies in the field—and disliked his job throughout the war. His vice president, Alexander H. Stephens, also accepted his job unwillingly. Actually, both he and Davis had done all in their power to block outright secession by the Southern states. During the frenzied period of secession, Stephens complained, "The people are run mad. They are wild with passion and frenzy, doing they know not what." The vice president was an old friend of Abraham Lincoln and secretly believed from the start that the Confederacy was doomed. With such leaders pessimistic about the South's future, is it any wonder that the Southern cause came to be known in history as "the Lost Cause"?

DRINKING WAS ALL HE HAD LEFT! (1861)

Lincoln, plagued throughout the war by generals too timid to fight, had a ready answer for associates who complained to Lincoln about Gen. Ulysses S. Grant's drinking habit: "Find out his brand and I'll order a keg for each of my other generals."

Lincoln was asked later if he really had said this, and he replied, "No . . . but it's a good story." Lincoln claimed that he had traced the story back to George II and Gen. James Wolfe. When people complained that General Wolfe was mad, George said, "I wish he'd bite some of the others."

Most of Grant's critics weren't aware of his virtues: he never swore, hated politics, disliked military pomp, and, unlike the president, refused to listen to off-color stories. One of his officers, in preparation for telling such a story, once looked around the table and remarked, "I see there are no ladies present." "No," replied Grant quietly, "but there are gentlemen."

FROM PLANTATION TO CEMETERY (1861)

In 1831 Robert E. Lee married Mary Custis, thus becoming heir to the beautiful Custis Mansion, built by George Washington's adopted son. The estate was originally part of the estate of George Washington. In 1861 Lee left this Arlington mansion to take command of the Virginia troops, never to return. Federal troops took possession, building a fort, establishing a hospital on the grounds, and paving the way for the famous Arlington National Cemetery now filling the plantation grounds. There had initially been no plans for a cemetery, but when the first patient, a Confederate soldier, died, officials decided to bury him on the grounds. Thus began the cemetery. Twelve years after the war ended, the U.S. government satisfied legal claims with George Washington Custis Lee, legal heir, with payment of $150,000.

DESTROYING HISTORICAL RECORDS (1861)

Shortly after the disaster of First Bull Run, it became necessary to make room in Washington to house the defending troops. Consequently, old storage rooms were cleaned out. In a long procession of sleighs, the records and papers from many years' storage were drawn to the Potomac and there disposed of. Many loose letters and papers were picked up by passersby—letters signed by Washington, Jefferson, Hancock, and others. The amount of irreplaceable historical material destroyed that day will never be known. Unfortunately, historical material is still being lost. One authority estimates that each day in America two thousand tons of historical material are lost not only through fires, floods, and decay, but also to a large extent through deliberate destruction by uncaring or unknowing owners.

GERM WARFARE (1861)

As Gen. William Tecumseh Sherman is credited with saying, "War is hell," and the Civil War was a prime example. In the fall of 1861, Confederate congressman Duncan Kenner received a letter from a Louisiana planter named R. R. Barrow, suggesting a type of germ warfare:

"I have been surprised that nothing has been done to carry the yellow fever into New Orleans. It could be done so easily by sending a man that had already had the disease to some yellow fever town and there procure fever corpse, wrap the dead body in Blankets and put in a metallic coffin. Bring the corpse over and then smuggle the blankets into New Orleans. Thus started the fever would soon become an epidemic throughout the city."

There is no evidence that this or any similar germ warfare plan was ever put into operation during the Civil War. It was practiced, however, as early as the colonial wars against the Indians. The same basic plan was used by sending blankets of smallpox victims to Indians, thus starting epidemics far more devastating than any wars the whites could ever conduct.

"QUAKER GUNS" (1861)

Dummy cannon, placed so as to deceive enemies into thinking they were facing real guns, are as old as cannon themselves, but the term "Quaker guns" originated in the United States. It refers to the doctrine of nonresistance taught by orthodox Quakers, or members of the Society of Friends, and was possibly coined by Washington Irving in 1809 in speaking of a "formidable battery of Quaker guns." The most famous "Quaker guns" in history were those used by the Confederate Army at Centreville, Virginia, in 1861. The Southern general Joseph Johnston, finding his army short of the real thing, ordered logs of wood put in position and painted so as to resemble cannon, successfully delaying Union attacks on their position. As late as 1943 the Italian coastal defense guns on Sicily were found to be made of wood, and in that same year a North Carolina congressman let out a howl when he discovered that the antiaircraft guns on the House Office Building on Capitol Hill were merely imitation guns served by dummy soldiers as decoys.

THE FIRST TO DIE (1861)

The first action of the Civil War centered on the nation's capital, open to possible Confederate attack. Responding to President Lincoln's appeals, volunteer units immediately poured into the city to protect it. One of the first regiments was led by a personal friend of the president, Col. Elmer Ellsworth, with his New York City Zouaves. Sent to secure the town of Alexandria, Virginia, Ellsworth's regiment found no Confederate soldiers, but he did see the Rebel Stars and Bars flying over the Marshall House Hotel. Unable to tolerate an "alien" flag flying over American territory, he raced to the roof and tore down the banner. On his way back down the stairs, he was met by the hotel owner, Marshall, with a shotgun. A Union corporal lunged at Marshall, but not in time to save his colonel, the first officer to be killed in the Civil War, ironically by a civilian.

SCOPE OF THE CIVIL WAR (1861)

When the War Between the States began in 1861, it is doubtful that anyone in the North or South could have envisioned the horror or scope of this great conflict. More than three million men served in the two armies, half of them becoming casualties. More than 2,200 engagements were fought from Vermont to the Arizona Territory. An average of 430 soldiers died each day of the four-year war. Eventually almost as many Americans died in this conflict as died in all of the nation's other wars combined. Materially, the war cost both sides $15 billion in destroyed property, burned towns and farms, and materials expended. No price tag could be placed, however, on such results as discrimination and bigotry, military and political excess and corruption, expansion of federal power at the expense of state sovereignty, and the cream of an entire generation destroyed.

BATTLE YELLS (1861)

Participants said they could tell which side was charging during Civil War battles by the cheers or battle yells—the two sides were distinctively different. The Union battle charge yell was a prolonged and nearly uniform hurrah, whereas the much publicized Rebel yell was a succession of jerky canine yelps with a shrillness up close that was intended to, and did, strike terror in Northern units. "The effect of the Enemy's peculiar cheer upon our raw men was very demoralizing," reported an Ohio sergeant after the fight at Mine Run. Primarily, battle yells are a natural and contagious method of relieving tension and instilling collective courage, although the Rebel yell was said to have been intentionally designed to put the Yankees to rout. No record shows that this high-pitched yell, first heard at Bull Run, ever succeeded in turning the tide of a battle, but there is really no way to judge psychological facts such as this.

FREMONT'S EMANCIPATION PROCLAMATION (1861)

John C. Fremont, one of the most controversial figures in American history and one of the most luckless, has several firsts to his credit. One of these occurred in 1856 when the newly formed Republican Party nominated him as its first presidential candidate. He lost to James Buchanan, allowing Lincoln to become the first Republican president. Interestingly, he attempted to precede Lincoln in another area but lost again to the man from Illinois.

During the Civil War, Fremont was military commander of the Union forces in Missouri. During the first year of the Civil War, the "Pathfinder" issued a proclamation freeing all slaves held by any residents of Missouri fighting for the South. Lincoln, feeling that this emancipation proclamation was premature and even politically harmful, reversed it. Two years later the president issued his own Emancipation Proclamation. Ironically, Fremont was a resident of Georgia.

FROM PRESIDENT TO TRAITOR (1862)

The only former U.S. president whose death the government took no official notice of was John Tyler, tenth president of the United States. The first man to assume the high office upon the death of the chief executive, Tyler served a not-too-conspicuous term other than also being the first president to have impeachment proceedings introduced by congressional leaders. The effort failed. After retiring in 1845 he lived quietly in his native state of Virginia until 1860. In that year he emerged as a strong voice urging moderation and careful deliberation in the South. In the following year he presided over the unsuccessful Washington Peace Conference, and only when all compromise seemed hopeless did he endorse secession. In 1861 he was elected to the provisional Congress of the Confederate States. Thus, when he died in January 1862, the U.S. government refused to acknowledge the death of a man considered a traitor. It was not until 1911 that Congress authorized a monument in his honor.

"LET THEM EAT GRASS" (1862)

It has been alleged that when starving French peasants pleaded with authorities for bread in the 1780s, Marie Antoinette replied with her infamous statement, "Let them eat cake"—words she was to later regret.

An interesting parallel is found in American history during the Civil War. When the U.S. government, supposedly lacking funds to meet its obligations, held up annuity payments and provisions, Native American demands grew bold and angry. When some Sioux Indians in Minnesota asked for an extension of credit from Andrew Myrick, an agency trader, he was reportedly said, "If they are hungry let them eat grass." Like the foolish queen, he also would live to regret such an unfeeling witticism. When the great Sioux uprising occurred in the summer of 1862, starting at the lower agency, agent Myrick was among the first to fall. Two weeks later when that part of the country was again made safe for whites, Myrick's body was found with a hay scythe thrust through his stomach and his mouth filled with blood-matted grass.

CUT NOSE SERVES A PURPOSE (1862)

One of the most memorable pictures in American history is that of thirty-eight Native Americans hanging en masse for the crimes they committed during the great Minnesota uprising of 1862. There is, however, a little-known postscript to this episode. After the bodies were cut down, they were buried in a common shallow grave. That night several frontier doctors, always eager to acquire cadavers for study, dug up some of the bodies. A doctor from the small community of LeSeuer happened to acquire the body of Cut Nose, probably the most infamous of those executed. He had admitted to twenty-seven killings, including children, and numerous rapes. His body was taken to the doctor's office, where the flesh was cleaned from the bones and the skeleton wired together for display and study. As a result of this unusual display, the doctor's two young sons developed an intensive interest in medicine and osteology. Eventually, they grew up to develop a fine medical facility in Rochester, New York. That obscure LeSeuer doctor who dug up Cut Nose and cleaned his bones was William W. Mayo, whose sons founded the famed Mayo Clinic.

ANGEL IN GRAY (1862)

One of the most tragic battles of the Civil War, from the Northern point of view, was Fredericksburg, fought on December 13, 1862. The inept Union general Ambrose Burnside futilely sent five Union divisions against Confederates entrenched behind stone walls at the foot of Marye's Heights. With cannon throwing shell at the Union soldiers from the heights above, everyone except Burnside realized that the charges were suicidal, and it was said that the senseless slaughter brought tears to the eyes of the firing Rebels. The following day the Union wounded were still lying in front of the Confederate positions, groaning and crying for help and relief from their pain and thirst. This was too much for Sgt. Richard Kirkland of the Second South Carolina Volunteers. Grabbing canteens from his buddies, he climbed the protecting wall and advanced into no-man's-land, giving words of comfort and water to the fallen enemy. The only response from the now-entrenched Union force was a cheer for Kirkland's humanitarianism, and for ninety minutes no shots were fired while the angel in gray moved among the dead and wounded. Within less than a year, Kirkland himself was to lie among the dead on the battlefield at Chickamauga.

A LEGEND IS MADE (1862)

The power of the pen is illustrated by the number of legends created by poets. As Henry Wadsworth Longfellow immortalized Paul Revere, John Greenleaf Whittier did the same for Barbara Fritchie.

In the poem "Barbara Fritchie," Whittier has the elderly Mrs. Fritchie rushing to her upstairs window in the small town of Frederick, Maryland, during an invasion by Confederate troops to save a Union flag from being riddled by rifle fire. "Stonewall" Jackson, impressed by her bravery, decreed death to any man who touched her head, and throughout the day the flag flew while the gray columns marched below.

Now, what was the truth? As near as can be determined, the old lady, aged ninety-six, feebly waved a small Union flag from her front porch six days after the supposed incident, when federal troops entered the town. Later testimony from both the Jackson and the Fritchie families indicate that the two heroes never saw each other.

"BEAST" BUTLER'S PROCLAMATION (1862)

The Union captured New Orleans early in the Civil War, and an army of occupation was sent into the town with Gen. B. F. Butler as military commander. There was naturally a great deal of hostility between the Southern citizens and the Northern troops, but General "Beast" Butler, as the Confederates called him, was particularly incensed by the insults to which the women subjected his troops. Knowing that the troops would be less likely to retaliate against women, even genteel New Orleans ladies taunted and spit on the Yanks they encountered in the streets. Shrewdly, Butler issued that most famous of Civil War orders, No. 28, to the effect that henceforth, any female showing contempt or insulting any Northern soldier would be treated as a woman of the town plying her trade. Needless to say, the order was effective, but it raised a storm of protest around the world, and by December, Butler had been removed from command.

SOUTH REACTS TO BLACK TROOPS (1862)

During the Civil War, nearly 180,000 African-Americans served in the Union army, the majority coming from Confederate territory. All of these soldiers were commanded by white officers. Southerners were so incensed over the use of black troops by the North that in December 1862 Jefferson Davis issued a proclamation to turn all captured leaders of black soldiers over to the states to be punished as "agents to excite servile war," which could normally mean the death penalty. The following year the Confederate Congress voted that white officers leading black soldiers who were captured should be put to death.

Immediately upon hearing of this vote, President Lincoln promised to execute one Confederate prisoner for every Union soldier so executed. There is no evidence that the South ever carried out the death penalty, although one of the most atrocious events of the war occurred when Rebels massacred black troops after capturing them in Fort Pillow, Tennessee. Southern historians tend to deny the massacre, suggesting that, although there was some needless killing after the capture of the fort, the heavy casualties in the black garrison resulted from their attempted escape from the fort. Most Northern historians disagree.

THE FATE OF THE IRONCLADS (1862)

Most students of history are familiar with the well-known battle between the two Civil War ironclads: the *Confederate Virginia* (*Merrimack* was its original name as a federal warship) and the *Monitor,* a "tin can on a shingle." Although the three-hour duel in Hampton Roads on March 9, 1862, seemed inconclusive, it marked the birth of steel navies.

Fewer students are familiar with the disposal of these two ships. A few weeks after the duel, the Confederate hoped-for super weapon was run aground and burned to prevent its capture by federals. The *Monitor* was equally ill-fated. On the final night of the same year, it sank in a storm off Cape Hatteras, North Carolina. Extensive efforts were made during the Civil War centennial to locate the wreckage. But it wasn't until 1974 that the ironclad was finally found.

CONFEDERATE SUBMARINE H. L. HUNLEY (1863)

Historians consider Bushnell's *Turtle* of Revolutionary War fame the first submarine, but the Confederate innovation, the *H. L. Hunley,* named after its designer and builder, was history's first tactical submarine and also its most frequently sunk sub. On its trial run at Mobile in 1863 it sank, but all hands escaped. It was rebuilt and shipped to Charlestown that summer, but it sank on its trial run there when a passing ship sent water down its open hatches. Eight of its nine crewmen drowned. It was raised and repaired, but it sank again for the third time three weeks later, with a loss of six more seamen. After it was raised again, Hunley himself took command and drowned along with eight others as the sub sank for the fourth time when its tanks burst on an experimental attack run. Despite the bad luck, it was raised once more, and a volunteer crew took it into action in February 1864 against the *USS Housatonic*. This federal blockader became history's first victim of a submarine attack. However, the *Hunley* sank in an ensuing explosion for the fifth and last time, taking all hands with it. No trace of the sub was ever found.

BLACK VALOR IN THE CIVIL WAR (1863)

A total of 178,895 African-Americans flocked to the colors of 120 regiments, 12 heavy artillery regiments, 10 light artillery batteries, and 7 cavalry regiments during the Civil War. Their numbers constituted 12 percent of the North's fighting forces, present in 39 major battles and 410 minor engagements. The death rate among black soldiers was high: 68,178 men, of whom 2,751 were killed in action. Most of the remainder died of disease. Fourteen black soldiers received the Medal of Honor, although Sgt. Anselmas Planciancois was not among that number. Just before the assault on Port Hudson, Planciancois received the regimental flag with a vow: "Colonel, I will bring back the colors with honor or report to God the reason why." Mortally wounded in the battle that followed, his last act was to hug the flag to his breast.

CAVALRY BATTLE (1863)

The greatest cavalry battle in the history of the western hemisphere, possibly the world, was fought at Brandy Station, Virginia, on June 9, 1863. Approximately 20,000 horsemen fought a pitched engagement for more than twelve hours in this "first true cavalry battle of the war." At the height of the battle, charges and countercharges were made continuously for almost three hours. Despite the numbers engaged, casualties were amazingly light, with 936 Yanks killed, wounded, and missing, to 523 Rebels. With numbers engaged equally divided, the Southerners gained a hard-fought victory, but the Northern horsemen earned from the Rebels a new respect for horsemanship. Previous to this battle most Southerners felt that any single one of their cavalrymen could outfight ten Yankee plow-boys.

JOHNNY REB BLOWS OFF STEAM (1863)

Not all of the derogatory comments made by Southern soldiers were directed at their Northern counterparts—outfits and officers of the Confederacy received much of the brunt. Virginia soldiers were known as the "Buttermilk Brigade" to other Southerners. South Carolinians were "Sand Lappers," Alabamians were "Yellow Hammers," and Georgians were "Goober Grabbers." Some of Johnny Reb's most caustic prejudices were directed at his officers, rather common in most armies but seldom expressed so graphically. A Louisiana sergeant told his wife that Gen. John C. Pemberton was "the most insignificant puke I ever saw." A Mississippi soldier described Gen. Rube Davis as a "vain, stuck up, illiterate ass." Actually, about one in three Southern soldiers was illiterate, and the writing of those who were literate left much to be desired. A soldier from Alabama described a Colonel Henry as "an ignoramus fit for nothing higher than the cultivation of corn." One of the most typical folksy witticisms came from a Florida soldier describing officers in general: "(They) are not fit to tote guts to a bear."

THE DIN OF BATTLE (1863)

The noise of a battlefield is difficult to describe to anyone who has never experienced it. Many Civil War veterans attempted to record the experience, and most of them agreed with a Confederate captain at Murfreesboro: "I cannot use language to Express the noise of this Battle. The Earth seemed to be in perfect commotion as if a heavy Earth Quake was on." A Virginia private at Petersburg said, "You couldn't hear your own gun Shoot, the Canon was roaring, bomb shells bursting, bullets whistling, men hollowing." Because of this noise and confusion, men in battle often failed to cap their guns after each shot, which resulted in their charging one load on top of another, thinking that they had fired the previous load. After the Battle of Gettysburg, 27,574 guns were picked up on the field of battle. Eighteen thousand of them contained two or more charges, and one had a record twenty-three loads in it.

THE MIRACULOUS BULLET (1863)

A Union doctor named Capt. L. G. Capers, who was acting as a field surgeon during an unnamed skirmish in a Virginia village on May 12, 1863, records something that modern authorities insist is possible. A soldier near Captain Capers was struck in the leg and scrotum by a stray bullet; that same bullet then proceeded to strike a young lady on the porch of a nearby house. The young lady, wounded in the abdominal area, was treated by a doctor and soon recovered. Several months after the incident, the doctor and his regiment were again in the same area, which allowed the doctor to call on his civilian patient. Astonishingly, he found her pregnant, shortly giving birth to an eight-pound boy that strongly resembled the young wounded soldier. As Captain Capers reconstructed the incident, he concluded that the young lady was impregnated by sperm carried on the bullet. Even the end of the story has a make-believe quality to it. The young soldier recovered, courted the girl, married her, and eventually produced two more children by a more conventional method.

BATTLE OF GETTYSBURG (1863)

Often referred to as the greatest battle fought in the Western hemisphere, Gettysburg was also one of the bloodiest of the Civil War, or of any war for that matter. For three days more than 163,000 men waged a vicious, unyielding fight along a four-mile front. In one fruitless charge by Confederate general James Longstreet (inaccurately referred to in history books as "Pickett's Charge"), 7,000 out of 15,000 men failed to return to the Rebel lines, adding the final blood to the already drenched battlefields. In only three days the two armies suffered more than 51,000 killed and maimed, the Confederate losses being about 5,000 greater than the Union's. The "high tide of the Confederacy" then began to recede, although it was not until after the Civil War that historians began referring to Gettysburg as the turning point.

THE GETTYSBURG ADDRESS (1863)

On November 19 of the year of the Battle of Gettysburg, dedication ceremonies for a new cemetery, planned by the governors of the Northern states, were held. The greatest orator of the times, Edward Everett, was invited to make the principal speech. Almost as an afterthought, President Abraham Lincoln was asked to attend. Lincoln worked on the draft of a short speech on the train from Washington and revised it at David Wills's house in Gettysburg the night before the ceremony. The next day Everett gave a two-hour oration before twenty thousand people, at the end of which the people were restless and noisy. By the time they had quieted down, Lincoln had finished his talk, less than three minutes long. As a result, Lincoln felt that his remarks were a complete failure and said to Ward Hill Lamon, the man who introduced him, "Lamon, that speech won't scour. It is a flat failure."

THE DRAFT RIOTS (1863)

The demonstrations opposing the war in Vietnam pale in comparison to the New York City draft riot of July 1863. Minor riots had occurred in Rutland, Vermont; Wooster, Ohio; Boston, Massachusetts; and Portsmouth, New Hampshire, but they were nothing like the one that began on July 13 at a New York draft headquarters. Policemen, firemen, militia, and private citizens were at the mercy of fifty thousand rioters who rampaged through the city for four days, burning, looting, hanging black men, and assaulting all who resisted. Before it was brought under control, the mobbing claimed a thousand casualties, at least seventy-five of them fatal. *A Pictorial History of the Negro in America,* by Langston Hughes and Milton Meltzer, states that the New York mobs blamed the black man for the war and "killed hundreds of them." Property damage totaled $1.5 million.

BANISHING A COPPERHEAD (1863)

The government is waging a "wicked, cruel and unnecessary war," claimed Copperhead Clement Vallandigham in 1863. This darling of the antiwar movement became so outspoken that President Lincoln had him arrested at his home in Dayton, Ohio, and turned him over to the South. Even his friends in the South snickered when he announced to a Confederate private, after walking across no-man's-land, "I surrender myself to you as a prisoner of war." The following year, as the Democratic candidate for governor of Ohio, he sneaked back into the United States with a pillow under his vest and fake whiskers pasted to his chin. Confederate authorities seemed relieved to be rid of their visiting sympathizer, and Lincoln ignored him when he returned. To top off his humiliation, he lost the election by a wide margin to the Republican candidate, John Brough.

BUT THE SENATOR APOLOGIZED (1863)

Probably no sitting president has suffered more vicious personal attacks on his character than did Abraham Lincoln. One such attack came in January 1863 by Democrat senator Willard Saulsbury of Delaware, speaking to the president of the Senate:

"Mr. President, you know how true it is that when a man is exalted in a high place, he seldom hears anything except the voice of flattery. The solemn words of truth never enter his ears. . . . Thus it has been with Mr.

Lincoln—a weak and imbecile man; the weakest man that I ever knew in a high place; for I have seen him and conversed with him, and I say here, in my place in the Senate of the United States, that I never did see or converse with so weak and imbecile a man as Abraham Lincoln. . . . If I wanted to paint a tyrant; if I wanted to paint a despot, a man perfectly regardless of every constitutional right of the people, whose sworn servant, not ruler, he is, I would paint the hideous form of Abraham Lincoln. If that be treason . . ."

Apparently the Senate thought it was, for threatened with expulsion by that body, Saulsbury apologized two days later for his remarks.

CARLETON'S EXTERMINATION ORDER (1863)

During the Confederate occupation of Arizona early in the Civil War, the military commander suggested as an answer to the "Indian Question" the extermination of all adult Indians and slavery of the children. The shocked Confederate president, Jefferson Davis, vetoed the suggestion. When the North took over the territory, Gen. J. H. Carleton, the Union commander, actually issued such an order with the blessing of the federal government: All Apache and Navajo males "are to be slain whenever and wherever they can be found." Women and children were to be taken prisoners. An alternative provision allowed the Indians to be confined to a reservation in central New Mexico, but for the most part this order was ignored as the government pushed a war of extermination beginning in 1863.

Flags of truce were used to entice Indians, bounties were paid for Indian scalps, friendlier Pima and Papago tribesmen were offered guns and leadership, and everyone went to work with enthusiasm. The program was a failure and finally ended after a massacre of eighty-five Aravaipa Apaches by a Tucson mob in 1871. The eight-year war of Indian extermination, according to a government investigator, "cost us a thousand lives and over forty million of dollars, and . . . the Indians are no nearer extinction." Ironically, the largest Indian population today is in the state of Arizona.

CIVIL WAR GUNFIRE (1863)

To fire a Civil War–era musket, eleven separate motions had to be made. The fastest a soldier could fire, according to regulations (seldom accomplished under battlefield conditions), was three shots per minute. It is thus amazing to learn that in a battle such as the one at Stones River, Tennessee, in January 1863, the federal infantry exhausted more than two million rounds in only three days. This number, incidentally, was in addition to more than 20,000 rounds of artillery shells, making a total projectile weight of 375,000 pounds.

Another interesting statistic, not necessarily relevant to all battles but often cited for the Battle of First Bull Run, is an estimate of 8,000–10,000 bullets fired for every man killed and wounded. Confederate losses of approximately 25,000 at Stones River figure out to only eighty bullets fired for every Johnny Reb killed or wounded. This number indicates either wildly inaccurate figures, effective artillery fire, or vastly improved marksmanship between Bull Run and Stones River. Perhaps a comparison might be made with World War I. It has been estimated that in that war the Yanks fired 7,000 times for every enemy soldier hit.

REBEL HUMOR (1864)

Humor is always an interesting subject in history, but some of the most revealing humor is found in the letters of Southern soldiers. One letter by a Rebel sums up the feelings of many soldiers months and miles away from their wives: "I don't feel much like a maryed man but I never forgit sofar as to court enny other lady. But if I should you must forgive me as I am so forgitful." Even the destitute condition of the Confederate army was the subject of Rebel humor. In describing the cows that the army killed for meat, one soldier wrote, "It takes two soldiers to holdup one beef to shoot it." Along a similar vein, another soldier near Atlanta in 1864 described how to tell officers apart: "In this army, one hole in the seat of the britches indicates a captain, two holes a Lt., and if the seat of the britches is all gone, the individual is a private."

THE JONES COUNTY UNIONISTS (1864)

When secession was put to a vote in many parts of the South, the people of Jones County, a relatively slaveless and wooded section of southern Mississippi, voted 376 to 24 to stay with the Union. The Confederacy, naturally, could not permit this and attempted to force the reluctant citizens into line. A backwoodsman named Newton Knight organized the county's Unionists and Confederate deserters into a company to fight for the freedom of

Jones County, bound by an oath never to surrender to the Confederacy. They never did and spent the rest of the war fighting off Confederate military authorities, defeating Lowery's Cavalry in one pitched battle. Women did as much as the men, raising food supplies for the Unionist company and poisoning bloodhounds sent to track down deserters. A tradition arose in the South after the war that Jones County had actually seceded from the Confederacy and set up the "Free State of Jones."

A MOST PECULIAR WAR (1864)

Cases of Northern and Southern soldiers fraternizing during Civil War battles are proverbial, but hundreds of them are well documented. One such unofficial truce involved a field of corn lying between the Union and Confederate lines and bisected by a deep ditch. A tacit agreement stipulated that this ditch constituted the dividing line in the ownership of the corn itself, each side gathering ears on its side of the ditch for roasting. While gathering corn, one Yank discovered a Reb on the Northern side with his arms full of roasting ears. When Johnny Reb refused to return the corn, a fistfight resulted, with soldiers from both sides forming a ring and cheering on the two fighters. After the Yank won, the two men shook hands and the men in gray retired to their side of the ditch in good humor. If this incident was typical of other truces, these same men soon went back to the business of killing each other.

LINCOLN'S COMPASSION (1864)

The president was extremely moved by the youthfulness of so many of the federal soldiers. He often wrote to his officers, "He is so young. Let him be sent back to his mother." He never actually witnessed any executions for desertion, but he often shed tears when he discussed executions with visitors: "It is shooting day over in Virginia. They are so young." Secretary of War Edwin Stanton lacked this compassion, often tearing up the cards Lincoln had written asking for pardons and postponements of executions. A rumor that hurt Lincoln deeply was the report that, to distract his mind from the mangled corpses he viewed while riding over the battlefield of Antietam, he had asked his friend Ward Hill Lamon to sing an amusing song. While hurt deeply by this malicious report, he kept his usual silence regarding the criticism. Lincoln was often criticized for telling his typical humorous stories while men were dying on the battlefield.

Friends defended the president by noting that Lincoln was so deeply saddened by all the bloodshed that humor was the only device that permitted him to keep his sanity.

LINCOLN UNDER ENEMY FIRE (1864)

In 1864, in an attempt to break General Grant's hold near Petersburg, Virginia, Gen. Robert E. Lee sent Gen. Jubal Early into Maryland to threaten Washington from the north. Early's forces were too small to make a direct attack on the strongly defended and fortified city, so he only demonstrated briefly against the outer defenses. While this fighting was going on, Lincoln rode to the front and watched part of the action from atop a federal parapet, thus becoming the only president ever to come under enemy fire. As his biographers Nicolay and Hay wrote, "Amid the whizzing bullets the President . . . stood . . . with that grave and impassive countenance . . . until an officer fell mortally wounded within three feet of him." Maj. Gen. Horatio Wright finally convinced the commander in chief to take cover. Earlier, in 1814, President James Madison risked enemy fire when he personally assumed command of a gun battery north of Bladensburg, Maryland.

ANOTHER OLD ABE (1864)

Any schoolboy knows that "Old Abe" is simply an affectionate nickname for Abraham Lincoln, but few are likely to recognize it as the name of a bald eagle. Old Abe was carried as a living battle standard by the 8th Wisconsin Regiment throughout the Civil War and was even wounded at Vicksburg, Mississippi. When a battle began, Old Abe was released to fly aloft, where he circled the battlefield, shrieking and flapping his wings, as if to rally his comrades. Southern guides at the Cyclorama in Atlanta today point out to visitors the picture of Old Abe high on a huge painting, circling and shrieking during the Battle of Atlanta.

After the war ended, Old Abe made a tour of the country, raising $80,000 for disabled veterans, finally dying in 1881 as one of the most honored, and certainly best known, veterans himself.

THE SKULKERS (1864)

Every army in history has been hampered by what are known as skulkers, but they especially weakened the Union army in the Civil War.

These were most often the bounty jumpers, substitutes, shirkers, and just plain cowards. Some Northern regiments forced these men into the front line of battle, often without muskets or means of defending themselves, with orders given to the veterans to shoot them if they ran. When the firing started, they would often grab the first musket available, quickly cured of their shirking and cowardice.

At many battles, pickets were deployed along the rear of an army to turn back stragglers or the faint of heart. In 1864 at the Battle of Cedar Creek, George Armstrong Custer's cavalry was assigned the job of turning back cowards; retreating men had to show their wounds in order to pass. Unless a soldier trying to pass through certain sentries "could show blood," he was to be shot down.

"HURRYING THEM TO GLORY" (1864)

In the Civil War, as in war today, chaplains were considered noncombatants, and most of them were; but apparently, according to records, many of these men of God could not resist the temptation to hurry a few men along to glory themselves. At Shiloh, Chaplain Tichenor of the 17th Alabama Regiment killed "with a rifle a colonel, a major and four privates." Another Confederate chaplain near Columbus, Kentucky, was reported to have shot two Yankees, cut the throat of a third, and pursued the retreating Northerners yelling, "Go to hell, you damned sons of bitches." During the siege of Vicksburg, a Union chaplain wrote in his diary that he had been out in the trenches taking potshots at the Rebs. "Five times," he records, "I fired deliberately, each time at a head which was incautiously exposed."

At the Battle for Atlanta, Chaplain Bennett of the 32d Ohio, was awarded "a gold medal of honor" for his gallantry during the fight. He had been so busy firing that he employed a private to load for him. Despite many charges of incompetence and cowardice against chaplains—and in general they were not of the best sort—Union records list eleven chaplains killed in combat.

HOW TO HANG A SHERIFF (1864)

One of the most notorious and best-organized outlaw gangs in the early West was that of Henry Plummer. Surrounding himself with approximately fifty other desperadoes, Plummer ravished the southern

Montana Territory almost at will during the Civil War, robbing and murdering at least 102 men in only a few months. What made it even more difficult to deal with the Plummer gang was that Plummer himself had been elected sheriff of both Bannack and Virginia City, so no help could be expected from the local law. Realizing this, the citizens of the territory, as so often happened in frontier towns, took it upon themselves to administer justice. Quietly a vigilante committee was organized, and a complete list of the Plummer gang was obtained. Starting out one night, the committee proceeded to round up the gang members, hanging them wherever they were caught. Twenty-four were hung, eight were banished, and the rest fled the territory. Henry Plummer was hung on gallows he had erected for others.

LINCOLN'S CHILDREN (1865)

Lincoln's oldest child was Robert, the only one of four sons to live to maturity. In later years he became the secretary of war. Lincoln's second son, Eddie, died at the age of three in Springfield in 1850. His father kept his grief to himself, writing to his stepbrother only to say, "We miss him very much." Lincoln's third son, Willie, was born that same year and became close and dear to his father. Willie's death twelve years later was almost more than Lincoln could bear. He is reported to have visited Willie's tomb twice to reopen the coffin and look at his son. He could not bear to leave him alone in the cold earth. Buried first at Georgetown, Willie's body was returned three years later to Springfield to be buried near his father—"the smallest one for me, the largest one for father," as Willie once wrote in a letter describing some things in a room he and his father once shared on a trip. The fourth son, Thomas (nicknamed Tad), was born with a cleft palate and thus a speech impediment. Lincoln loved him dearly as well. He outlived his father by six years, dying at the age of eighteen after returning from a trip to Europe. All three sons apparently died from respiratory infections.

LINCOLN'S FUNERAL EXPENSES (1865)

As sorrowing and tearful as the participants were at Lincoln's funeral, there was a mercenary limit. The undertaker's charge came to $7,459. The government, of course, was billed for mourning clothes for the White House staff. One typical bill was $125 for a black suit for a footman named Peter. All members of the Senate, House, and departments charged the government for their black armbands and badges. Those who draped the rotunda Tuesday and Wednesday nights charged overtime. Even the public gardeners who supplied the flowers from public grounds put in their bills for flowers, even padding the requisitions heavily. Hundreds of hack (horse for hire) owners put in their claims for eight dollars, the standard price for a full-day rental of a hack. Even Chief Justice Salmon P. Chase put in a bill for eight dollars for the use of his carriage in the procession. The total Washington funeral bill came to exactly $30,000. Lincoln's contemporaries were deeply grieved by his death, but it appears that their grief would have been deeper still had it meant any kind of personal sacrifice for them.

LINCOLN'S LAST WORDS (1865)

After the assassination, Mrs. Lincoln was questioned several times about her husband's last words. She is reported to have given two entirely different versions. In the first version, while leaning over his chair at the theater, she is reported to have asked her husband, "What will Miss Harris think of my hanging on to you so?" (Miss Clara Harris was one of their two guests for the evening.) Lincoln, according to this version, replied, "She won't think anything about it." In her later version the president turned to her just before Booth's shot and said, "How I should like to visit Jerusalem sometime!" This seems less likely because the play they were watching, *Our American Cousin,* was a comedy and hardly the thing to prompt this line of thought. We do know the last words he heard. They were said by Harry Hawk, the comic lead in the play. He was alone on stage and, in referring to a scheming English matron, said, "You sockdologizing old mantrap." John Wilkes Booth timed his shot to coincide with the anticipated laughter.

FORD'S THEATER (1865)

After Lincoln's assassination, the theater was never opened for another performance. The federal government bought it later from its owner, John Ford, and used it for storing Confederate records. Even later it was turned into the Army Medical Museum. The most popular exhibit in this museum, ironically, contained several vertebrae of John Wilkes Booth, vertebrae that had been pierced by the bullet that killed him and were removed from his body during an autopsy.

The theater was used next by the Record and Pension Bureau, and it was during this period that a second—and to many people, greater—tragedy occurred. On the morning of June 9, 1893, all three floors of the old theater, burdened with heavy desks and files, collapsed and fell into the basement, killing twenty-two people and injuring sixty-eight. The theater was later turned over to the National Park Service, which reconstructed it almost as it was in 1865 and reintroduced theatrical plays. The only major difference in the reconstructed theater was in the seating. Because Americans were becoming too broad to fit into the nineteenth-century seats, they were made proportionately larger.

STANTON—THE UNSTABLE ONE (1865)

After the assassination of Lincoln, Secretary of War Edwin Stanton ran the country, single-handedly conducting conspiracy investigations. His strange conduct in these proceedings may have resulted from some degree of guilt or perhaps instability. Thirty-two years before, when a young girl in his boarding house had died of cholera and was buried, Stanton attempted to dig her up, not believing she could really be dead. When his young daughter Lucy died in 1841, Stanton ordered her body exhumed, and he kept the coffin in his room for two years. When his wife died three years later, the future secretary of war dressed and redressed her in her wedding clothes and late at night would roam about the house asking, "Where is Mary"?

It seems ironic that a man whom death would affect so strongly would later be placed in a position in which it became his duty to oversee the deaths of many others.

GRANT'S ABSENCE AT FORD'S THEATER (1865)

Some historians have speculated as to the reason Ulysses S. Grant, invited to the theater on that fateful night in April 1865, lamely begged off going. Some have even hinted at his possible involvement in the assassination plot. The truth lies in nothing more than female jealousy. Lincoln and Grant had grown close during the final years of the war but not so Mrs. Grant and Mrs. Lincoln. As a matter of fact, Mary Todd Lincoln had temper tantrums of jealous rage when she heard that the president had so much as even seen Mrs. Grant alone. Thus Grant was absent, and with his absence came the absence of additional protection the general would more than likely have taken with him. But for a fluke of pettiness, Grant might have been able to save the president. Or Grant himself might have been a victim. Whatever the case, Mrs. Lincoln may have been responsible in more ways than one for the evening ending so tragically for her husband.

LINCOLN REJECTS PEACE PROPOSAL (1865)

Seldom mentioned in history textbooks—probably because it failed—is the peace negotiation meeting in February 1865 involving Lincoln, Secretary of State William Seward, and three Confederate officials, including Vice President Alexander Stephens. At this meeting, on board the *River Queen* at Hampton Roads, the Confederates suggested that the "two nations" conclude a peace treaty for the purpose of joining together in a war against the French in Mexico, a technical enforcement of the Monroe Doctrine. Stephens insisted that history was full of examples of warring nations joining together against a common foe. Lincoln was plainly not interested, replying that he knew nothing of history and was interested in peace under two conditions only: restoration of the Union and the conclusion of slavery. The Southern officials refused to even consider these demands, and the meeting ended, as did the war itself, two months later.

THE MCLEAN HOUSE (1865)

Twice in the early days of the Civil War, fighting swirled around the home of Wilmer McLean at Manassas, Virginia. Determined that their home would not be part of a battlefield for the third time, the McLean family moved into the interior of the state, where they hoped they would be remote from the horrors of war. Remote it seemed until April 1865, when the sound of gunfire announced the worst. The remains of Lee's army was approaching with the mighty army of the Potomac in pursuit. Around 2 P.M. on Palm Sunday, April 9, Generals Lee and Grant met in the front parlor of a farmhouse at Appomattox to arrange final surrender terms—the farmhouse of Wilmer McLean.

CIVIL WAR CASUALTIES (1865)

One of every five participants in the Civil War, North and South, died in service. More Americans died during the Civil War than in World

War I and World War II combined—126,000 and 407,000, respectively. In the Civil War, 618,000 died. The North lost 360,022 men, of whom 67,058 were killed in action and 43,012 died of battle wounds. Confederate records are incomplete, but at least 258,000 Rebels died of all causes in the war. About 94,000 of these were battle fatalities. Sickness, however, was the greatest killer. About 300,000 men from the two armies combined died from diarrhea, dysentery, measles, smallpox, chicken pox, typhoid fever, pneumonia, and gangrene. More than 57,000 Yankees died from intestinal disorders alone. The Union army was, in general, better fed and cared for, but nearly four times as many Yanks died of disease as their Southern counterparts. Prison deaths were another major factor in Civil War casualties. Andersonville and Libby Prisons have come to be synonymous with Southern cruelty and Union sacrifice. So it comes as a surprise to many to learn that, with all its resources, the North allowed almost as many Southerners to die in Northern prisons as Yanks were allowed to die Southern prisons—26,000 to 30,200.

REGIMENTAL CASUALTIES (1865)

The Light Brigade's Charge at Balaklava, as immortalized by Tennyson, is usually recounted as not only an example of military stupidity but also of the extremely high casualties suffered by armies in combat. In that Crimean battle, the Light Brigade suffered losses in killed and wounded of 36.7 percent. In the Civil War, however, 115 regiments—63 Northern and 52 Southern—sustained losses of 50 percent or more in a single engagement. The First Texas Regiment had more than 80 percent casualties at Antietam, as did the First Minnesota at Gettysburg. At the latter battle, the 26th North Carolina claimed the highest losses of any regiment on either side throughout the war. On the first day's battle, its Company F reported 100 percent casualties, and Company E ended the day with two men alive and unhurt out of eighty-two.

The First Maine Heavy Artillery lost all of its men in battle within a period of ten months, most of them from suicidal frontal assaults. At Petersburg the First Main charged with about 900 men in line (about the same as the Light Brigade) and lost 632 of them (twice that of the Light Brigade). Unfortunately, America had no Tennyson to immortalize its Civil War battles.

CIVIL WAR—FIRST MODERN WAR (1865)

The American Civil War deserves the title as the first modern war because of the number of "firsts" it introduced:

- First practical machine gun
- First repeating rifle used in combat
- First use of railroads for warfare
- First extensive use of trenches and field fortifications
- First large-scale use of land mines
- First naval mines or torpedoes
- First combat ironclad ships
- First multimanned submarine
- First organized care of wounded on battlefield
- First portable use of telegraph units
- First aerial reconnaissance (balloon)
- First draft in the United States
- First voting for national elections by men in field
- First income tax to finance war
- First photograph taken in combat
- First Medal of Honor

CIVIL WAR WEAPONS (1865)

The Civil War was innovative in many ways, most dramatically in giving people a glimpse into the hell of future wars and the harvest of death they would reap. On Little Round Top at Gettysburg, the Rebels mistook a hundred Yankees for two regiments because of the destructive firepower of the two new machine guns the Yankees were using. Early in the previous year, soldiers of the 28th Pennsylvania Regiment, fighting near Harpers Ferry (Middleburg, Virginia), used one of these "coffee mill guns" to kill the first soldier ever by a machine gun. We are all familiar with the new breech-loading rifle, mines, iron warships, and aerial balloons, but few of us are aware of the new weapons that were being developed and that would emerge in future conflicts: armored vehicles, incendiary rockets, submarines, and increasingly effective explosives. It is possible that Gen. B. F. Butler of the Union army used a flame-thrower in a battle in 1865. As Henry Adams, concerned about such weapons, prophesied in a letter to his brother, "Some day science may have the existence of mankind in its power, and the human race commit suicide by blowing up the world."

"CRAZY" WILLIAM SHERMAN (1865)

The revered Northern general the South learned to hate passionately as the man most responsible, next to Grant himself, for bringing the South to its knees, came very close to missing all the adulation and notoriety. Redheaded William T. Sherman, after the tragic defeat of the Union at First Bull Run, was sent to command military forces in Kentucky. There his mental health deteriorated quickly, and he developed a neurotic suspicion of all newsmen, imagining himself poised against overwhelming enemy forces and distrusting his own ability to command.

Characterized as "Crazy" Sherman by a hostile press, his military career appeared over, except that Gen. Henry Halleck, and later Grant, still recognized in Sherman a military genius. They gradually coaxed him back to normal confidence in himself—too much so perhaps. With the war over and the defeated Southerners beginning to forgive his depredation as part of the cost of war, he wrote his autobiography. Supremely confident of his own military prowess, he proceeded to belittle Southern generalship, one thing the defeated South still looked to with pride. For this, Southerners could not forgive him, and for the next fifty years any misfortunes in Georgia or South Carolina were blamed on him.

LEW WALLACE: AUTHOR AND JUDGE (1865)

Gen. Lew Wallace, author of the well-known book *Ben Hur,* never let Christianity or its precepts interfere with his pursuit of military justice, or more aptly, revenge. He was one of the military judges at the trial of the Lincoln conspirators, throughout which he showed a consistent lack of both brotherly love and justice. In fact, Judge Wallace so consistently showed his bias against all the accused that Edwin Stanton, secretary of war, rewarded him by appointing him president of the military court that hanged Capt. Henry Wirz, the former commandant of Andersonville Prison, in Georgia. The gross unfairness of Wallace and the court moved the defense attorney to later state that if allowed the same biases, he could easily condemn and hang every member of the military commission on any charge whatever. The injustice of the Andersonville trial might have forever blackened the name of Lew Wallace had not that model of forgiveness, Jesus, offered the general a plot for an all-time best seller.

MILITARY EXECUTIONS (1865)

In the early stages of the Civil War, the death penalty was seldom enforced in the Union army, and when it was, as in the case of desertion, Lincoln often set it aside. As desertions increased with the Gettysburg campaign in 1863, the firing squad came more and more into use. Executions were carried out rapidly and publicly, witnessed by whole brigades in order to make a deep impression on the other troops.

Novels and popular histories, in speaking of Civil War executions, usually associate them with the common offense of sleeping on sentry duty. Many men were found guilty of this offense and were sentenced to be shot, but records fail to show a single such execution being carried out. Records, as usual, are lacking for the South, but nearly complete Union records list 267 wartime executions broken down as follows:

- Desertion 141
- Murder 72
- Rape 23
- Mutiny 20
- Theft or pillage 4
- Spying 3
- Others 4

FAMOUS PEOPLE IN THE CIVIL WAR (1865)

Their claim to fame rests in other areas, but the following famous people served in the Civil War:

- Sidney Lanier, poet, served as a private in the 2d Georgia Battalion. He was captured and imprisoned in Maryland.
- Albert Pike, New England poet, commanded the Confederate Department of Indian Territory. He wrote stanzas for the Southern version of "Dixie."
- Lew Wallace, author of *Ben Hur,* served as a Union general defending the Northern Capitol.
- Mark Twain joined a Missouri company but left it before it was ever mustered into service.
- Henry M. Stanley of "Doctor Livingstone" fame, served with the South at Shiloh, was captured, and later joined the Union army.
- Elias Howe, wealthy sewing machine inventor, joined a Massachusetts Regular as a private. He met regular payroll with his own money when the state became negligent.

- George Westinghouse, of air brake fame, ran away from home and joined the Union army at age fifteen.
- George Dewey, of Manila Bay fame, served as lieutenant under Union Adm. David Farragut at the Battle of Port Hudson. Dewey's ship was the only one lost in the engagement.
- Chris "Kit" Carson commanded the 1st New Mexico Union Volunteers and fought against Comanche, Navajo, and Apache Indians during the war.
- Jesse James served under William Quantrill as one of the notorious Confederate raiders.

AGE OF UNION SOLDIERS (1865)

Wars are always decided by old men but fought by a nation's youth. The Civil War was no exception. Of the 2.3 million men in the Union army from 1861 to 1865, 70 percent were under twenty-three years of age. Approximately 100,000 were only sixteen, and an equal number were only fifteen. Even more inconceivable by modern enlistment standards, three hundred were thirteen or less, and records show that twenty-five were no older than ten. There is no reason to believe the South was less prone to use young boys. If anything, because of a manpower shortage, the Confederate army enlisted a larger percentage of children. The average federal soldier was twenty-five years old, but the largest single age group was eighteen. Above eighteen the numbers in each group decreased until age forty-five—beyond which no enlistment was legally accepted. One boy from Michigan, John L. Clem, enlisted in the Union army at age nine, eventually becoming a major general.

ERA OF THE GUNMAN (1866)

It usually comes as no surprise to those raised on a diet of TV westerns to hear someone like A. M. King, one of Wyatt Earp's deputies, saying, "All of our gun fighting took place in about twenty years." Most western historians are aware that the killers and peace officers so familiar to western Americana buffs operated between 1866 and 1885. Actually, a walk through Boothill in Tombstone, Arizona, will reveal a period of violence much shorter—at least for Tombstone. Most of the markers show a death date between 1880 and 1885. According to King, "The gunfighter was a product of the Civil War," and by 1885 most of them were dead. Their life spans were brief:

Jesse James died at thirty-five, "Wild Bill" Hickok at thirty-nine, King Fisher at thirty, Doc Holliday at thirty-five, Curly Bill Brocius at thirty, John Ringo at thirty-one, Billy the Kid at twenty-one, and Luke Short at thirty-nine. Two outstanding exceptions were Wyatt Earp and Bat Masterson. Earp spent his declining years selling real estate in California and died peacefully at the age of eighty. Masterson wound up in New York working for the New York Telegraph and died at sixty-seven.

PUNISHING THE SOUTH (1866)

The worst enemy former Confederates faced during Reconstruction was the leader of the radical Republicans in the House of Representatives, Thaddeus Stevens. He had his own private plans for the "damned rebel provinces": Carve them up and fill them with new settlers as you would Indian lands. The large estates belonging to the Rebel leaders were to be cut into forty-acre parcels and sold to former slaves at $10 per acre. "I have never desired bloody punishments," he said, "but . . . strip a proud nobility of their bloated estates . . . send them forth to labor . . . and you will thus humble the proud traitors." If they didn't like this, he suggested, they could go to any other country they liked. Thousands didn't wait for such a plan to be enacted—they fled to Canada, Mexico, and South America, where many of them planned to carry on the hopeless fight for Southern independence.

LEE TAKES COMMUNION (1866)

Billy Graham has told the story of an unusual communion service that took place soon after the Civil War in a fashionable church in Richmond, Virginia. A black man dared not only to attend church service, but when time for the communion came, he also proceeded to the front of the church and knelt at the altar. As shock and rising anger swept the congregation, a distinguished member of the church walked to the front and knelt beside him to share the communion. Impressed by this brotherly spirit, the rest of the congregation soon followed suit. In war or peace, the Southern people felt that Robert E. Lee could do no wrong, and where he led they would follow.

JOHNSON'S HUMILIATION (1866)

In the latter part of 1866, President Andrew Johnson made a tour of the East and Midwest, attempting to rally public opinion against the radical Republicans who demanded harsh treatment for the former Confederate states. The president's treatment at the hands of the crowds whom he addressed was an insult to the office—no president ever received greater disrespect that he did throughout the tour. Grant, Farragut, and Secretary of State William Seward were with him, and most of the favorable treatment went to Grant. Johnson, on the other hand, was booed down in almost every city. Before the tour was completed, Johnson knew that the Lincoln plan of peaceful restoration of the South was dead and that future generations would reap the whirlwind of the hate Johnson had experienced.

"UNCLE BILLY" BUYS AN EMPIRE (1867)

Perhaps it was prophetic that the American secretary of the navy, upon the arrival of the Russian fleet in New York Harbor in 1863, should record in his diary, "God bless the Russians." Late one evening four years later, while Secretary of State William Seward was playing cards, the Russian minister to America stopped in to see him, informing the American official that Czar Alexander II was willing to sell all of Russian America for $7,200,000. Never a man to postpone decisions, Seward offered to close the deal at once. When the Russian pointed out that the State Department office was closed, Seward said to report to his office anyway before midnight. By 4 A.M. Baron de Stoeckel had put his signature to the deal, turning over 375 million acres for less than two cents per acre.

For more than a century the Soviet government accused the United States of stealing this vast Russian empire through underhanded work, once suggesting that Seward got the Russian minister drunk before making the deal. In one sense it was a steal. In 1969 alone, the sale of oil leases on the North Slope brought $900 million into the state of Alaska.

CODY GETS A NEW NAME (1867)

The hunting deeds that earned William Cody the nickname of "Buffalo Bill" are familiar to most Americans, but the actual hunting statistics, when revealed, become somewhat staggering to the imagination. Cody, who became the man in his family at the age of eleven in 1857, was adept with both a gun and a horse. At the age of fourteen, he was a Pony Express rider, and when he was sixteen, he was the protégé of Marshal

James "Wild Bill" Hickok of Hays, Kansas. At the age of twenty-one, he at last found himself when the Kansas Pacific Railroad hired him at the unheard-of wages of $500 per month to furnish 1,200 track layers with buffalo meat. His quota was set at twelve buffalo a day, utilizing, according to his own autobiography, only the humps and hindquarters. Within the next eighteen months he killed no less than 4,280 of these Great Plains animals. His reputation as "Buffalo Bill" assured him success as the first and greatest "Wild West" entertainer, with his name and show known around the world. He started with his own show in 1883 and made his last appearance with the Miller Brothers Show in 1916.

UNITED STATES HAS NO CITIZENS (1867)

After the Civil War, Confederate president Jefferson Davis was tried before Salmon P. Chase, chief justice of the U.S. Supreme Court, on a charge of treason against the United States. The case against him was dropped for the following and most interesting supposition. The chief justice asked the question, "Could a person be accused of treason against the United States if he were not a citizen of the United States?" The obvious answer was, "No." Chase then pursued this line of thought by asking where in the Constitution there is mentioned any such thing as a citizen of the United States. The answer was again, "No such thing." It was agreed that a person was legally only a citizen of his own state. Thus, Davis went free in 1867 because constitutionally there is no such thing as an American citizen. Several cases of treason have been tried since 1867, but there is no recorded case of a similar defense.

IF JOHNSON HAD BEEN REMOVED (1868)

Many of us today shudder at what the removal of Andrew Johnson would have meant to America: the impotency of the office of president and the destruction of the system of checks and balances. Conviction in the impeachment proceedings could have had more drastic, immediate effects than this, however. Had Johnson been ousted from office, the next man in line for the highest office in the land was the president pro-tem of the Senate, Sen. Ben Wade. If his words bespoke his true thoughts, a bloodbath following his ascension to office was not inconceivable: "There is no doubt that if by an insurrection [African-Americans] could contrive to slay one half of their oppressors, the other half would hold them in the highest respect and no doubt treat them with justice." Such sentiments, expressed by the nation's chief executive, might well have encouraged land-hungry and revenge-seeking former slaves to institute a reign of terror against their former white oppressors. Ben Wade, fortunately, never became president.

ARRESTING A PRESIDENT (1868)

Ulysses S. Grant delighted in racing fast horses. He owned several, including a fast pacer named "Jeff Davis." As president he once raced down a street a few blocks from the White House. A police officer, not recognizing the driver, ran into the street and grabbed the team, bringing the horses to a halt. When the arresting officer realized whom he had stopped, he attempted to apologize. Grant stopped him, saying, "Officer, do your duty," whereupon the patrolman drove the horse and rig back to his station house while an amused president walked back to the executive mansion. The speeding charges were never pressed.

Grant was not the only president to run afoul of the law while in office. President Franklin Pierce came close to being arrested when one of his horses ran down an old woman. Actually, presidents are immune from arrest while in office unless they voluntarily submit.

TWO BILLION OR CANADA (1869)

During the Civil War, several Confederate ships were built or armed by Britons, resulting ultimately in the destruction of much Northern shipping and the driving up of insurance rates. After the war the United States entered claims against the British government for damages wrought by eleven Confederates ships, totaling approximately $19 million. Most of this loss was caused by the Confederate cruisers *Alabama* and *Shenandoah*. When England failed to respond to American demands, Sen. Charles Sumner gave a speech in which he blamed England not only for the damage to Northern shipping but also for lengthening the war by more than two years through her support of the South. Considering the actual cost of the war, he estimated the total bill owed America to be more than $2 billion. He felt that such a demand could only be met by the cession of Canada. Such demands ceased when an international tribunal awarded the United States $15.5 million in gold, which both the British and the American governments agreed to.

"PREMIUM PIGS, PREMIUM MEN" (1869)

"Every race-horse, every straight-backed bull, every premium pig tells us what we can do and what we must do for men." Thus began the first organized experiment in human eugenics by John Humphrey Noyes and his Oneida Community.

Members of the communal society in upstate New York believed that the second coming of Christ had occurred centuries before and that mortal men could consequently be perfect here and now. Part of this perfection was love and sex free of passion, sin, or shame: "The marriage supper . . . is a feast at which every dish is free to every guest." In addition to the complex marriage aspect with "dishes" passed around for the consummation of all, it was recommended that older women initiate young men into the art of love while mature men guided the maidens. As if these "ethics of the barnyard" were not more than enough for their more Puritan neighbors, Noyes went one step further in 1869 with his "stirpiculture," or controlled breeding program. The selected matings (at first by Noyes and later by committee) were based on physical, spiritual, moral, and intellectual suitability. Outside pressure finally forced the abandonment of the experiment but not before Noyes himself had fathered nine children.

HIGH COST OF EDUCATION IN NEW YORK CITY (1870)

William Marcy Tweed's list of public robberies in New York City is fairly common knowledge—the selling of $50 desks from his own furniture company to the city for $5,000 each, submitting to the city outrageous street-cleaning bills from his nonexistent street-cleaning companies, and so forth. The ultimate perhaps was a bill from Tweed's Manufacturing Stationary Company for supplies furnished to the cities' schools in April 1870.

For six reams of paper, twenty-four pen holders, four ink bottles, twelve sponges for blotting ink, three dozen boxes of rubber bands, and six rulers, the city received a bill for $10,000, which School Commissioner William Marcy Tweed promptly paid. Even 130 years of inflation hasn't yet caught up with such prices.

WOMAN SUFFRAGE OR SUFFERING MEN! (1870)

Few people recognize the name Esther Morris, much less associate it with women's suffrage. The truth is, half a century before women received the right to vote, Esther Morris almost single-handedly brought it about in Wyoming, the first state to enact legislation allowing women to vote. Mrs. Morris used anything but gentle tactics, however, in bringing this about.

Her efforts started, appropriately enough, in the gateway to the West, South Pass City. When Mrs. Morris first approached the subject, she received the expected cold shoulder from the town's leadership and the local delegate to the territorial legislature in Cheyenne. Suddenly every woman in town, from the most pious housewife to the joy girls at Magnolia and Fatty's place, turned prim—and remote. The local power structure got the message, and when William Bright, the local delegate, introduced a bill for women's suffrage in Cheyenne at the next legislature, the legislators had already heard about it. When the territorial legislature showed resistance, the women of Cheyenne made a trial run of no suppers and extreme tiredness. The legislature knuckled under, and women's suffrage became law.

THE GREATEST BRIBE OFFERS (1872)

That boss of all corrupt city bosses, William Marcy Tweed, whose "ring" controlled New York City after the Civil War, essentially owned the nation's greatest city and state, with puppets in the governor's mansion, state legislature, municipal offices, and courts. His standing rule that all bills submitted to the city and counties of New York were to be at least 50 percent fraudulent, and similar corrupt practices, allowed him to misappropriate no less than $30 million and possibly $200 million from the taxpayers of New York before he was finally indicted and found guilty on 204 out of 220 counts in 1872. The "Boss" was brought to justice largely because a few men could not be bought. One was George Jones of the *New York Times,* and the other was Thomas Nast, who drew cartoons for *Harper's Weekly,* and to whom Tweed offered five million dollars and half a million dollars, respectively, to stay silent. They weren't for sale.

AN HONEST PRESIDENT (1872)

America has had presidents who, in their early years, found it necessary to kill other men in war or in duels, but only one was put in a position of having to personally execute criminals. As sheriff of Erie County,

New York, from 1871 to 1873, he could have delegated such official duties as hanging criminals, but he carried them out himself. In 1872 he sprang the trap on Patrick Morrissey, convicted of killing his mother; and the following year he did the same with Jack Gaffney, a gambler who killed a man during a card game.

Grover Cleveland's sense of duty as sheriff was a portent to what was expected of him in later years when he became president. "Henceforth I must have no friends," he declared when he became president. Probably more so than any other president, he lived up to his beliefs in absolute honesty. Some of his former Democrat cohorts said that this hardworking, 260-pound president behaved as though he had never heard of the Democrat Party.

ECOLOGY—EARLY WESTERN STYLE (1872)

Richard Irving Dodge describes a typical western hunting expedition of the late 1800s southeast of Fort Dodge, which he recounted as "the most delightful hunting of this kind I have ever had." Within twenty days, Dodge, another American officer, and three English gentlemen bagged 1,262 animals for sport, including the following:

- 127 buffalo
- 17 herons
- 2 badgers
- 2 deer (red)
- 6 cranes
- 7 raccoons
- 11 antelope
- 187 quail
- 11 rattlesnakes
- 154 turkeys
- 32 grouse
- 143 meadow larks, doves, and robins
- 5 geese
- 84 field plover
- 33 yellow legs (snipe)
- 45 mallard ducks
- 12 jack snipe
- 3 shell-ducks
- 49 shovel-bill
- 1 pigeon

- 57 widgeon
- 9 hawks
- 38 butter-ducks
- 3 owls

INVENTION OF TRAIN ROBBERY (1873)

Train robbery, the standard crime in countless western movies, is reputed by some historians to have been invented by the James brothers on July 21, 1873. A short distance out of Adair, Iowa, the James gang loosened a rail of the Rock Island Railroad and attached a rope to it. As the train approached, they pulled the rail aside, causing the train to wreck and killing the engineer. The gang then looted the cars of $3,000—not bad for a day's work. They could have done much better, however, had they not miscalculated the schedule. An express carrying $75,000 was scheduled for twelve hours later.

Careful historians credit the James-Youngers with the first bank robbery, in 1866, but not the first train robbery, which also occurred in the year 1866. The credit, most historians claim, should go to the Reno brothers, who robbed their first train at Seymour, Indiana, on October 6, 1866, and got away with $13,000. Approximately twenty trains were robbed between 1866 and 1873, when the James brothers made their first attempt.

BONE PICKING (1874)

In the latter years of the nineteenth century, an unusual occupation developed on the Great Plains. Men with wagons started harvesting the plains for buffalo bones for shipment to fertilizer factories. The supply seemed endless as a result of the great slaughter during the preceding years. The Santa Fe Railroad alone reported shipping out ten to twenty tons of bones each day, and other railroads were shipping even more. In 1874, a *New York Daily Tribune* correspondent reported some unusual rewards in this strange business:

"In sorting bones for market, strange discoveries are sometimes made. It is no uncommon thing, for instance, to find Indian skulls, legs, and arms; and in some cases the skulls and vertebrae of women and children have been picked up. The latter are usually tossed aside as a sort of rude reverence for the helpless and innocent; but no such respect is paid to the bones of an Indian. The Indian skull is said to be worth $1.25 for combs, and the Indian thigh makes knife handles that are beautiful to behold."

ANDREW JOHNSON'S COURAGE (1875)

After President Johnson's fateful term in the White House, he decided to run for the U.S. Senate, if for no other reason than to vindicate his character. It took courage, for threats on his life were common. Informed that a speech by him attacking his opponent would be a signal for his assassination, Johnson mounted the soapbox before the courthouse in Columbia, Tennessee, and thundered in defiance, "These eyes have never yet beheld the man this heart feared! I have said it and I repeat it now, Jesus Christ had his Judas, Caesar had his Brutus, Charles I had his Cromwell, Washington had his Benedict Arnold, and I have my Edmond Cooper." Pistols could be heard clicking to full cock in the crowd, but none was fired. In 1875 the state legislature, on the 52d ballot, elected Johnson to his old senate seat—the only former president ever to succeed. Johnson was at least vindicated by his own state.

THE JUKES (1875)

"The Jukes" is the alias given to a family in New York State in 1875— a family that was the subject of a sociological study by R. L. Dugdale because of its extremely high rate of crime, pauperism, and degeneracy. Information on 709 of the 1,200 descendants of Margaret Jukes, the "Mother of Criminals," turned up 140 who had been imprisoned for crime, 280 paupers, 50 common prostitutes, and 30 who had been prosecuted for bastardy. A large proportion of the rest were licentious or had sexually transmitted diseases. A follow-up study of the same family forty years later found that out of 748 scattered members that could be traced, 323 were found in the same debased categories.

This family study has been frequently contrasted with studies made of the descendants of Jonathan Edwards, the early American minister who had twelve children. The number of worthy and important descendants those children produced has become proverbial.

"COMANCHE" (1876)

Two days after the Battle of the Little Big Horn, U.S. Army troops, in gathering together the dead, discovered a horse standing in a ravine.

The horse had several wounds from bullets and arrows, and it was nearly dead from loss of blood. Soldiers removed the arrowheads and bullets, and then they dressed the animal's wounds. "Comanche," the "clay-bank sorrel" charger belonging to Capt. M. W. Keogh, who perished with his entire troop in the battle, soon became the special charge of the entire 7th Cavalry, and orders were given that no one should ride him again. One man was detailed to feed and care for Comanche thereafter and to lead him, draped in black, in all future dress parades. Comanche finally died twelve years after Little Big Horn at Fort Riley, Kansas, where the 7th Cavalry was stationed at the time.

CUSTER MASSACRE SURVIVOR (1876)

One of the most intriguing episodes in American history involves the Col. Custer massacre on the Little Big Horn and the controversy over survivors. Most historians tend to agree that the only possible survivor of the actual battle was Comanche, one of the horses. Others, however, believe that a man named Curley, one of Custer's Crow scouts, also survived. Forty-four hours after the battle, Curley arrived at the mouth of the Little Big Horn and reported to the steamer *Far West* news of the massacre. He claimed that being an Indian enabled him to escape in the confusion of the battle. For years his detailed description of the battle was the only eyewitness account heard by the whites until the stories of the former hostiles were related. When the Sioux told their side of the battle years later, Chief Gall dismissed Curley's story of escape as impossible, and historians have agreed. Perhaps it is more romantic to believe that a horse was the sole survivor.

DEAD MAN'S HAND (1876)

"Wild Bill" Hickok was responsible for the phrase "d ead man's hand," used in poker to refer to a hand consisting of a pair of aces (some say jacks) over eights—a full house. Wild Bill reportedly held such a hand at the time Jack McCall shot him in Deadwood, South Dakota, on August 2, 1876. Some poker players maintain that a dead man's hand is lucky and seldom beaten. In certain wild games it wins over everything, even a royal flush. Hickok died because, momentarily forgetting the habits of a lifetime of caution, he allowed himself to sit with his back to an open door. He was shot through the heart from behind and died almost instantly.

Despite this fact, he had his gun halfway out of his holster before he hit the floor.

"WE DIDN'T MEAN THIS LONG!" (1878)

In 1878 a starving band of Arapahoe Indians appealed to the U.S. Army for a place to stay in peace. Washakie, chief of the Shoshone tribe on the Wind River Reservation, reluctantly granted the army permission for their former Arapahoe enemies to stay until spring. But they stretched their stay into years, to the bitter protests of the Shoshones. Finally, Washakie asked the army to put on paper his official protest: "I don't like these people; they eat their dogs. . . . If you leave them here there will be trouble. . . . When the grass comes again take them off my reservation. . . . I want you all to sign as witnesses to what I have said. . . . I have spoken." Washakie was no fool. Fifty years later, partly because of this official complaint, a court decision awarded the Shoshone nation $4.5 million for suffering the presence of the "dog-eating" Indians. The same Shoshone chief is noted for one of the shortest Indian speeches on record. In 1887, after listening for hours to his minor chief and Indian Bureau officials debate small-truck farming, he rose and cut the debate short with the most majestic simplicity: "G– damn a potato!"

THE MASTERSONS (1880)

The truth about the so-called western hero Bat Masterson has been difficult to uncover after decades of glorifying fictionalized accounts. One of the most dramatic examples of historical distortion is revealed by the U.S. Census Report for June 1880 in Dodge City, Kansas:

> James Masterson, age twenty-four, City Marshal of Dodge City,
> Dwelling with Minnie Roberts, age sixteen, occupation concubine.
> Bat Masterson, age twenty-five, occupation laborer, dwelling
> With Annie Ladue, age nineteen, occupation concubine.

Interestingly enough, Bat Masterson was a friend of Teddy Roosevelt, who said he admired men with "guts." Offered a job as U.S. marshal of Arizona, Bat turned it down and instead accepted from Roosevelt a position as deputy marshal of New York. He moved to New York, and for the last seventeen years of his life he worked on a newspaper there. He died with his boots off and a pen in his hand—certainly not the Bat Masterson of television fame.

WESTERN "VIOLENCE" (1880)

The United States is a violent country—ask any European who watches American television. And the reason usually given is the presence of an ever-expanding and violent frontier. However, just how violent was the American West?

Western historian Robert West Howard estimates that between 1865 and 1900, Native American raids and army campaigns took a total of not more than 5,000 lives—Indian, African-American, and white. One source listed exactly 2,571 white men, military and civilian, killed and wounded. The army estimated 5,519 casualties. In the year 2000, auto accidents in the United States claimed nearly 42,000 lives. Barroom brawls, shoot-outs, and violent crimes "caused not more than two thousand, probably closer to one thousand murders." That compares to 15,517 murders in the United States during the year 2000.

According to Howard, the violence-prone Western heroes and anti-heroes are not the least bit typical—any more than Lizzie Borden was a typical New Englander. Of people like Wyatt Earp, Buffalo Bill, Calamity Jane, the Pony Express riders, the mountain men, it has been said, "In all, one hundred to two hundred men form the prototype of the nineteenth-century Westerner."

A CRIPPLED CHIEF (1881)

The exploits of Cochise and Geronimo are legendary, partly because the names themselves are catchy and romantic. The name Nana just doesn't rank with the great Indian heroes' names. And yet this proud but crippled old Chiricahua chief, for a few short months in 1881, exceeded the exploits of any other Indian leader. With a tiny group of warriors—no more than fifteen of his own tribe, together with less than twice that many Mescaleros—he fought a campaign against the military and civilian establishments of both Mexico and the United States. He fought an average of one battle a week, winning against a thousand U.S. troops, Texas Rangers, civilian possees, and Mexican military and police. At this time Nana was between seventy and eighty years old and so crippled from old injuries and rheumatism that he had to walk with a cane.

Four years later Nana broke from a reservation at Turkey Creek, Arizona, because military authorities tried to prevent the Apaches from following the tribal custom of beating their wives. Upon leaving, Nana said,

"Tell the Stout Chief (the military commander) that he can't advise me how to treat my women. He is only a boy. I killed men before he was born."

GARFIELD: LAST "LOG CABIN" PRESIDENT (1881)

James Garfield, who moved into the White House in 1881, started life at the lowest possible level. Like Lincoln, he was born in a primitive log cabin and was the last U.S. president to be born into such surroundings. The year was 1832. When James was only two, his father died fighting a forest fire that threatened their small log cabin, leaving the courageous pioneer mother alone to raise her "four young saplings." Young James was doing a man's work when he was only ten, working as a bargeman, farmer, and carpenter. He still managed to get an education, leading any class he was in. Seeing her son rise from log cabin to the White House, his aged mother lived to see her son inaugurated and, four months later, die at the hands of an assassin.

Ironically, Lincoln, the first president to be assassinated, started Garfield along the same route to his similar fate. During the Civil War, Garfield was serving the Union as a major general when an Ohio constituency elected him to Congress. He had no intention of serving, but Lincoln persuaded him to resign an army commission to serve as a congressman. This move was the beginning of a national political career that led him to eventually follow Lincoln to the White House and violent death.

GARFIELD'S PROLONGED DEATH (1881)

James Garfield, the fourth president to die in office and the second to die by assassination, was shot in a Washington railroad station on July 2, 1881. The assassin, Charles Guiteau, was caught, convicted, and hung, but he caused Garfield to suffer a slow, painful demise before death claimed him on September 19. At one point Alexander Graham Bell was called in to help locate the bullet that physicians were unable to find. He devised a metal detector, but it was unsuccessful because of the metal bedsprings on which the president lay. Finally, two and a half months after being shot in the spine, Garfield died from infection and internal hemorrhage. Modern medical practices such as X-rays, surgery, and antibiotics would undoubtedly have saved Garfield. His spent his last moments of life wondering about his place in history. Ironically, the remembrance accorded him is usually concerned only with the tragedy of his death.

FENCE OR DE-FENCE? (1883)

From America's earliest colonial days, Europeans looked upon the American custom of building fences as further evidence of barbarism. Fields in Europe were set off with hedges or ditches, and cows were tended by shepherds. But in the Colonies, fences, derived from the word "defence," became predominant. The origin of the fence led Europeans to remark that Americans were more concerned with inhospitably keeping people out than keeping cattle in.

As an indication of U.S. fence-building mania, the Iowa Agricultural Report of 1883 stated that the United States had six million miles of rail fences built at a conservative cost of $325 per mile, which totals $2 billion for the entire country. Considering the purchasing power of the dollar in those days and the fact that $2 billion was also the size of the national debt, the importance of the now picturesque rail fence becomes evident. It should also be evident that a great deal of first-growth forest went into all this fencing. In many cases it was not worn-out soil that prompted western migration as much as it was lack of fence materials.

HE MUST HAVE BEEN REPUBLICAN (1883)

Every year Lake City, Colorado, reenacts the trial of Alfred Packer, who was tried and convicted on charges of cannibalism and murder in 1883. While stranded in the mountains that year, Packer killed and ate five companions, for which he was sentenced to be hung. The judge later commuted his sentence to forty years in prison. Fifteen years later the *Old Denver Post* got him a parole and hired him as a doorman. He worked there until his death in 1907—old, free, and by then full of memories. A local legend says that when the judge pronounced his sentence, he made the observation, "There was seven Democrats in Hinsdale County, and you et five of them."

GRANT'S TOUGHEST BATTLE (1885)

After retirement from the presidency, Ulysses S. Grant discovered that he was no more adept in business than in controlling the corruption in his presidential administration. By 1884 he was penniless and

in ill health. Friends, including Mark Twain, persuaded Grant to write his memoirs. (Twain would later publish them.) Dying at this time of cancer, Grant retired to a secluded home in upstate New York and valiantly struggled to finish the massive task of writing. Not wanting to leave his family penniless, he hurried toward completion in the spring of 1885, although each day was more torturous. When cancer had destroyed his voice and he could no longer dictate to a stenographer, he huddled under blankets and scribbled on sheets of paper. Finally, his pain-wracked body could take no more, and he succumbed in July 1885, only seven days after completing his memoirs. He won his last great battle, however, and his family received half a million dollars from the general's efforts.

PART THREE

A NEW CENTURY
(1886–1950)

THE YOUNGEST FIRST LADY (1886)

Friends couldn't understand why the new president, Grover Cleveland, was so irritable. Gorging himself on steaks and chops for breakfast and huge beef and cabbage dinners, the 260-pound bachelor was hiding his frustrations and love for an attractive girl just out of college. In 1885 he apparently felt brave enough to propose—and was accepted. The youngest first lady, Frances Folsom Cleveland, was only twenty-one when she moved into the White House. Her marriage to the forty-nine-year-old bachelor in 1886 marked the only wedding ceremony of a chief executive in the Executive Mansion. On the day of the wedding, Cleveland did a full day's work before the 7 P.M. ceremony, in which the president deleted the word "obey" from the bride's vows. During the president's second administration, Mrs. Cleveland became the first wife of a president to give birth to a child in the White House.

APACHE JOURNEY (1886)

When Geronimo, the last of the fighting Apache chiefs, was shipped to Florida in 1886 with seven hundred of his warriors aboard a train, one of the prisoners escaped just after they passed St. Louis. The sole thought of this lonely and frightened Apache was to return home to

Arizona, almost two thousand miles away—and he did it. He escaped from the prison train in a thickly settled part of the country and made his way across Illinois, Missouri, Oklahoma, Texas, and New Mexico. He was without any weapons or maps, and he had to find food each day. His instinct guided him straight to his home in Arizona, which he reached in the fall of 1887 without a single human eye being laid on him during that entire time and distance. Only an Indian could accomplish such a feat—and his story ended like any other Indian story. After a series of one-man raids and kidnappings, he was reportedly killed, and to this day his identity is unknown.

"TO THE LAST MAN" (1887)

The history of the American West is a history of conflicts among various occupational groups, but the most vicious of all the conflicts were the cattle-sheep wars. The nature of sheep grazing, the invasion of what was considered private land, economic competition, and even race all contributed to the antagonism between cowboys and sheep men. In 1902, while the wars were still raging, a writer in *The Outlook* quoted an authority as saying that in the previous ten years, cowboys had killed 600,000 sheep, and "five hundred man-killings have annually accompanied the sheep-killings." On the other hand, a state official in Wyoming denied these estimates, saying, "In all the sheep killings by cowboys during these thirty-six years the number will not exceed twenty five thousand . . . and the killings . . . will not exceed fifty." The truth most likely lies between these estimates.

The bloodiest of all these feuds lasted from 1887 to 1892 in Arizona. The Tonto Basin War was between the Tewksbury family, which had hired their guns to some sheep men, and the Graham family, who were cattlemen. Within that five-year period, one authority listed thirty-three victims, including eleven innocent people. As Zane Grey described in *To the Last Man,* the war ended only when the males on both sides had been virtually eliminated.

"THE MAGIC CITY" (1889)

At noon on April 22, 1889, the "city" of Guthrie, Oklahoma, consisted of a small station house, a Wells Fargo Express shanty, and a Government Land Office. By nightfall it was a city of ten thousand people, completely laid out with streets, staked lots, and the start of buildings. This "magic city" was the result of the greatest race for land in American history. When the signal was sounded at noon that day, 100,000 people who had lined the borders of the Oklahoma district surged forward on horseback, in wagons and trains, and even on foot pushing wheelbarrows. A few hours later there was no land left for claiming; at Guthrie, as across the territory, thousands squatted at night on property that at forenoon had been virgin prairie. Paradoxically, the city of Guthrie today has almost the same population it had within twelve hours of its founding more than a hundred years ago—a living monument to American organizational ability and enterprise.

HARRISON THE TRADITIONALIST (1889)

In 1889, one hundred years after Washington took the oath of office as president, Benjamin Harrison returned to the site at old Federal Hall in New York City to reenact the nation's first inauguration. Impressed by the show of flags along Wall Street, Harrison started the custom of flying the national colors from all public buildings.

America's twenty-third president is also credited with the establishment of another even more delightful custom. Four men have been given credit for the solid entrenchment of the Santa Claus legend in America. Washington Irving started the whole trend in America with his *Knickerbocker's History of New* York in 1809. In 1863 Thomas Nast started drawing annual Christmas pictures of Santa Claus for *Harper's Weekly.* In 1882 the Rev. Clement C. Moore wrote a poem that initially shamed him—"The Night Before Christmas." Santa Claus was assured American immortality, however, in 1891 when Benjamin Harrison told a news reporter, "We shall have an old-fashioned Christmas, and I myself intend to dress up as Santa Claus for the children. If my influence goes for aught in this busy world, I hope that my example will be followed by every family in the land."

THE LAST BATTLE (1890)

The last few days of 1890 saw the final pitched battle between Indians and whites in the United States. The 7th Cavalry, guarding a captured band of 200–350 Hunkpapa Sioux at Wounded Knee Creek, South Dakota, attempted to disarm the braves. A minor disturbance erupted into a full-scale slaughter, with the surrounding troops firing Hotchkiss guns into the Sioux camp. The shooting continued as long as any Indian men, women, or children moved; some women were pursued as far as three miles before they were caught and killed. More than two hundred Sioux were gunned down, whereas the whites lost only twenty-nine. Many of the wounded froze to death in a blizzard the next day. Appropriately, the Indian wars had closed with another atrocity by the whites. Also appropriately, in that same year the U.S. Census Bureau discovered that there was no longer a distinct frontier line, and the frontier was declared closed. The last of the Indian barrier vanished with the frontier.

EIGHT GEORGE WASHINGTONS (1899)

Exactly one hundred years from the date of George Washington's second inauguration, in 1799, the roster of the Fifty-Third Congress found eight congressmen with the Christian name of George Washington:

- George Washington Smith, Illinois
- George Washington Fithian, Illinois
- George Washington Ray, New York
- George Washington Houk, Ohio
- George Washington Hulick, Ohio
- George Washington Wilson, Ohio
- George Washington Shell, South Carolina
- George Washington Murray, South Carolina

This was either an amazing coincidence, or the name Washington was still quite a political asset.

"THE MOST PROFANE CALLING" (1895)

Shaking out logs in the great Northwest was primarily the job of bull teams driven by that most important man of the woods, the bullwhacker. The authority on the subject, Stewart Holbrook, refers to this job as the most profane calling in North America:

"His profanity long ago became legendary in the Western woods. When he raised his voice in blasphemous obscenity, the very bark of the smaller fir trees was said to have smoked a minute, then curled up and fallen to the ground. No sailor, no truck driver, no logger who hadn't driven bulls could hope to touch its heights of purple fluidity. And when both goadstick and profanity failed to rouse the plodding oxen to their best, the bullwhacker might leap upon the animals' backs and walk the entire length of the team, stepping heavily with his caulked boots and yelling like all the devils in hell."

HE JUST LIKED TO JUMP (1896)

The Olympic Games, of course, go back to ancient Greece, but their modern counterpart was not reestablished until the spring of 1896, with eight countries taking part. The cooperating American team consisted of only eleven athletes, nine of them sponsored by the Boston Athletic Association. Two others joined the team independently, one a discus thrower from Princeton and the other a jumper from Harvard. The first scheduled event in the modern Olympics was the hop, step, and jump, and when the event concluded that afternoon in Athens, it was the young Harvard student who had won the olive wreath of victory with a combined jump of forty-five feet. When the playing of the "Star Spangled Banner" had ended, King George read the name of the first modern Olympic champion, James B. Connolly of South Boston. But it was his city and his country that proudly accepted the credit, not Harvard. Harvard had expelled him for attending the games.

TEDDY AND THE SPANISH-AMERICAN WAR (1898)

After the sinking of the battleship *Maine* in Havana Harbor in February 1898, Spanish officials did everything in their power to avert war with the United States, but American imperialists and yellow journalists such as William Randolph Hearst were whipping up the war fever. One of the leaders of the war hawks was Assistant Secretary Teddy Roosevelt. When President William McKinley balked at sending a war message to Congress, Teddy raged, "McKinley has no more backbone than a chocolate eclair." Pressure from the country, but especially from men of influence such as Roosevelt, who called McKinley a "white livered cur," finally forced the reluctant president's hand. Teddy reveled in the resulting war, raising his own regiment and personally leading them in combat.

It is another irony of history that this same devoted follower of the Mahan school of imperialism and war, the same "Big Stick" advocate who secretly delighted in the early victories of the Japanese over the Russians in 1904 because "Japan is playing our game," became the first American president to win the Nobel Peace Prize in 1906 for negotiating peace between Russia and Japan in 1905.

INFORMING THE ENEMY (1898)

Teddy Roosevelt and his Rough Riders assured the Battle of San Juan Hill a lasting place in the annals of American military history. A little less glorious is an interesting sidelight of that particular battle. With the Cuban Expeditionary Force was a Signal Corps detachment that possessed a large observation balloon. Both sides had used these in the Civil War with some success. In Cuba, however, the use of one balloon was little short of a fiasco.

The Americans advancing on the San Juan heights, aware of only one approach through the dense growth, marched along the Santiago Road in closely packed formations. Actually, the road was more of a trail, and the Spaniards had it zeroed in with their artillery. This could have spelled disaster, but to compound their military ineptitude, the Signal Corps sent its one balloon aloft, controlled and moved by men on the ground. To better view the Spanish positions, it was moved into position on the trail with Roosevelt's advancing and horseless cavalry. The balloon accurately marked for the Spanish the exact location and position of the Americans, who recoiled from the resulting enemy fire until the balloon itself was brought to earth by the Spanish fire.

SELLING PAUPERS (1899)

An early American custom called for local authorities to auction off people with no homes, relatives, or means of support to the lowest bidder for a term of feeble service and meager keep. This usually took place at the local tavern and consisted of young children and aged folk. Apparently, the custom was still around as late as 1899, at least in Pike County, Pennsylvania. A seventy-seven-year-old woman, Mrs. Elmira Quick, who had three living sons and a daughter, was put on the auction block at Rowland Station by the overseer of the poor. When the lowest bid of $1.50 a week was made by a backwoodsman, Mrs. Quick bid $1.25 a week, assuring authorities that she could maintain herself on such an amount—eighteen cents a day. The sale papers were drawn up, but the records don't show how well she lived on that princely allowance.

AND CONGRESS LAUGHED! (1899)

As the nineteenth century came to a close, Congress saluted it with a series of typical speeches. That of John J. Fitzgerald of Massachusetts was one of these:

"Think for this moment what a hundred years has brought forth. This century received from its predecessor the horse; we bequeath the bicycle, the locomotive and the automobile. We received the goosequill; we bequeath the typewriter. We received the sickle; we bequeath the harvester. . . . We received the cotton and wool loom; we bequeath the factory.

"We received gunpowder; we bequeath nitroglycerine. We received the tallow dip; we bequeath the arc light. We received the flintlock; we bequeath the automatic firing gun. . . . We received the old-fashioned sailing ship; we bequeath the ocean greyhound. . . .

"Perhaps with the coming of the twentieth century airships may be invented to sail from this country to other parts of the world." A hearty legislative laugh followed such an outrageous prediction.

NEAR EXTINCTION OF BUFFALO (1900)

When the first whites landed on the East Coast, the American bison was there to meet them. It has been estimated that in 1600 there were as many as a hundred million bison, herds stretching from Maryland to Florida to the West Coast. According to archaeologists, bison had supplied the Indian with his basic necessities for at least ten thousand years. By 1900 there were only about 20 wild bison left in the United States, another 100 in captivity, and perhaps as many as 250 in Canada. The disastrous decline to near extinction is a sad but well-known story.

In 1845 alone an estimated two million bison were taken by commercial hunters. One hunter, known as "Sharpy" and working out of Dodge City, hired fifteen skinners to keep up with his kills. He claimed a record of 1,500 in one week and 250 in one day. Many hunters recorded season kills of more than 3,000. One surveying party records finding 6,500 skinned carcasses rotting on the prairie. The American Fur Company recorded 110,000 robes and 25,000 tongues sent to St. Louis in 1848.

Today the bison is safe. About 15,000 roam on 200 ranges and 450 private ranches in forty-six different states, covering about the same geographic area they did three hundred years ago.

INDIAN USE OF BISON (1900)

One of the things that infuriated the Indians about the whites was their senseless waste of buffalo, often using no more than the delicate tongue. To all Indians, every pound of the great animal was used. They never hunted it for sport, and wasting any portion of it was a sin against the Great Spirit. Indians ate every edible portion, and they made the skins into bull boats, tepees, beds, robes, and winter clothing, from moccasins and leggings to cloaks. Bladders and paunch linings made water bags and storage containers. Ribs became knives and sled runners. Horns were turned into utensils, bows, and ornaments. Sinews were made into bow strings and thread. Bone splinters became awls and needles. Boiled hoofs were made into glue. Tasseled tails became decorations and fly swatters. Gallstones were ground into medicine. The thick neck skin of the old bulls made shields so tough that they turned away arrows, lances, and glancing rifle balls. Rawhide strips, applied wet and then allowed to dry, held whatever they lashed with iron-clamp tightness. Even buffalo droppings, called "chips" by white settlers, furnished excellent fuel on the woodless plains. Finally, unborn buffalo boiled in its own fluid sac was a particular delicacy.

THAT DAMNED COWBOY! (1900)

Political boss Tom Platt, wishing to remove Governor Roosevelt from the scene of scandals in New York for fear Teddy would expose him, managed to push the governor out of New York in 1900 and into the vice presidency, despite the protests of President William McKinley's manager, Mark Hanna. With the assassination of McKinley, Roosevelt, forty-two years old, became the nation's youngest president.

"Now look," moaned Hanna, "that damned cowboy is President of the United States."

Hanna, who had put $100,000 of his own money into making McKinley president, couldn't be blamed for his bitterness. Besides, he was right: Teddy Roosevelt was a cowboy!

In 1884 when both his wife and mother died within hours of each other, Roosevelt decided to leave the scene of his sorrow to take up the strenuous life he had always advocated. He moved to the Badlands of the Dakotas, and for the next two years wore out his grief living the hard life of a cowboy. He practically lived in the saddle, learning roundups, hunting, and running down cattle thieves. Years later when he formed his famous Rough Riders, many of his troops were former cowboy friends and admirers.

YOU KNOW HOW TO HURT A MAN, J. P. (1901)

In 1901 J. Pierpont Morgan decided to form one of the world's largest trusts by organizing the U.S. Steel Corporation. To create this gigantic trust, Morgan not only had to buy Minnesota's Mesabi iron mines from John D. Rockefeller but also the entire steel business of Andrew Carnegie, which at that time was the largest steel-producing company in the world. Two years before Morgan approached him, Carnegie had offered to sell his business for $157,950,000. Now that Morgan wanted it so badly, the Steel King upped his price to $447 million—and got it immediately. Like many sellers whose price is accepted so quickly, Carnegie felt to the day he died that he could have gotten more out of Morgan. He was still thinking of this missed opportunity when he happened to sit next to Morgan one morning for breakfast on an ocean liner. "I find I made a mistake. I should have asked you for another hundred million," Carnegie remarked good-naturedly to Morgan. Morgan's reply wasn't designed to offer the former Steel King much consolation. "If you had, I should have paid it," he said.

MCKINLEY'S BIGGEST FAN (1901)

Most politicians' wives are their biggest fans, but most don't make it quite as obvious as Mrs. McKinley. When anyone referred to the president's resemblance to Daniel Webster or Napoleon, Mrs. McKinley would wave the compliment aside as one that did not honor her husband as much as it did the other man. At a White House dinner, a young English visitor admitted that as much as she enjoyed America, she still loved England best. Overhearing the remark of the young English girl, Mrs. McKinley looked at her severely. "Do you mean to say that you would prefer England to a country ruled over by my husband?" The First Lady was completely serious and waited for an answer that did not come.

PRESIDENT ALMOST LEAVES COUNTRY (1901)

With modern presidents making whirlwind world tours, it is difficult to imagine a president actually fearful of crossing the national boundary.

Yet, this was exactly the case with President McKinley, and ironically enough, he exhibited this reluctance on the day he was assassinated. On September 6, 1901, McKinley visited Niagara Falls and the International Bridge. Here he encountered his problem. As any tourist knows, the best view of the falls is from the Canadian side, but no president had ever left the United States while in office (although technically, Cleveland had once passed beyond the three-mile limit while on a fishing trip). President McKinley solved his problem by making his way almost to the center of the bridge, from where he viewed the falls and then returned without ever leaving the country. It remained for his successor, Teddy Roosevelt, to be the first president ever to visit a foreign country while in office. In 1906 Roosevelt visited Panama for four days.

A GOOD THING FOR THE COUNTRY! (1901)

According to historians John and Alice Durant, "No more devoted or more pathetic couple than the McKinleys ever dwelt in the White House." Three years after their marriage in 1871, Mrs. McKinley lost her mother and two baby daughters; afterward she developed severe epilepsy. For the rest of her life, her husband did everything possible to shield her, taking her with him almost everywhere, never knowing when she would fall unconscious.

On September 6, 1901, the president was shot by the anarchist Leon Czolgosz at Buffalo's Pan-American Exposition. As the fatally wounded president was cradled in the arms of one of his aides, he whispered, "My wife—be careful . . . how you tell her—oh, be careful." From his jail cell, Czolgosz said, "I thought it would be a good thing for the country to kill the President."

WAS HE REALLY JINXED? (1901)

Shortly before he went to Ford's Theater, where he was shot, President Lincoln invited his son Robert along. Just returned from General Lee's surrender at Appomattox, Robert pleaded weariness and retired early, fortuitously missing the president's assassination. On July 2, 1881, Robert Lincoln, then secretary of war, arrived at the Washington railroad station moments after President James A. Garfield was shot by Charles Guiteau. Twenty years later, on September 6, 1901, he arrived at the Pan-American Exposition only moments after the chief executive was mortally wounded by Leon Czolgosz. After the third assassination, Lincoln would no longer accept invitations to attend events where the president was present, fearing he was a jinx. The superstitious might make something of the fact that Robert Lincoln's father was killed, his mother went insane, and three of his brothers died in their youth.

The Myth of Flying (1901)

It is fortunate the Wright Brothers didn't believe everything they read in the papers or periodicals. Midway through their experiments and only two years before their successful flights at Kitty Hawk, the September 1901 issue of *McClure's* appeared with an article exploding the myth of the flying machine. Nationally known astronomer Simon Newcomb agreed with a host of other so-called experts that flying was something that mankind would never be able to do. "The example of the bird does not prove that man can fly. Imagine the proud possessor of an aeroplane darting through the air. It is his speed alone that sustains him. How is he ever going to stop?" Of course, the Wrights weren't experts and never thought about such details as stopping.

Wrights Inform the World! (1903)

Thursday, December 17, 1903, came and went, and the world would never be the same—only the world didn't know it. That afternoon the Wright brothers had the pleasant task of informing the nation and world of their triumph. They wired their father to inform the press of their successful flights, but the press wasn't interested, even their hometown *Dayton Journal.* The first paper to print the story was the *Norfolk Virginian-Pilot,* its farsighted editor obtaining the story through a leak in the local telegraph office. Efforts by the *Pilot,* however, to sell the story were almost unsuccessful: only five papers in the country bought the item. Even those who did run the story didn't quite know how to handle the news or even where to place it in the paper. The well-known *New York Tribune,* which eventually printed the story, carried the item on the sports page—right beneath a story of a sandlot football game in Brooklyn.

Horseback Dinners (1905)

Author Walter Lord terms the early 1900s as the era of the Golden Circus, with wealthy socialites like the Astors, the Guggenheimers, and the Vanderbilts trying to outdo each other with lavish and bizarre parties. The Stillmans installed a waterfall in their dining room for one party; the Guggenheimers stocked the Waldorf's Myrtle Room with nightingales; Mrs. Stuyvesant Fish invited Norfolk society to a reception for a foreign "prince"—a monkey in full evening dress. One of the most bizarre gatherings was put on by Cornelius K. G. Billings, who staged a horseback dinner at Sherry's. Livery stable horses were brought up to the grand ballroom by the freight elevator, where honored guests mounted them and dined in the saddle from precariously balanced trays. The dinner was served by waiters dressed as grooms, while the real grooms hovered nearby to clean up.

"BATTLE OF THE FLAGS" (1905)

In 1905, when Teddy Roosevelt was president, he decided to return Confederate battle flags, which the War Department had stored since 1865. This act was acclaimed throughout the North as generous and graceful, although the same act, when attempted by President Grover Cleveland eighteen years before, was viewed somewhat differently. In 1887 Cleveland had to quickly revoke his decision when a furor erupted in Congress and throughout the North. A small battle began in Congress between the northern Democrats and the Republicans, but the greatest threat occurred when the Grand Army of the Republic (Union veterans) threatened to march on Washington to prevent such a national disgrace. The most ironic aspect of this "battle of the flags" was that no one in the South had ever asked for their return.

ALICE'S HONOR (1906)

To many students of American history, it seems ironic that Teddy Roosevelt, of all people, should receive the Nobel Peace Prize, which he did in 1906 for the Treaty of Portsmouth and for settling a dispute between Germany and France. When American interests were involved, however, Teddy proved to be not quite so peace loving. Probably the epitome of his chip-on-the-shoulder attitude involved an incident with Chinese nationalists in 1905–6.

When the United States renewed the Chinese Exclusion Act of 1883, the Chinese replied with street demonstrations and a boycott of American goods. Unfortunately for the Chinese government, one of the American tourists insulted during a street demonstration was Alice Roosevelt, who was on a tour of the Far East. To Teddy this was the rice straw that broke the cooley's back. The American president, in reply to the insult, sent the battleship *Oregon* to the China coast and threatened to follow it with an expeditionary force. Rather than face such seemingly fateful consequences, the emperor issued an edict condemning further expressions of antiforeign sentiment. Teddy was satisfied.

THE JUNGLE BACKFIRES ON SINCLAIR (1906)

In 1906 a socialist writer named Upton Sinclair published a now-famous novel called *The Jungle.* In it he described the horrors of the meat-packing industry in Chicago, how government inspectors were bribed to pass tubercular animals dying of cholera, how poisoned rats were shoved into meat-grinding machines, and how filth scraped from the floor each night (which the protagonist of the novel did for 17½ cents an hour) was turned into "potted ham." The book was an immediate best seller. For a year it outsold all other American books. A clamor immediately arose, with the public demanding strict laws for meat inspection. President Roosevelt read the book and hit the White House roof; Congress responded with a tight inspection law and a new Pure Food Act. Sinclair, however, was not happy. He had ended his novel with a socialist orator shouting from a platform, "Organize! Organize! Organize!" He had hoped that millions would rush to join the American Socialist Party. Instead, they demanded reform through the major parties and got it. He sadly summed it up with, "I aimed at the public's heart and hit its stomach."

HOW TO SPEND MONEY! (1906)

It's hard for the average wage earner to comprehend the problem of having too much money to spend, but that seemed to be the case with some of the rich at the turn of the century. William Vanderbilt's palace on Long Island had a garage for a hundred automobiles. His brother George hired more men to care for his North Carolina estate than the Department of Agriculture hired for the entire United States. J. P. Morgan spent more than $1 million in one year on his hobby of collecting old scrolls and tapestries. This helps us understand John Jacob Astor's statement that "a man who has a million dollars is as well off as if he were rich." Astor's wife, incidentally, had a bathtub cut from a two-ton block of marble. The Belmonts bedded their horses down at their estate in Newport with linen sheets embroidered with the family crest. In that same town the Fahnestocks decorated the trees around their house with artificial fruit made of 14-carat gold.

THINGS DO CHANGE! (1906)

The year 1906 means one thing in American history: the year San Francisco burned down; or perhaps more accurately, fell down. At exactly 5:12 A.M. on April 18, the ground under San Francisco ripped and heaved "like a man shakes a rug" or "like a dog shakes a rat," according to some descriptions. For the next three days what the earthquake didn't destroy, the resulting fires seemed intent on doing. Three days later, when the fires finally burned themselves out, the staggering statistics started pouring in. For all practical purposes, the San Francisco that everyone knew was gone. Four hundred ninety blocks were smoldering ruins, 25,000 buildings were in ashes or rubble, 225,000 people were homeless, more than 450 lives were lost, and property damage was estimated at $500 million. A member of the Metropolitan Opera Company, baritone Giuseppe Campanari, paused long enough on his flight out of the city to give an interview. When asked about his impression of the earthquake, he replied with the all-time classic understatement: "It is such a change."

LAUGH IT TO DEATH (1906)

Congressmen have discovered that it is possible at times to ridicule a bill to death. This happened in 1906 when Washington, D.C., police disclosed that in the previous two years 508 cases of wife-beating had occurred in the nation's capital. Angry congressmen immediately rushed a bill into Congress that would punish "any male person in the District of Columbia who shall beat, bruise or mutilate his wife, with thirty lashes laid on his bare back." The bill was apparently not taken as seriously as the authors intended.

Mr. Sims: "I do not think it is good enough to administer just anywhere. . . . We should build a platform on top of the Washington Monument so that people . . . will see that at least in whipping wife-beaters we give them a square, open deal."

Mrs. Stanley: "There are more of them that are in pain because they are unmarried than are in pain because they are married and are beaten. . . . I want to offer an amendment that a like punishment shall be inflicted not only on those who are guilty of wife-beating, but those who feloniously refuse to take one." Unfortunately for many, the wife-beating bill did not pass.

THE GREAT WHITE FLEET (1907)

Wishing to impress potential enemies of the United States, especially in Asia, with American naval might, Teddy Roosevelt decided to dispatch sixteen gleaming white battleships on a fourteen-month world cruise in 1907. Congress, which he was trying to persuade to authorize funding for two battleships, refused to authorize expenditures for the cruise. Teddy, perfectly in character, responded by telling Congress that he had enough fuel to take the fleet halfway around the world. If Congressmen wanted the fleet back home, they would have to authorize funds to provide the fuel for the return trip. They did.

NOW THAT WAS A FUNERAL (1907)

Jessica Mitford never recorded the following funeral in her *American Way of Death,* but she should have. Before his death, Arthur Haine of Vancouver, Washington, had provided in his will for a most nontraditional funeral:

"Know everybody by these presents that I, Arthur Haine, knowing what I am about, make this my last will and testament. . . . My funeral is to be of the cheapest kind and I don't want my body to be transported but buried in the vicinity where I may die. As I have lived an Infidel, I must be buried as such without any monkey business."

He probably would have been pleased with the results that came in 1907. To the accompaniment of popular tunes played by a band, his body was carried to the cemetery in a beer truck along with several beer kegs for the refreshment of friends and spectators. His epitaph was equally nontraditional: Haine Haint.

TO PLEASE A WOMAN (1908)

It is well-known that Teddy Roosevelt had the power and the popularity to name his successor in the White House, so he did, naming William Howard Taft. How he did so is not as well known. It happened at a small White House dinner in January 1908. Sitting in his easy chair, President Roosevelt threw back his head, closed his eyes, and intoned, "I am the seventh son of a seventh daughter. I have clairvoyant powers. I see a man standing before me weighing three hundred and fifty pounds. There is something hanging over his head. I cannot make out what it is; it is hanging by a slender thread. At one time it looks like the Presidency—then again it looks like the Chief Justiceship." "Make it the Chief Justiceship," replied Taft, whose real aspirations were in that direction. "No!" cried Mrs. Taft. "Make it the Presidency!" Against his own judgment, Taft agreed to his wife's desires and spent four very uncomfortable years in the White House.

Finally, in 1921, he realized his fondest dream, accepting an appointment as chief justice of the United States—without asking his wife's advice.

GOLF IS FATAL! (1908)

At the end of his second term, Teddy Roosevelt flatly declined another term, handpicking his successor. When he gave his blessing to William Howard Taft, he put himself on record as not wanting to interfere in the coming campaign; he didn't plan to be "officious or busybody." Yet politics was in Teddy's blood, and he couldn't keep himself from offering advice throughout the 1908 campaign. "Stay in hotels. . . . Stop citing court cases." (Taft's first love was the judiciary.) "Say nothing, not one sentence that can be misconstrued. . . . Let the audience see you smile always." (No one could smile like Teddy.)

Near the end of the campaign, Teddy sent a special message to his friend, warning him that many people had sent him letters objecting to Taft playing golf: "I myself play tennis, but that game is a little more familiar; besides, you never saw a photograph of me playing tennis. I'm careful about that; photographs on horseback, yes; tennis, no. And golf is fatal." Considering his disillusionment with Taft four years later, perhaps he should have added one further bit of advice: "Stop breathing!" It would have been in character.

GERONIMO'S FINAL ESCAPE (1909)

The most ferocious of all the Indian tribes American troops faced in the taming of the West was the Apache. As a matter of fact, *Apache* was so identified with terrorism that as far away as Paris, France, the word came to be applied to that city's worst criminal element. The best known and most elusive of all Apaches was Geronimo, war chief of the Chiricahuas, who for many years led Mexican and American troops and authorities on fruitless chases all over the Southwest before he finally surrendered and was sent to prison in Florida. Later, much subdued and Christianized, he was relocated to Fort Sill, Oklahoma.

Geronimo spent his final years traveling to fairs and exhibitions, where he posed for tourists, filling his pockets with change that he spent on whiskey. In February 1909, drunk from a resulting spree, he fell off his horse and lay all night in a patch of weeds, fatally contracting pneumonia. In death, the chief who so often had escaped his white enemies made a final escape, but it wasn't known until 1943. An old Apache revealed that Geronimo's body was not in his presumed grave at Fort Sill, but many years before, it had been moved by some of his former warriors to a secret place off the white man's reservation.

REACHING THE NORTH POLE (1909)

"We will plant the Stars and Stripes—at the North Pole." So spoke Robert E. Peary on the morning of April 7, 1909, when, after four different observations, he was convinced that he was at the North Pole. With him to share some of the glory were four Inuits and "Matthew Henson, colored," as Peary listed him on a record he left at the pole. Other members of the expedition had been stationed at camps along the trail north.

Unfortunately for Peary, another explorer, Dr. F. A. Cook, returned from an Arctic trip before Peary, claiming to have reached the pole first. History has proved him a fraud, but he was able for a time to create a hostile press for Peary, the "second" man to return and claim victory. Some of the press attacked Peary for not only trying to steal the glory from Cook but also for not taking any white companions along on the final dash to the pole. At least Peary was honest. When asked why he didn't have a white companion with him at his final goal, he replied, "Because after a lifetime of effort I dearly wanted the honor for myself." It was universally conceded at the time, the liberal press included, that black people didn't count.

TAFT'S WEIGHT (1909)

America's largest president was William Howard Taft, who, according to his mother, was born in 1857 "a fat and smiling boy." Fat he remained all his life. By the time he graduated from Yale, he weighed 243 pounds. He eventually reached 340 pounds, despite attempts at dieting and exercising. As civil governor of the Philippines between 1901 and 1904, he would dine on such simple lunches as "crabs or small lobsters or shrimp, beefsteak, cheese and salad, banana fritters or griddle cakes and fruit." Then to lose weight he would go for a horseback ride. After one such trip he cabled Secretary of War Elihu Root, "STOOD TRIP WELL. RODE HORSEBACK TWENTY-FIVE MILES TO FIVE THOUSAND FEET ELEVATION." Back came Root's famous reply, "REFERENCE TO YOUR TELEGRAM . . . HOW IS THE HORSE?"

Sitting in a theater, Taft once told his brother, "Horace, if this theater burns, it has got to burn around me." Yale still cherishes the gargantuan chairs made to make Taft comfortable, as well as the story of the time he got the train to stop at Hicksville, a water tank whistle stop, by telegraphing the conductor, "STOP AT HICKSVILLE. LARGE PARTY WAITING TO CATCH TRAIN."

NO ONE SUSPECTED "ALBERT" (1911)

Automobile accidents weren't that uncommon, even though the year was 1911, so an accident in which Albert Cashier was injured wasn't newsworthy. That is, at first. As a veteran of the Civil War, Albert was sent to a veteran's hospital, and there it was discovered that Albert wasn't an Albert. He, or rather she, was really Jennie Hodgers, a woman who had been drawing a Civil War pension since 1899. Like her counterpart of Revolutionary War fame, Deborah Sampson, Jennie had posed as a man, enlisted in the Union army, fought four years throughout the war, and received an honorable discharge. She was apparently successful in hiding her gender from her fellow soldiers the entire time. The most intriguing aspect of the whole episode, however, occurred thirty-four years after Appomattox. In 1899, when she applied for a veteran's pension, she was required to be examined by a doctor. It is too bad that history hasn't recorded that examination because the physician apparently never discovered her true gender either.

THE *TITANIC* AND WOMEN'S RIGHTS (1912)

The big day was planned for May 4, 1912, only three weeks away. It was to be the largest women's suffrage parade New York City had ever seen, right up Fifth Avenue with the whole country watching. And then suddenly came the news of the sinking of the *Titanic,* which for a time threatened to squelch the entire suffrage movement, including the parade. Why? The whole country had been so impressed with reports of the gallantry of the men who gave up their seats in lifeboats to women and died as a result. "I think," said Lida Stokes Adams, a leading suffragette, "the women should have insisted that the boats be filled with an equal number of men." The women hadn't, though, and at a time like this most people wondered how women could still demand equal rights. The founder of Barnard College, Annie Nathan Meyer, returned her pledge card noting, "After the superb unselfishness and heroism of the men on the Titanic, your march is untimely and pathetically unwise." But the parade went on as planned, five times larger than any previous suffrage parade, with the women demanding their rights as planned.

"THE STRENUOUS LIFE" (1912)

As a child, Teddy Roosevelt had to struggle against ill health. When his father told him he had the mind but not the body to sustain a worthwhile career, he replied, "I'll make my body." Through years of constant and strenuous exercise and sport, he built a strong body and became a lifelong advocate of the rugged outdoor life of the sportsman. An example of the strenuous life he led comes to us from his description of a visit to Rock Creek Park in 1908, where the ice had just broken: "We did the usual climbing stunts at the various rocks, and then swam the creek; and it was a good swim, in our winter clothes and with hobnail boots and the icy current running really fast." He also exhibited his physical fitness when he was shot in the chest by a fanatic while campaigning in Milwaukee during the 1912 campaign. He insisted on giving his campaign speech before being taken to the hospital. "This bullet is in me now," he told his audience, "so that I cannot make a very long speech." He recovered from the wound but lost the election to Woodrow Wilson, and he never did regain the robust health of which he was so proud.

"ACORN" TAXES (1913)

Americans have had little but bad experience with the income tax, not only in paying it but also in getting it passed. It was first passed by Republicans during the Civil War, and the Supreme Court ruled that it was constitutional. But the war ended, as did the tax. Thirty years later, in June 1894, a Democrat Congress enacted a 2 percent tax on incomes of

$4,000 or more. The Democrats hailed it as "the dawn of a brighter day, with more sunshine, more songs of birds," whereas the Republicans hailed it as "socialism, communism, devilism," forgetting their own Civil War tax. A Republican Supreme Court this time declared the tax unconstitutional. Nineteen years later the country tried again when Delaware, with an affirmative vote, put the Sixteenth Amendment into effect. Once again conservatives howled when they discovered their taxes could run as high as 2 percent on incomes of $20,000–$50,000 a year. A married man in 1913 making $20,000 dollars, for example, owed the federal government $160—less than 1 percent. Truly, "Oak trees from little acorns grow."

WILSON THE LOVER (1915)

To most men, President Woodrow Wilson appeared aloof and scholarly—a cold computer. Not so to women, however. They found him witty and attractive, and he was constantly seeking out their company. Before he was elected to the presidency, his home was a fortress of femininity, being surrounded and pampered by an adoring wife and three devoted daughters. After he gained the presidency, his wife died, but within a year he had sought out and fallen in love with an attractive Washington widow fifteen years his junior. At the age of fifty-eight, Wilson put younger men to shame with his courting, sending his love flowers each day and installing a private telephone line between her house and the White House. Although World War I was then underway, he put aside all but the most urgent affairs of state to be with her. They were married a week before Christmas in 1915.

WILSON'S INTENDED RESIGNATION (1916)

Until Richard Nixon, no president in American history had ever resigned from office, although Woodrow Wilson came close. It occurred just two days before his reelection to a second term in November 1916. Conscious of the inherent inabilities of a lame-duck president, particularly at such a critical time in world history, Wilson decided that if he lost the 1916 election, he would not be such a president. Accordingly, he wrote Secretary of State Robert Lansing of his plans to put would-be president-elect, Charles Evan Hughes, into office sooner.

"I feel it would be my duty to relieve the country of the perils of such a situation at once. The course I have in mind is dependent upon the consent and cooperation of the Vice President; but if I could gain his consent to the plan, I would ask your permission to invite Mr. Hughes to become Secretary of State and would then join the Vice President in resigning, and thus open to Mr. Hughes the immediate succession to the presidency."

Wilson had reason to plan this drastic action: his electoral majority was only a little more than 52 percent, but it was enough.

Bathtubs and H. L. Mencken (1917)

The origin of the bathtub was the subject of a hoax dreamed up by H. L. Mencken in 1917. In an article he wrote that year, he stated that the first American bathtub was installed in 1842 in a home in Cincinnati. He detailed that the construction of the tub was mahogany and lead. He said the owner of the house was Adam Thompson and that the unveiling event was a stag party at which the guests took turns trying out the new invention. The whole story was a fabrication, as Mencken admitted several times, but it still continues to appear in reputable publications as historical fact. Truth is stranger—not stronger—than fiction.

Congresswoman Votes Against War (1917)

On March 4, 1917, Jeannette Rankin of Montana took her seat as the first congresswoman in history—just in time to vote against the U.S. entry into World War I. Although only thirty years old and a gifted speaker, she lost a reelection attempt in 1918. The Montanans didn't like her antiwar vote. Twenty years later this had been forgotten, and Montana returned her to the House of Representatives in January 1941—once more in time to vote against U.S. entry into another world war. Hers was the only negative congressional vote on December 8, although the Japanese had attacked the United States the day before. Needless to say, she was not returned to Congress again. She apparently had never read Santayana: "Those who ignore the lessons of history are condemned to repeat them."

"Big Bertha" (1918)

On July 4, 1917, the first battalion of American troops ever sent to Europe marched through the streets of Paris, secure far behind Allied lines. In March 1918 the city was still far behind Allied lines—seventy-five miles, to be exact—but no longer secure. The Germans were shelling Paris, killing civilians and Allied troops alike with an unbelievable weapon. One shell alone struck a church on Good Friday, killing eighty and wounding sixty-eight. Allied troops could not locate the monstrous gun, nicknamed "Big Bertha." It was not until the Germans began their retreat in August 1918 that the gun was discovered. Several guns, in fact, were located in a forest seventy miles from Paris, each weighing more than 150 tons. If stood on end, each gun would have been as tall as a ten-story building. The carriages for the giants were twenty-five feet high. The ball bearing used in the revolving bases was as large as a bowling ball, and the shells, weighing 250 pounds each, reached an altitude of twenty-five miles in the course of their flight. So long was the flight of these death-dealing missiles that the curvature and rotation of the earth had to be considered in aiming and firing the guns.

THE "MOST DECORATED" BIRD (1918)

One of the most unusual exhibits in the Smithsonian Institution is a stuffed pigeon that stands on one leg. It is the only bird in American history to receive a special medal for gallantry. Its name is Cher Ami ("dear friend"), and it was a member of the famed Lost Battalion in World War I. Surrounded by the German enemy in the Argonne Forest, 550 troops of the American 77th Division not only came under intense fire by the Germans but also found themselves under fire from their own artillery. To stop the growing number of casualties (only 194 of the 550 walked out after five days), Maj. Charles Whittlesey, using carrier pigeons, attempted to get word through to American lines to halt the barrage. Each bird sent up was immediately shot down by the Germans until only one, Cher Ami, was left. Sent aloft, it too was hit and dropped, but it recovered and struggled homeward. Thirty minutes later it landed at division headquarters twenty-five miles away. He suffered from a shattered leg, a badly injured wing, and a broken breastbone, but the message was intact, dangling from the shattered leg. Despite the best of medical care, Cher Ami never recovered, dying in 1919.

THE FORD SUCCESS STORY (1919)

Henry Ford's formal education ended at age fifteen, after which he held several jobs involving machinery. At age twenty-nine he built his first gasoline-powered buggy, and eleven years later he founded the Ford Motor Company, which between 1908 and 1927 produced $15 million worth of Model Ts. Ford experienced such incredible financial success that, on the twenty-first birthday of his son Edsel, Henry presented him with a gift of $1 million in gold. The Ford Motor Company was one of the dramatic success stories in American business enterprise. A story is often told about Rosetta Hauss, sister of the company's first business manager, James Couzens. Couzens had tried to sell his reluctant sister $200 worth of his own Ford Motor Company shares. Finally she invested $100. Over the next sixteen years, she received $95,000 in dividends, and when Ford bought her out in 1919, her $100 share was worth $260,000.

THE YEAR OF THE MOB RULE (1919)

In 1918 the United States completed the job of making the world "safe for democracy." The following year Americans lynched eighty-three people, several of them black veterans in uniform. The African-American community did not take this violence passively. Twenty-five major race riots occurred within seven months in 1919. In the nation's capital, mobs prowled the city streets for three days before they were brought under control. At about the same time in Chicago, thirty-eight people were killed in rioting, six hundred were wounded, and a thousand families were burned out. In Omaha, Nebraska, a black man was dragged through the streets, shot more than a thousand times, and hanged on main street.

In 1922 the NAACP inserted a full-page advertisement in the *New York Times* with the following information: "Do you know that the United States is the Only Land on Earth where human beings are BURNED AT THE STAKE? In four years, 1918–21, twenty-eight People were publicly BURNED BY AMERICAN MOBS. 3436 People Lynched, 1889–1921."

A STRIKE MAKES A PRESIDENT (1919)

In September 1919 a dispute over pay and working conditions led to a walkout of at least three-quarters of the Boston police force. Unprotected, the city was immediately subjected to widespread rioting, looting, robberies, rapes, and other forms of violent disorder. Before the strike, the governor of the state was asked to intervene but refused. With the city now under control by mobs, Mayor Andrew Peters was forced to call out the Boston militia, declaring, "There is no right to strike against the public safety by anybody, anywhere, any time." This strong stance in favor of law and order by the mayor gave the governor a reputation that pushed him into the vice presidency in 1920 and eventual succession to the presidency. Cal Coolidge had played it cool.

A FORETASTE OF PROHIBITION (1920)

Prohibition, contrary to most history books, did not go into effect with the passing of the Eighteenth Amendment. It went into effect six months previously as the result of a wartime act that provided that no alcoholic beverages were to be sold after June 30, 1919, because of the need to conserve grain. The war ended in 1918, but the law still went into effect on July 1. The Anti-Saloon League, in fact, had tried to shame America into being dry throughout the war by pointing out that liquor was the Kaiser's greatest ally in America; and besides, weren't beer and pretzels both German?

Enforcement of the Volstead Act (National Prohibition Enforcement Act) became the big joke of the 1920s, but its doom should have been foreseen even before it went into effect. Americans knew well ahead of time that Prohibition was to be enforced beginning in January 1920. In the three months preceding that time, $500,000 worth of liquor was stolen from guarded government warehouses.

WHICH ONES WERE UNTOUCHABLE? (1920)

The Alice in Wonderland picture of enforcing national Prohibition becomes fairly obvious when we glance at a few statistics of the period. The Anti-Saloon League, when asked by Congress to estimate the cost of enforcement, suggested $5 million per year. So that's what was allotted. And yet, within the first four years of Prohibition, one Chicago mobster alone, Johnny Torrio, amassed more than $50 million from illegal booze. Congress provided around 1,500 agents for a nation of 105 million people, with more than 18,000 miles of coast and two long borders. That's about one agent for every 70,000 people—and agents were paid less than $40 per week. As proof of how ineffective this spartan enforcement proved to be, the New York police commissioner estimated at the end of the 1930s that there were 32,000 speakeasies in that city alone.

HARDING THE "SOFTHEARTED" (1921)

President Warren G. Harding has been portrayed in American

history as one of the nation's weakest presidents, and ironically, it was partly because he was such a nice guy. He was extremely popular with his hometown folks in Marion, Ohio. He was a successful, genial, small-town businessman who wanted more than anything else to be liked by his fellowmen. These attributes put him ahead in a small town, but they were not an asset in the White House. He could not believe that there was evil in any man, although it flourished under his nose in the presidency. In thirty-six years as publisher of the *Marion Star,* he never dismissed a single employee. He allowed himself to be advised on important matters by his wife, the "Dutchess," who often based her advice on consultations with an astrologer. "I cannot say no," he once told a press club friend. "It is a good thing I am not a woman. I would always be pregnant."

HARDING'S LOVE LIFE (1923)

Presidents are human like everyone else, but Harding was probably more human than most presidents. For fifteen years before he ran for the highest office in the land, he carried on a love affair with Carrie Phillips, the wife of one of his best friends, Jim Phillips of Marion, Ohio. In 1968 the Phillips family sued Francis Russell, author of a biography on Harding, for $1 million for revealing this information. Russell had discovered love letters from Harding to Carrie Phillips.

As president, Harding carried on another love affair with Nan Britton, thirty-five years younger than he and the daughter of a Marion, Ohio, friend. Apparently unwilling to control his sex urge, President Harding made love to Nan Britton in such places as the floor of a White House closet. She conceived his daughter and, three years after his death, wrote a best seller of the times called *The President's Daughter.* She dedicated the book to "all unwed mothers, and to their innocent children whose fathers are usually not known to the world." A picture of her daughter, along with her famous father, were on the frontispiece to the book.

"SILENT CAL" COOLIDGE (1924)

Calvin Coolidge rightfully earned the title "Silent Cal," given him by both friends and enemies. He was close-mouthed, shy, and rarely smiled. Once when a guest at an official affair told him that she had made a bet that she could get him to say more than two words, his only comment was, "You lose." He once told Bernard Baruch why he said so little: "Well,

Baruch, many times I say only 'yes' or 'no' to people. Even this is too much. It winds them up for twenty minutes more." At the laying of a cornerstone, Coolidge said nothing during the entire ceremony until it came time for him to turn a spadeful of earth. Then he picked up a small clod and, as the crowd waited expectantly, remarked, "Good dirt."

WE'LL NEVER KNOW (1925)

Edward L. Tinker claims in the *Bookman,* February 1925, that in a great New York library, letters and documents of George Washington were deliberately destroyed because the lady who was in charge of them felt that they were smutty. "I did not want them to become public and destroy the ideal of Washington that had flourished for so long," she told Tinker. "It was only a question of money. Could we afford to pay the price and then destroy our investment? We could and did."

In 1923 a friend of Robert Lincoln visited him in his Manchester, Vermont, home. There he found Lincoln before the fireplace, burning private papers and letters belonging to his father. Unable to restrain him, the friend called N. M. Butler, president of Columbia University. Butler arrived the next day and found Lincoln with another box of family papers he intended to burn. Butler convinced Lincoln that his father's letters and papers belonged to the public; subsequently the son turned the remainder over to the Library of Congress. How much and what was destroyed, we will never know.

MONKEY TRIAL SIDELIGHTS (1925)

The trial of John Scopes on charges of teaching evolution contrary to the laws of Tennessee is fairly well known to most students of American history, but there are some interesting little-known sidelights. Scopes was found guilty and fined $100, but he never paid the fine. (He also never actually taught evolution.) The Tennessee Supreme Court ruled that the fine had been improperly levied.

William Jennings Bryan, the prosecuting attorney, died only five days after the trial, many attributing his death to humiliation at the hands of Clarence Darrow. More likely, it was heat exhaustion and too much food. (He was a diabetic but disregarded his diet during the trial.) The Tennessee Supreme Court advised the district attorney to never bring to court again what it considered bizarre cases. After the trial a dozen states introduced "monkey bills" to prohibit the teaching of evolution, but politicians found expedient ways to avoid taking stands. In Delaware the bill was referred to the Committee on Fish, Game, and Oysters, and heard of no more.

THE POPE'S ON HIS WAY (1928)

The Ku Klux Klan had many targets, but in the 1920s a chief target was the Catholic Church and the Pope. One story the Klan circulated declared that the Pope was coming to Washington, D.C., to lead an uprising against the United States. The KKK even circulated pictures of the Protestant Episcopal Cathedral of Sts. Peter and Paul located on Mount Alban in Washington, depicting them as actual pictures of the new Vatican in the process of construction. The Klan claimed that the structure was being built four hundred feet above Washington to enable field guns to be fired from it directly upon the Capitol and White House. The climax of these charges occurred at the college town of North Manchester, Indiana, when a speaker told the crowd that the Pope could be expected at any time. "He may even be on the northbound train tomorrow," the agitator shouted. The next day some 1,500 persons met the northbound train, from which a lone male traveler alighted. Seeing the huge crowd in an ugly mood, he tried to flee but was grabbed and forced to identify himself as not being the Pope.

THE LAST INDIAN RAID (1930)

Although it occurred south of the U.S. border, the incident described in the following news story is so closely connected with Southwestern history that it might easily be called the last Indian raid.

"Tucson, Arizona, April 22 (INS)—Riding out of their wilderness hideout high in the Sierra Madre Mountains, a band of wild Apache Indians scalped three Persons April 10, in a settlement near Nacori Chico, Sonora, Mexico, it was reported today by V. M. White, a mining engineer. The three victims were Mexicans who opened fire on the marauders while the latter were looting the village. Armed parties immediately set out to trail the painted savages and attempt to engage them in battle before they reached their impregnable and historic cliffs.

"The Apaches are believed to have been led, White said, by Geronimo III, the grandson of the Geronimo who was chased by the United States

Army for three years during the '80s in Arizona."

AMERICANS IMMIGRATE TO RUSSIA (1931)

In the 1930s Russia found itself short of skilled workers for expanding industries, while in the United States the Great Depression had put thousands of skilled workers out on the street. A logical solution appeared in an ad sponsored by the Amtorg Company in 1931 asking for applicants for "six thousand skilled workers to work in Russia." The result, according to *Business Week,* was 100,000 applicants for the jobs, everything from barbers and funeral directors to engineers and teachers. About 85 percent of those applying were citizens of the United States, although 60 percent were foreign born. The main reasons given for wanting to go to Russia were the need for a job, disgust with conditions in the United States, and an interest in the Soviet experiment, communism.

Most of the emigrants stayed to become citizens of Russia, but two who didn't were Victor and Walter Reuther. They returned to the United States, where Walter Reuther, making use of his anticapitalistic ideas acquired in the Soviet Union, became the head of United Auto Workers, one of the largest labor unions in the world.

FOOTLOOSE BUT NOT SO FANCY (1932)

Americans have always been a mobile people, but a new kind of mobility took place during the 1930s—a movement of homeless, jobless, poverty-stricken citizens uprooted by drought, dust storms, and unemployment. The *New York Times* reported in an article in 1932 that "at least twenty-five thousand families in our country and more than two hundred thousand boys and young men" belonged to the transient army. It admitted that "the actual count, beyond doubt, is several times the reported figures."

Just one railroad, the Missouri Pacific, took official notice in 1931 of 186,028 transient trespassers found on its trains and property. Multiply this by the number of railroads, and count those not traveling by rail, and the numbers reach astronomical proportions. In that same year the railroad reported that 125 transients were killed on railroad property and and 247 were injured—many of them boys and girls. These figures cannot begin to illustrate the misery associated with this national phenomenon, especially when whole families were involved. In one western town in

1921, thirty-five seriously ill people, many in advanced stages of pneumonia, were removed from box cars.

"BROTHER, CAN YOU SPARE SOME TOOTHPASTE?" (1932)

When Franklin Roosevelt declared a bank holiday on March 6, 1932, the repercussions were unusual, to say the least. Millions of people, caught without any ready cash, had to make do for several days in a strange carnival-like atmosphere of goodwill. Piggy banks were broken open, friends borrowed from friends, and merchants who had never done it before took IOUs. When people became unsure of how long the bank holiday would last, they turned to a system of barter. Madison Square Garden took canned goods, shoes, and even foot ointment in exchange for fight tickets. In Salt Lake City tubes of toothpaste and silk stockings were traded for transit fares. One Midwest newspaper advertised a year's subscription for ten bushels of wheat. Mexican pesos started circulating in the Southwest, and one major company even paid its workers with its own coins stamped from a metal alloy. The holiday didn't last long, but in just a few short days, the nation was on its way to the barter economy that existed in colonial America. In view of later events, the Depression might have been less severe had it continued.

THE PRESIDENTIAL "CLUB" (1933)

The "log cabin to the White House" tradition or "any child can be president" belief has become a cherished part of the American Dream. To an extent, the dream is still possible, but in reality the relatives or offspring of presidents stand a far better chance of moving into 1600 Pennsylvania Avenue than does the unknown boy from Podunk Center, Nebraska. History proves this point.

The nation's third and sixth presidents were father and son. John Scott Harrison, who served two terms in Congress, was the son of one president and the father of another. Millions believe that only an assassination prevented Robert Kennedy from following his brother's footsteps into the White House. And, of course, President George Bush is the son of another President George Bush. Probably the most overwhelming proof of a tendency toward dynastic succession in the White House came to light in 1933 when Franklin D. Roosevelt became the thirty-second president. He was related by blood or marriage to no fewer than eleven former presidents: Washington, both Adamses, Madison, Van Buren, both Harrisons, Taylor, Grant, Theodore Roosevelt, and Taft.

OF COWS AND WAR (1934)

Emma Tiller and her sharecropper husband, like millions of others, shared the degrading poverty of the Great Depression of the 1930s, but unlike others, Emma was one of the few black sufferers to set down on paper her experiences and feelings:

"What bothered me about the Roosevelt time was when they come out with this business that you had to plow up a certain amount of your crop. . . . And seein' all this cattle killed. Bein' raised with stock, to me it was kind of a human feelin' we had toward them. . . . They didn't have the food to feed these cattle, and there was drought, so they had these cattle drove up and killed by the hundreds of head. . . . To me it was sorta like human beings, because they would just groan and go on—when they was killin' 'em and they wasn't dead . . . and all of a sudden it hit me. I seen the war. When I listened to those cows . . . then I seen how terrible wars were. I thought then: why do they have wars? To me, those cows were like women moanin' over their husbands, their children and the starvation. . . . I ran up to the house and I sit up there a long time and then I went to cryin' because they was doin' these cows this way."

THE "KINGFISH" FILIBUSTERS (1935)

It was not the longest, but it was one of the zaniest. The year was 1935, and Huey "Kingfish" Long was filibustering against the National Recovery Act. Starting shortly before noon one day in July, the "Kingfish" talked for 15½—until nearly 4 A.M. the next day. He did more than just talk or read telephone directories, as some senators do. His was an act that no senator has ever been able to match. He was witty, sarcastic, funny, religious, angry, and serious as he touched on all possible topics. He talked about the baptism of his uncle, his political enemies, and his own honesty. He gave out elaborate recipes for frying oysters, making Roquefort cheese dressing and potlikker. He did all of this after stating, "I desire the Senators to understand that I am not doing any filibustering. I am speaking on this bill." The Supreme Court, incidentally, had already declared the NRA unconstitutional.

The Prisoner Presidents (1938)

FDR was crippled by infantile paralysis, but he was able, with special controls, to drive a small Ford Phaeton on his estates at Hyde Park and Warm Springs. A favorite pastime of the president appeared to be to get into his car and try to escape from the ever-present Secret Service men. It eventually became a game with his official protectors, and they would wait a while before starting to look for him. He would eventually return like a disappointed little boy whose parents hadn't missed him.

President Woodrow Wilson once tried to escape from the White House without his Secret Service agents spotting him; they caught up with him several blocks away. President Calvin Coolidge made a futile attempt to shake off his official companions while vacationing at a beach in Massachusetts. Harry Truman was heard to mutter occasionally about the White House being no less than a prison. Today it is highly unlikely that a president would even consider trying to elude the men so essential to keeping him alive. We have moved a long distance from the early days of the Republic when presidents could go for rides in the country—alone.

The "Good" Old Days (1939)

One day in 1939 a door at Alcatraz swung open and a helpless and pale paralytic was helped down to a waiting boat. Thus began the final days of life for the once great Al Capone, a far cry from the days when he owned one of the largest cities in Illinois. That was back in the early 1920s, and Al was on his way up in the rackets. He decided to mix politics with crime—not an unusual combination—and his first move was to take over Cicero, the largest city in Cook County. Al and his men campaigned for the reelection of Mayor Joseph Klenha, and not being a man who likes to lose, he made sure of the election by intimidating voters, beating up and kidnapping election workers who wouldn't go along with his crooked deals, and raiding polling places to make sure that only the right people voted. After Klenha won, Capone turned Cicero into a playground for the underworld with saloons running openly, despite Prohibition. Capone ruled the city so completely that he once knocked the mayor down publicly in front of City Hall. On another occasion Capone sent his henchmen to beat up some city council members during their meeting and send them home because they were considering a city ordinance he didn't like.

RULES FOR A CONGRESSMAN (1940)

Every profession has its own rules and regulations, but none like those Luther Patrick of Alabama submitted to the House of Representatives in 1940. Here's a sampling:

"1. Entertain with a smile constituents, their wives, their sons, sons' wives, etc. Go with them to the White House; show good reason why you are unable to personally have them meet the President; take daughters to meet midshipmen at Annapolis."

"5. Be a cultured gentleman, a teller of ribald stories, a profound philosopher, preserve a store of 'Confucius say' gags; be a ladies' man, a man's man, a he-man, a diplomat, a Democrat with a Republican slant, a Republican with a Democrat viewpoint, an admirer of the Roosevelt way, a hater of the New Deal, a new dealer, an old dealer, and a quick dealer."

"7. Have the dope on hot spots in town, with choice telephone numbers for the gay boys from back home."

"ENTERTAINING THE ENEMY" (1941)

The U.S. government's treatment of American citizens of Japanese descent, in sending them to the well-known "detention camps" at the outset of World War II, is in sharp contrast to the treatment accorded the actual enemy temporarily detained in this country after Pearl Harbor. The Japanese "peace envoy" of Saburo Karusu and Ambassador Kichisaburo Nomura, together with about 250 other Japanese officials, were moved into the famous Homestead Hotel at Hot Springs, Virginia. There, at the expense of the American taxpayer, the "prisoners" had the entire 650-room resort hotel to themselves and were served by 700 maids, waiters, gardeners, porters, chauffeurs, chefs, bakers, craftsmen, masseurs, and so on. So as not to offend the guests, the FBI ordered the removal of the large American flag in the lobby. The Japanese were later exchanged for American officials detained in less sumptuous quarters in Japan.

SUMIO NICHI: PATRIOT? (1942)

The following is part of the testimony of a second-generation Japanese-American who, along with thousands of others, was forcibly removed to an internment camp after the Japanese attacked Pearl Harbor:

"We had a big farm near Salinas, California. Lettuce, celery, cauliflower, broccoli. . . . In 1936, I bought four trucks and trailers for $24,000. We had our own packinghouse. . . . The day I was to report to the assembly center, in 1941, we brought that mortgage down to $9,875. The day I left for the internment camp, I walked into the bank, paid them $9,875. We had an inventory of $80,000 worth of equipment. . . . They set up appraisers. I got $6,000 for it.

"After the war I wound up in the army, counter-intelligence, would you believe it? I took a trip back to Salinas. I couldn't lease one acre of land. Nothing available. The people who took over the place. They're doing quite well. So I came to Chicago and here I am.

WOODEN GUNS AND WOODEN HEADS (1943)

In the early stages of World War II, the military mounted Quaker antiaircraft guns on the roof of the Capitol. When members of Congress discovered the guns, a furor arose in the House of Representatives.

Rep. Crawford said, "I am not concerned about how many wooden guns, but how many wooden Congressmen they have around here."

Rep. Cooley added, "I think the time has come when the Members of this House ought to know what is being done around this city of Washington. It is unfortunate that this city, the capital of the greatest republic of the earth, is being protected by wooden guns and decoy soldiers."

Rep. Brown opined, "We have heard a good deal about wooden guns and wooden soldiers, but is not the real danger from wooden heads?"

NAZIS COPY BENEDICT ARNOLD (1943)

During the Second World War, a Nazi spy ring was uncovered in Brooklyn, and during the course of the trial, reference was made to a secret code that was the same as that used by Benedict Arnold in his dealings with the British in the Revolution. The secret code the traitor used was based on Blackstone's law book. To send a secret message, Arnold first located each word somewhere in the book, and then to indicate that word he used three numbers. The first number referred to the line, the second indicated the page, and the third revealed the position of the word in that line. To decode the message the British simply needed a copy of the same book. It was extremely simple and almost foolproof—almost—for it brought Arnold eternal disgrace.

"BULL" HALSEY (1944)

Adm. William Halsey, South Pacific naval commander in World War II, was not a man known for his defensive tactics. Ten days before Pearl Harbor was attacked, he told his superior, Adm. Husband E. Kimmel, that if he found so much as one Japanese sampan between Pearl Harbor and Wake Island, he would sink it. Later, during the course of the war, upon hearing that the Japanese were wondering "Where is the American Fleet," Bull Halsey replied, "Send them our latitude and longitude."

In another instance in 1944, upon being told that the Japanese claimed that most of the U.S. Third Fleet was either sunk or "retiring," Halsey issued the following radio message: "Our ships have been salvaged and are 'retiring' at high speed toward the Japanese fleet."

NO MAN IS THAT GOOD! (1945)

Henry Ford enjoyed authority and exerted it over everyone except his wife, Clara. Through fifty-nine years of marriage they were devoted companions, observing birds from the back porch of their estate in Dearborn, Michigan, or sitting around the radio listening to "Amos 'n' Andy" or "The Quiz Kids." At other times she would read aloud to him such books as *The Yearling, Bambi,* or *Gone With the Wind.* Their major concern seemed to be to make each other happy.

Upon being invited by Franklin Roosevelt to have dinner at the White House with the King and Queen of England, Ford sent his regrets because his wife's garden club was meeting that day. In 1929 he gave a huge testimonial dinner for Thomas Edison, the total cost of which came to more than $1 million. He later commissioned an artist to do a painting of the dinner. The finished painting was seven feet high by seventeen feet long and showed 266 recognizable portraits of the guests. One day Ford ordered the artist to remove one of the portraits in the painting—the wife of a Ford company official—because "Mrs. Ford doesn't like her."

COMMUNISTS ACKNOWLEDGE HOOVER (1946)

At the end of World War II, Harry Truman asked former president Herbert Hoover to conduct a world study of food supply and needed relief. Hoover's trips through Europe brought out thousands, who remembered and cheered him for his relief work at the end of World War I. A member of Tito's cabinet in Belgrade publicly acknowledged that he was alive because of Hoover's work in Serbia thirty years before. In Warsaw, Poland, a woman physician proclaimed at a conference that she was one of millions whose life had been saved by Hoover and his American organization a generation earlier. At this point she turned to some rather glum Communist officials at the conference table. "Own up," she demanded, "that but for Mr. Hoover's food you too wouldn't be here." Reluctantly they admitted this fact.

THE LAST ENCAMPMENT (1949)

From a peak membership of 409,489 in 1890, the Grand Army of the Republic, or GAR (Union veterans of the Civil War), declined until 1949, when the survivors decided that that year would be their last encampment. The following year only nine members were still living. In 1953, when James Albert Hard died at the age of 111, he was listed as the last combat veteran of the Union army. Albert Wolson still lived, but he had only served the last six months of the war, as a musician. Eighteen years later, on October 15, 1971, a controversy arose when a former slave, Sylvester Magee, died at the age of 130. Many historians have become convinced that "Slave" Magee, who ran away from a Mississippi plantation to join the Union army, was indeed the last Civil War veteran. Whether it was Hard or Magee, the survivor exceeded the ages of death of any previous American war veteran. The last veteran of the Revolutionary War, Daniel Bakeman, died in 1869 at the age of 109; the last veteran of the War of 1812, Hiram Cronk, died in 1905 at the age of 105; and the last veteran of the Mexican War, Owen Edgar, died in 1929 at the age of 98.

"MEDDLING WITH THE DEVIL" (1949)

One of the best works published on the Salem Witchcraft Trials is a 1949 book by Marion L. Starkey titled *The Devil in Massachusetts*. Those readers inclined to the supernatural might find interest in the author's report of some natural phenomena connected with the book. On the very hour that Starkey began research for the book (from Kittridge's *Witchcraft in Old and New England*), a small windstorm came through, toppling every tree in Miss Starkey's yard, blowing in through an open window in her house, and wrecking the room where she was researching. It even toppled the steeple of the East Saugus Community Church, visible in the flashes of lightning from her window. On the evening of the day she shipped off the manuscript, a violent lightning storm struck directly over her house. Lightning hit several neighbors' homes but missed hers. Meddling with the devil in Massachusetts is dangerous work, even in this day and age.

. . . AND BY 1950? (1950)

"Probably before 1950 a successful aeroplane will have soared and come home safe and sound." So spoke a prophet of the future in one of the national newspapers as 1899 drew to a close. Ray Stannard Baker, a top reporter who was optimistic about the solution to the "traffic problem," wasn't so prescient.

"It is hardly possible to conceive the appearance of a crowded whole-sale street in the day of the automotive vehicle. In the first place, it will be almost as quiet as a country lane—all the crash of horses' hoofs and the rumble of steel tires will be gone. And since vehicles will be fewer and shorter than the present truck and span, streets will appear less crowded."

H. G. Wells was amazingly accurate in his predictions of air conditioning, detergents, throughways, and the "do-it-yourself" mania, but he was somewhat off on his concept of future wars. Accurately, he believed there would still be wars, but he predicted that victory on land would depend on balloon power.

SOURCES

Aaron, Daniel, ed. *America in Crisis*. New York: Alfred A. Knopf, 1952.

Adams, James Truslow. *Album of American History*. Chicago: Consolidated Book Publishers, 1944.

The American Heritage History of the 20s and 30s. New York: American Heritage Publishing Co., 1970.

Andrews, Wayne, ed. *Concise Dictionary of American History*. New York: Charles Scribner's Sons, 1962.

Armstrong, Virginia Irving. *I Have Spoken*. New York: Pocket Books, Inc., 1972.

Beebe, Lucius, and Charles Clegg. *The American West*. New York: E. P. Dutton & Co., 1955.

Bishop, George. *The Booze Reader*. Los Angeles: Sherbourne Press, Inc., 1965.

Boatner, Mark M. *The Civil War Dictionary*. New York: David McKay Co. 1961.

Boorstin, Daniel J. *The Americans—The Colonial Experience*. New York: Random House, 1958.

Branch, E. Douglas. *The Sentimental Years*. New York: Hill and Wang, 1965.

Brooks, Van Syck. *The Confident Years*. New York: E. P. Dutton & Co., Inc., 1952.

Brown, John Hull. *Early American Beverages*. New York: Bonanza Books, 1966.

Bruce, Philip Alexander. *Social Life in Virginia in the Seventeenth Century*. Williamstown, Mass.: Corner House Publishers, 1907.

Calhoun, Arthur W. *A Social History of the American Family*. 2 vols. New York: Barnes and Noble, Inc., 1945.

Chinard, Gilbert. *Thomas Jefferson*. Ann Arbor, Mich.: University of Michigan Press, 1963.

Chitwood, Oliver Perry. *A History of Colonial America*. New York: Harper & Brothers, 1948.

Congdon, Don, ed. *The 30s, A Time to Remember*. New York: Simon & Schuster, Inc., 1962.

Cook, Fred J. *What Manner of Men*. New York: William Morrow & Co., 1959.

Doten, Dana. *The Art of Bundling*. Woodstock, Ver.: The Countryman Press and Farrar and Rinehart, 1938.

Dunlop, Richard. *Doctors of the American Frontier*. Garden City, N.Y.: Doubleday, Inc., 1965.

Earle, Alice Morse. *Customs and Fashions in Old New England*. Williamstown, Mass.: Corner House Publishers, 1969.

———. *Home Life in Colonial Days*. New York: The MacMillan Co., 1922.

———. *The Sabbath in Puritan New England*. Williamstown, Mass.: Corner House Publishers, 1969.

Edmonds, Walter D. *The Musket and the Cross*. Boston: Little, Brown and Co., 1968.

Furnas, J. C. *The Americans*. New York: G. P. Putman's Sons, 1969.

———. *Goodbye to Uncle Tom*. New York: William Sloane Associates, 1956.

Flexner, James Thomas. *The Benedict Arnold Case.* New York: Collier Books, 1962.

Freidel, Frank. *Our Country's Presidents.* Washington, D.C.: National Geographic Society, 1968.

Garraty, John A., ed. *The Unforgettable Americans.* Greatneck, N.Y.: Channel Press, 1960.

Glubok, Shirley. *Home and Child Life in Colonial Days.* Toronto, Ontario, Canada: Collier-MacMillan Co. Canada, Ltd., 1969.

Hamilton, Edward P. *The French and Indian Wars.* Garden City, N.Y.: Doubleday and Co., Inc., 1962.

Hawke, David. *The Colonial Experience.* New York: Bobbs-Merrill Co., Inc., 1966.

Hinds, William Alfred. *American Communities.* New York: Corinth Books, Inc., 1961.

Holbrook, Stewart H. *Dreamers of the American Dream.* Garden City, N.Y.: Doubleday and Co., Inc., 1957.

Holliday, Carl. *Woman's Life in Colonial Days.* Williamstown, N.Y.: Corner House Publishers, 1922.

Holt, Sol. *The Dictionary of American History.* New York: MacFadden-Bartell Corp., 1963.

Hoogengoom, Ari, and Olive Hoogengoom, ed. *The Gilded Age.* Englewood Cliffs, N.J.: Prentice-Hall, Inc., 1967.

Howard, Robert West. *The Great Iron Rail.* New York: Bonanza Books, 1962.

Hughes, Langston, and Milton Meltzer. *A Pictorial History of the Negro in America.* New York: Crown Publishers, Inc., 1956.

James, Marquis. *The Raven.* New York: Paperback Library, 1971.

Jones, Cranston. *Homes of the American Presidents.* New York: Bonanza Books, 1962.

Johnson, Clifton. *Old-Time Schools and School Books.* New York: Dover Publications, Inc., 1963.

Kane, Harnett T., ed. *The Romantic South.* New York: Coward McCann, Inc., 1961.

Kane, Joseph Nathan. *Facts about the Presidents.* New York: Permabooks, 1960.

———. *The Pocket Book of Famous First Facts.* New York: Pocket Books, 1970.

Kull, Irving S., and M. Nell. *A Short Chronology of American History, 1492–1950.* New Brunswick, N.J.: Rutgers University Press, 1952.

Kunhardt, Dorothy Meserve, and Philip B. Kunhardt Jr. *Twenty Days.* New York: Harper and Row, 1965.

Lamb, Harold. *New Found World.* Garden City, N.Y.: Doubleday Inc., 1956.

Lingeman, Richard R. *Don't You Know There's a War On?* New York: G. P. Putnam's Sons, 1971.

Lord, Francis A. *They Fought for the Union.* New York: Bonanza Books, 1960.

———. *The Good Years.* New York: Harper and Brothers, 1960.

Meirs, Earl Schenck, ed. *The American Story.* Great Neck, N.Y.: Channel Press, 1956.

McDowell, Bart. *The Revolutionary War.* Washington, D.C.: National Geographic Society, 1967.

McMillen, Wheeler, ed. *Harvest.* New York: Appleton-Century, 1965.

Middleton, Lamar. *Revolt U.S.A.* New York: Stackpole Sons, 1938.

Miller, John C. *The First Frontier: Life in Colonial America.* New York: Dell Publishing Co., Inc., 1966.

Mowry, George E., ed. *The Twenties: Fords, Flappers & Fanatics.* Englewood Cliffs, N.J.: Prentice-Hall, 1963.

Narcy, Randolph B. *The Prairie Traveler, A Handbook of Overland Expeditions.* Franklin Square, N.Y.: Harper and Brothers, 1959.

O'Meara, Walter. *Daughters of the Country.* New York: Harcourt, Brace & World, Inc., 1968.

Peterson, Harold L. *The Book of the Continental Soldier.* Harrisburg, Penn.: The Stackpole Company, 1968.

Platt, Rutherford. *Wilderness.* New York: Dodd, Mead & Co. 1961.

Porter, C. Fayne. *The Battle of 1,000 Slain*. New York: Scholastic Book Services, 1968.

Quarles, Benjamin. *The Negro in the American Revolution*. Chapel Hill, N.C.: University of North Carolina Press, 1961.

Ruxton, George Frederick. *Life in the Far West*. Norman, Okla.: University of Oklahoma Press, 1964.

Scheer, George F. *Private Yankee Doodle*. New York: Little, Brown and Co., 1963.

Shannon, David A., ed. *The Great Depression*. Englewood Cliffs, N.J.: Prentice-Hall, Inc., 1960.

Shyrock, Richard Harrison. *Medicine and Society in America*. Ithaca, N.Y.: Cornell University Press, 1962.

Smith, Marie. *Entertaining in the White House*. New York: MacFadden Bartell Corp., 1970.

Stampp, Kenneth M. *The Peculiar Institution*. New York: Alfred A. Knopf, 1956.

Starkey, Marion L. *The Devil in Massachusetts*. New York: Alfred A. Knopf, 1949.

Stewart, George R. *Ordeal by Hunger*. New York: Ace Books, Inc., 1960.

Stimpson, George. *A Book about a Thousand Things*. New York: Harper and Brothers, 1946.

Swanson, Neil H. *The Perilous Fight*. New York: J. J. Little and Ives Co., 1945.

Terkel, Studs. *Hard Times*. New York: Random House, Inc., 1970.

Thornton, Willis. *Fable, Fact and History*. New York: Greenberg, N.Y., 1957.

Vaughan, Alden T. *New England Frontier: Puritans and Indians*. Boston: Little, Brown and Co., 1965.

Viereck, Phillip. *The New Land*. New York: The John Day Co., 1967.

Ward, Christopher. *The War of the Revolution*. New York: The MacMillan Co., 1952.

Watkins, T. H. *Gold and Silver in the West*. Palo Alto, Calif.: American West Publishing Co., 1971.

Webster's Guide to American History. Springfield, Mass.: G&C Merriam Co., 1971.

Wellman, Paul I. *Spawn of Evil*. New York: Pyramid Publications, 1965.

Wharton, Anne Hollingsworth. *Social Life in the Early Republic*. Williamstown, Mass.: Corner House Publishers, 1970.

Wiley, Bell Irvin. *Embattled Confederates*. New York: Harper and Row, 1964.

Wiley, Bell Irvin, and Hirst Milhollen. *They Who Fought Here*. New York: Bonanza Books, 1959.

Willison, George F. *Behold Virginia!* New York: Harcourt, Brace & Co., 1951.

———. *Saints and Strangers*. New York: Reynal and Hitchcock, 1945.

Woodward, William E. *The Way Our People Lived*. New York: Washington Square Press, Inc., 1963.

Zweig, Stefan. *Amerigo*. New York: The Viking Press, 1942.

INDEX

B

G

N

O

P

T

Z

ABOUT THE AUTHOR

George W. Givens spent twenty years teaching American history in schools in upstate New York, Arizona, and Virginia before opening what became the largest family-owned bookstore in Virginia. He and his wife, Sylvia, spent several summers in Nauvoo, Illinois, as in-house historians. They are the parents of eight children.

George is the author of *In Old Nauvoo, The Nauvoo Fact Book, Out of Palmyra,* and *The Hired Man's Christmas.* He is also the author of *500 Little-Known Facts in Mormon History, 500 More Little-Known Facts in Mormon History,* and *The Language of the Mormon Pioneers,* published by Cedar Fort.

George passed away in 2004.